THE VEHEMENT PASSIONS

PHILIP FISHER

THE VEHEMENT PASSIONS

PRINCETON

UNIVERSITY

PRESS

PRINCETON

AND OXFORD

Published by Princeton University Press, 41 William Street, Princeton, New Jersey 08540

In the United Kingdom: Princeton University Press, 3 Market Place, Woodstock, Oxfordshire OX20 ISY

Library of Congress Cataloging-in-Publication Data

Fisher, Philip, 1941–

The vehement passions / Philip Fisher.

p. cm.

Includes bibliographical references and index.

ISBN 0-691-06996-4 (alk. paper)

I. Emotions (Philosophy) I. Title.

BI05.E46 F57 2002

128′—dc2I   200I055I93

British Library Cataloging-in-Publication Data is available

This book has been composed in Centaur with Gill Sans

Printed on acid-free paper. ∞

www.pup.princeton.edu

Printed in the United States of America

10 9 8 7 6 5 4 3 2 I

FOR ELAINE SCARRY

AND MARK FISHER

CONTENTS

ACKNOWLEDGMENTS

This book was completed during a year as a Senior Scholar at the Getty Research Institute, where the warmth and energy of Michael Roth and the aid of the remarkable library and staff made the daily life on the Getty's sunny hilltop a great pleasure. My thanks to the Getty Foundation for including me in a yearlong project and scholar's seminar on the passions.

Three sections of this book in a compressed form were presented as Christian Gauss Seminars at Princeton. I am grateful to Michael Wood, the director of the seminars, for his very gracious and humane hosting of my time in Princeton. His friendship and wide-ranging conversation made every part of these events a delight. The audience at Princeton brought out, through their questions and comments, a welcome set of fresh lines of doubt and speculation. George Kateb's rigor and his probing engagement were of particular importance to me, as was the intellectual challenge of Alexander Nehemas and Albert Hirschman.

I would like to thank the John Simon Guggenheim foundation for a fellowship year during which a very many-sided project took its final form. During that year the Center for Advanced Study in the Behavioral Sciences at Stanford, through the generosity of its Director, Neil Smelser, and its Associate Director, Robert Scott, provided me with an office and with the company and stimulation of the forty scholars in residence. The beauty of the Center's spartan work quarters on the hillside above Stanford give a rugged and informal energy to every day's work there.

The earliest stages of work on this project took place thanks to a generous fellowship for a year's residence in 1987 at the Wissenschaftskolleg (Institute for Advanced Study) in Berlin, where I have had the good fortune to return many times in the decade that followed. The chapters on fear were first given as an evening lecture at the Kolleg at the invitation of the Rektor, Wolf Leppenies. All of my work since my first encounter with this truly unique international institution has benefited from the ever-changing conversation that from morning to night, year after year, modifies and enhances the work that each of us thinks of as individual acts of writing, but that we find, as we reach the final pages, has thrived in the atmosphere of the pleasure of the mind as it often can best be seen in the unusual intensity of a community of other quite striking projects that keep taking us away from our own, only to return us to it from a fresh path impossible to locate alone

Richard Poirier and *Raritan* published sections of several chapters in earlier versions, and I am pleased that it was in this journal that the first appearance of parts of this larger project appeared. Robert Nozick read and commented on the two chapters on fear, and I am grateful for his acute questioning, as I am for his friendship and engagement as a colleague. Allen Grossman, with whom I stood under the spell of conversation throughout my years at Brandeis, will recognize within this book the opportunity for thought that his creation at Brandeis of a unique kind of humanities core curriculum opened out for all of us who joined him in this enterprise. In the editing and manuscript preparation I was aided by two assistants, Mark Greif and Shane Slattery-Quintanilla, both of whom gave their energy and care to the final details of this book.

THE VEHEMENT PASSIONS

Could any pair of words seem as natural together as the words "dispassionate knowledge"? Yet in at least one case the passions were always understood to be essential to the search for knowledge. Descartes, in naming wonder the first of the passions, described wonder as an impassioned state that makes learning possible. In wonder we notice against the background of a lawful and familiar world something that strikes us by its novelty and by the pleasure that this surprising new fact brings to us. Each of us has at every stage of our lives a distinct but provisional horizon separating the familiar from the unknown and the unknowable. Any one experience of wonder informs us about the momentary location of this horizon line. The horizon line a red balloon reveals as it rises in the air before the eyes of a small child marks a different line from the one revealed when, as an adult astronomer, she sees for the first time in human history a pattern in the distribution of galaxies.

The passion of wonder has always been described by scientists and mathematicians as the heart of the experience of the search for new knowledge. At the same time, the very details of wonder might seem to rule out even more strongly any similar claim for anger, fear, grief, shame, and the other vehement passions. If it is only scientific knowledge that we are concerned with, then anger or mourning would seem to preclude clear thought, the pursuit of a continuous chain of thought and experiment, and the preservation of the calm atmosphere in which order and rationality make possible long and arduous projects.

As I hope to show in this book, wonder is not an exception. Each of the strong emotions or passions designs for us an intelligible world and does so by means of horizon lines that we can come to know only in experiences that begin with impassioned or vehement states within ourselves. The part played by wonder in scientific thought, both in the moment of attention that leads to a first discovery and in the final ordered knowledge that we call science, is played by anger in discovering or marking out for us unmistakably the contours of injustice and of unjust acts in certain moments of time. In this case as well, the concrete and ordered form that those local discoveries sponsored by anger lead to in the end is the nuanced legal system that is both codified and altered over time by newly discovered paths of anger and outrage, sometimes at individual acts that in their aftermath lead to new or stronger laws; at other times the outcome is the retraction of laws that in their workings lead to cases that arouse angry demands for redress.

That we are often surprised by wonder or surprised by anger is one clue to the fact that something new is disclosed to us in states of vehemence. The object's demand for attention that makes up one detail of wonder lets us see that we do not choose the objects we end up thinking about. Something, as we put it, catches our attention. Descartes describes how we find ourselves delighted, puzzled, and then drawn to pause and to think about what is new and strange to us.[1]

Wonder is located at that promising line between what we already know—our familiar world—and all that it would be pointless to think about because we personally lack, or our historical moment as a whole lacks, the skills and framework of knowledge that would let us profitably spend time thinking here and now at this location. Wonder occurs at the horizon line of what is potentially knowable, but not yet known. We learn about this horizon line when we find ourselves in a state of wonder. Surprise has guided us to something where we can invest energy and time in a profitable way. The same is true for anger, although it will take many chapters of this book to make plausible this claim about anger.

Scientific discovery and the demand for justice might seem, even if shown to be grounded in wonder and anger, to have saved these two vehement states at the expense of many others: distress (the Stoic's encompassing term that includes grief and mourning), shame, and, above all, fear. But in at least the case of fear, the deep and intrinsic connections between fear and aesthetic experience have been known in a restricted way since Aristotle's work on tragedy, where pity, fear, surprise, recognition, and suffering, along with a certain shudder of terror, were for the first time systematically described as states of pleasure. It is by means of the relations between fear and pity that a civic component enters into the highly self-centered and self-defining vehement states, and does so most clearly in the aesthetic experience of a spectator at a play or film, or the reader of a novel. An important parallel experience occurs in law courts where, as jurors, we are placed as observers and judges of opposed stories told by the prosecution and the defense about a set of events.

By using modern work in philosophy, economics, and game theory, I will develop a nuanced geography of fear with the goal of showing that in this case as well, the experience of extreme fear discloses, by means of a kind of horizon line found within the moment of experience itself, a necessary wealth of details that articulate an intelligible world. Here it will be the realms of aesthetics, storytelling, and, once again, the cases or stories told in courts of law that will be the domain of experience for fear that parallels the territory of wonder in science or the territory of anger within justice—both formal justice as we know it embodied in courts of law, judges, juries, prisons, and codes of statute law, and informal, everyday justice between neighbors or brothers or children who play together day after day in a city playground.

The uses of shame and grief I will not describe in advance except to say that, in combination with fear and anger, these two passions announce to us the presence within ongoing life of the fact of mortality, and that they do so by marking the contours of the limited radius of our will by means of the injuries and humiliations of that will that are signaled to us by the moments when we find ourselves in a state of vehemence—that is, in an impassioned state. The workings of the passions will be my subject in the pages that follow, and not the problems posed by their excess. Nor will I be concerned with their trivial misuse, therapeutic irrationality, and prolonged fixity in those lives where anger or fear, shame or mourning might be excessive, fixed, arbitrary, and irrational. Instead, my concern will be the common sense of the vehement passions and just how the sensible mechanisms within the passions work within experience to map out the geography of an individual, intelligible world for each of us at every moment. The passions, as one of the longest uninterrupted, most intricate and necessary descriptive problems in the intellectual life of Western culture, have had time to accumulate waves of damage both from absent words and from the bad surplus of overlapping, once technical, but now informal vocabulary. Along the path of this almost three-thousand-year history the language that we now use, or find ourselves lacking, has been frozen into place at surprising moments. The word "pathology," which would exactly suit the study of the passions (*páthema*, in Greek), serves instead, when we look in a medical dictionary, for the study of abnormality, the study of diseases: "anatomic and physiologic deviations from the normal in the tissues of animals and plants that are manifested as disease."[2] In English the word "affection" means a mild, benign feeling of goodwill or liking, but the word is still linked to the philosophical term "affect," which is used to translate *affectus* or *páthe* in philosophical works where rage or grief, shame or terror is more likely to be the state implied.

Our words often have behind them a single salient case that steers response from behind the curtains of time. When capitalized, ever since the Middle Ages, the word "Passion" is listed first in English dictionaries as denoting the sufferings of Jesus on the cross, or in the period between the Last Supper and his death. With this overwhelming central instance in Christianity, passion in ordinary life is touched by suffering, and it is also passive, after the model of Jesus on the cross.

Our word "passionate" reaches us along a different route and holds on to a core meaning that we can trace back to Homer's *Iliad*, where we might think first of someone easily roused to anger, someone in a state of vehemence. By extension, "passionate" refers to strong states of any emotion, but on the model of anger. To have a leading edge of anger as the path along which to understand any other highly aroused state, as the word "passionate" insists, would bind us back to Plato, Aristotle, and the Greek ethical and legal traditions. The word "passionate" understands anger as a positive state, the very essence of an aroused and dynamic spirit. Hector and Achilles sit in the shadow of this word, while Jesus on the cross stands offstage near the capitalized word "Passion."

The Hellenistic philosophers of Greece and Rome, and above all the Stoics, endowed our civilization with a Latin vocabulary for the emotions and the inner life that seeped into every European philosophical tradition; Aquinas, Descartes, Spinoza, Hobbes, and Kant translated, modified, or reversed a standing list of Latin terms that reached back to the time of Cicero. But Stoicism was at war with the passions and viewed them as suffering rooted in false belief. The Stoics contrasted passions with actions, bending an earlier history back against itself.

In modern French or English the word "passion" in isolation would most often suggest sexual passion, while the plural "the passions" might sound archaic because most of the cargo associated with that term has now been transferred to "the emotions," where a different organization and set of implied edges, meanings, and core instances design the topic in a new way. Once a new category, like the emotions, has taken over, our thinking and talk are liberated from the backstage presence of the Passion of Jesus, the anger of Achilles, but they are liberated as well from the remarkable success of what we might call low-level, everyday Stoicism in all later European culture, and from the medical language of diseases that appeared, even to Cicero, to draw too strong an analogy between the diseases of the body and those states of the soul—grief, fear, anger, shame—that seemed to be diseases of the spirit or soul, needing treatment, therapy, and purgation.[3]

We can see in mid-eighteenth-century English philosophy and rhetoric the banishing of the term "passion" and its replacement by the new term "emotion." At least on the surface this change of vocabulary seems to have rinsed out the deformations and preferences tacitly built into the earlier history of thought about the passions. What remained unchanged, when the passions came to be called the emotions, were the words for the specific passions or emotions. We still speak of the emotion of fear, or the emotion of anger, or of angry feelings and jealous feelings. If the full specificity of fear and anger and jealousy is preserved, what difference can it make to have gone from speaking of fear as a passion to regarding fear as an emotion or feeling? The answer lies, in part, in what would count as salient or typical examples of fear when one is speaking of a feeling of fear or an emotion of fear or of fear as a passion. A fear of mice or a phobia about sticky tactile surfaces (to use a Freudian example) might seem useful as instances of emotions. Such modern, quirky, therapeutic instances often govern twentieth-century discussions of inner states. But when describing the passions, Aristotle went at once to the single greatest, universal fear: the fear of imminent death, as a soldier might experience it on a battlefield, or as a trembling passenger might on a ship that seems about to sink. The inflection given to our tacit understanding of fear by what seem to be natural or colorless examples is often the most revealing snapshot of the shift from a vocabulary of passions to one of feelings, emotions, or moods.

What does it mean to speak, as we often do in the twentieth century, as though moods were our preferred version of inner states?

Passions, moods, emotions, and feelings are profoundly different configurations of the underlying notion of a temporary state of a person. Each term makes plausible a very distinct template. Boredom, depression, nostalgia, and anxiety might be natural first instances of what we mean by mood, but such states could never have been plausible examples of passions. Rage and wonder, central to any idea of what the passions are, seem out of place with the low-energy conditions generally meant by the term "mood." Just as the English term "the passions" defines a different domain from the German *Leidenschaften*, which would be its translation, or from the French term *passions* or the Greek term *páthema*, so too within English itself we need to regard passions, emotions, feelings, moods as different languages with overlapping but also strongly differing accounts of what might count as a typical, a central, or an excluded inner state.

In spite of the limitations and confusions of language that I have hinted at, the stubborn, consecutive, rich thinking about the passions is one of the best arguments that we have for cultural memory, for a sustained core account of human nature in spite of the constructions of culture, power, and historical moment, and for the deep structural grasp on certain themes within the changing episodes and local design or redesign that can be traced in our three-thousand-year record.

What we know or how we think about the passions was, from the beginning, a complex product of overlapping and sometimes mutually encumbering work in philosophy, in literature—especially epic and tragedy—in medicine, in ethics, in rhetoric, in aesthetics, in legal and political thought. In our own time, new work in evolutionary biology, psychology, anthropology, and most recently in the neurobiology of the brain, along with work in game theory and economics, and, above all, in philosophy, continues the interwoven texture of shared, interdependent, sometimes interfering, even damaging, and sometimes enhancing collaborative thought. I will be speaking about some features of game theory and modern political philosophy when I speak of the new model of fear in chapter 6, and of legal philosophy and legal procedures when I speak of anger and justice in chapters 8 and 9, but above all, throughout this book, I will be drawing on the intersection of philosophy, literature, and aesthetics.

Philosophical analysis of the passions in its crucial early phase was, in fact, the analysis of certain literary examples, both small-scale events within tragedies and the Homeric epics, and also profound accounts of those kinds of works of art, formally and as a whole. It is not because passions come up in literature at certain moments, felt by certain characters whose fate and motives concern us, but because, first of all, the nature of having an experience, per se, has close ties to what we mean by a passion, as the Greek word *páthe* shows in meaning both passion and experience. A second, equally important reason lies in the fact that many of the larger, formal features of complete literary works, on a certain temporal scale, map temporal features of the passions.

In literature, the passions are not present merely as incidents; that is, as certain kinds of moments alongside other important moments like choosing, perceiving, remembering, talking, or acting. Key passions determine genres or literary kinds; large and ordered systems of aesthetic practices that generate the form of the whole. Elegy is a literary kind determined by mourning or grief. In its details the form known as elegy is generated by the details of mourning, including the way that mourning lasts, but then comes to an end, and including as well the larger darkening of the world in grief as though interest in life itself will never return. Above all, elegy makes clear the presence in any grief that we feel at the death of another person of an anticipation of our own death. A kind of grieving in advance for ourselves takes place in any grieving for another. Finally, in elegy, we commonly find near the end a resolve that seems for a while to increase the value of the time remaining in life, a resolve produced by this imaginative brush with our own death that has been occasioned by the death of another. The literary form that we call elegy, in its many features, takes the shape that it does through an implicit anatomy of grief and mourning.

Tragedy, as Aristotle defined it, is both a certain kind of action and a work characterized by fear and pity, two passions intimately related to one another, as he showed. Fear, along with a set of forms generated by fear, reappeared once the novel became the central narrative practice in Europe. The gothic novel, which first appeared in the late eighteenth century, continues to be one of the most important popular genres, down to the novels of Stephen King and the terrifying movies of this year, last year, and every year. The gothic novel is in fact a form generated by the experience of fear. By describing fear, it induces fear in its reader or in an audience by means of step after step of graduated doses of fear. Edmund Burke listed many of the aesthetic features of any form based on fear: the representation of isolated persons, danger, night, and obscurity. Events in fear-centered stories have an abruptness and unexpectedness. Burke noted the part played by sounds, by animals, by confusion, and by the rapidity with which the action unfolds. In his book on our ideas of the sublime and the beautiful, Burke devotes distinct sections to darkness, vastness, difficulty, sound and loudness, blackness, intermittence, the cries of animals, stenches, bitters, and pain.[4]

Like elegy in its elaboration of the details of grief, the gothic or any other fear-based form uses most of the inner details of the fear experience, among them suddenness, surprise, dilated experiences of time, and nearly unbearable suspense in the moments of pause before the dreaded thing at last happens. The shape of time within fear-based forms is entirely different from the shape and pace of time within forms based on mourning or grief. That difference follows from the familiar arc and pace of time within the vehement states themselves. Wonder, anger, grief, and fear reveal different ways that time is rushed, dilated, ordered, and used up. Works of art modeled on those states follow distinct recipes for the use of time.

In aesthetic experience only certain forms create, as the gothic novel or the modern fright film does, the duplication in the reader of the aroused state of the central character. Pornography does this with sexual arousal. The reader of a pornographic novel is meant to experience sexual arousal and orgasm while reading about characters experiencing sexual arousal and orgasm. But when we see works depicting rage, the audience reacts, as Aristotle claimed was true for tragedy, with fear. Wrath is so unpredictable and so potentially violent a passion that when we see it begin, even in a work of art, we know that we are about to move into a wildly volatile and violent set of events. The spectator of rage feels fear when confronted with this prospect, not an anger that runs parallel to the central figure's rage. The counterpoint between the passions that are dramatized or read about and those quite different passions aroused in us when we witness those vehement states raises one of the most complex aesthetic questions about the passions. We are terrified or angry or sorry for Desdemona and disgusted with her husband while witnessing Othello's mistaken and, finally, murderous jealousy. What he feels and what we feel watching him in his impassioned state are interwoven, but distinct, adjacent states of arousal.

Of all the larger forms that translate the details of one passion, it is the working out of anger that has been most important. The epic as we know it through Homer's *Iliad*, Virgil's *Aeneid*, Milton's *Paradise Lost*, or Melville's *Moby Dick* not only turns on the subject of anger but relies on the pitch, the process, and the speed of anger, along with its generation of consequential action such as killings, curses, and abrupt violence of word and deed.

To add one final, important modern instance, the novel in its many varieties captured the fanatic loyalty of readers by means of works that were state-based: fear in the case of the gothic novel of the late eighteenth century; pity and tears in the sentimental novel that has lasted at full strength from Richardson and Rousseau at the start of the modern novel, to Dickens and Stowe, down to the films, novels, and television serials of the present.

From the side of literary culture, as these examples show, the passions are not important mainly as momentary situations within works. They are not only occasions where some character or another feels shame or anger, love or sorrow. Instead, wonder, pity, mourning, fear, anger, grief, and shame legislate what we mean by genre and by form in many of the most profound and culturally important works that we have.

Literature shares with the legal realm of cases, trials, rulings, and the formal codification of the law the highest importance because it is in these two domains that deeply thought out human experiences over dozens of centuries reveal the contours of the vehement passions. The aesthetic, legal, and scientific legitimacy of the workings of the strongest passions, along with the underlying features of felt mortality and spiritedness, unfold within our experience the fact that aroused or impassioned states create a third condition within everyday life, as far in one direction from our ordinary or settled state as the condition of sleep is in the other.

Passions, Strong Emotions, Vehement Occasions

In *The Expression of Emotions in Man and Animals*, Charles Darwin in 1872 began with a description of the physical expressions of four of "the stronger sensations and emotions." His four examples are rage, joy, terror, and the agony of physical pain.[1] Ten years later in William James's essay "What Is an Emotion?," in which we find the elements of what came to be known as the James-Lange theory, James took for his examples what he called the "coarser" or the "strong" emotions: grief, rage, fear.[2] The neurobiology of our own time, studying the results of brain lesions, has located in the medial temporal lobe known as the amygdala the physical component of the emotion system: disgust, surprise, and, above all, anger and fear. In fact most brain-emotion research involves, first and foremost, the study of fear.[3]

These coarse or strong emotions carve out the territory once known to philosophical psychology, to ethics, to medicine, to rhetoric, and to literature as the passions. Twenty-five hundred years ago Aristotle's *Rhetoric* and *Nicomachean Ethics* inaugurated and set the grounding terms for the formal, complex, detailed analysis of states of the soul or, to use a less religious word, the spirit. The second part of Aristotle's *Rhetoric* began with anger, giving a richly elaborated, pattern-setting, full, structural description of the state of necessary anger and its conditions. The analysis of the virtues in *The Nicomachean Ethics* began with fear, the ground on which the virtue of courage arises. Behind Aristotle's close, phenomenological descriptions we notice again and again the pervasive offstage presence of Homer's *Iliad*. The anger of Achilles, in its profound relation to war, to justice, to mourning and loss, and to the militant defense of self-worth is Aristotle's implicit example in the *Rhetoric*. He refers to the *Iliad* six times in four pages. In the case of fear and courage, in the *Ethics*, it is the battlefield where the soldier must face and then move forward toward what threatens him with imminent death that Aristotle takes as his only central case. Once again the descriptions of battle in the *Iliad* provide his offstage model. Offering as it did a storehouse of minutely described moments of experience, Homer's *Iliad* provided the best available widely known accounts of a wide range of fundamental human states in time, among them anger, fear, wonder, and grief.

Fear and anger are what I want to call templates for the many briefer descriptions of other passions in Aristotle's two works. Examined in detail and listed first, they model or set out the domain of features for the diverse states that can be given much briefer analysis because the primary features of any state whatsoever have been presented in the first passion he examines. As memorable, rich first instances, anger and fear hover over and measure what follows, just as certain facts about the *Iliad* underpin what Aristotle himself says. As templates, fear and anger shape more than these chapters or books of Aristotle. They dominate the long analytic history of the passions— and, later, the emotions—that follows, replicating, enriching, opposing, or varying Aristotle's work in fields as diverse as rhetoric, the law, medicine, philosophy, ethics, and literature down to the work of Heidegger and Freud in the twentieth century.

It is usually easy to see, for any later theory of the passions that we examine, whether it is, in the end, fear or anger that spells out first and most deeply just what is meant by the category of the passions per se. Fear and anger sponsor opposite accounts of just what the larger category of the passions amounts to and how it is valued or devalued.

In anger an outward-streaming energy, active, fully engaging the will and demonstrating the most explosive self-centered claims on the world and on others, makes clear the relation of the passions to spiritedness or to high-spiritedness, to motion, to confidence, and to self-expression in the world. No one thinking of the passions by means of the template of anger could ever think of the passions as passive or opposed to action.

With anger's close relation to courage—Hobbes defines courage as "sudden anger"—the underlying topics of mortality, danger, imminent death, and the smaller everyday mortalities of diminution or loss rise to the surface.[4] Behind these topics, we see the third passion that has closest links in all analysis to either anger or fear: the passion of grief or mourning (distress, as the Stoics called it).

Within impassioned states like anger two highly significant secondary features occur: obstinacy and irritability. This pairing should be taken as a clue to the fact that the inner material of anger is, finally, the will, and that the spirited or passionate self provides a description allowing us to see the closest relation of the soul to immediate action, and to what would later come to be called the will in Western thought after Augustine. Obstinacy is the rigid pursuit of what has been willed, while irritability is the response of the will when it is baffled and unable to achieve its goal. The obstinacy of Achilles or of King Lear is one of their primary traits. Here we can see one of the crucial secondary motives hidden behind the use of templates like fear or anger. Obstinacy and irritability are two features of the passions in general that become immediately visible in the passion of anger.[5] When one thinks of the passions, or of the spirited self as a whole, by means of the local example (or template) of anger, features like obstinacy and irritability occur as natural-seeming descriptive features of the larger category.

When fear, rather than anger, is taken to be the template for inner life, the underlying frame is quite different. Accounts of the passions displayed by means of a template of fear are preliminary to a therapeutic description of how the passions might be minimized or eliminated from experience. When we think first of fear, the passions are, as Cicero claimed, diseases.[6] Where fear is used as the template, as it was in Stoicism, the passions are taken as disturbances of the self, rather than internal material of the self. No one ever wished to have been more often or more thoroughly terrified than he actually was in his life. The template of anger, on the other hand, sponsors a fundamental claim for a model of human worth and dignity, inseparable from the passions and nearly equal to the worth and dignity of reason. In anger, a high-spirited, active, energetic response to the world is placed at the heart of what we mean by impassioned states.

With fear we can see at once the logic of the Stoic conclusion that passions are passive and opposed to action or to any active state of the self, such as careful thought. In fear we are overwhelmed by something outside ourselves or by something that we believe may damage or destroy us. What is feared defines for us the very opposite of all that we will or choose or desire, and for that reason it is the negation of our own self-understanding. With fear we are the victim or potential victim of something coming toward us in the world, something that undermines, for at least the moment, our capacity to think of ourselves as agents. It is a very small step from wishing that what threatens us did not exist to wishing that our own impassioned state did not exist and that we would never in the future feel anything similar.

Where we build a template for the passions out of fear, each of the features that I have just described is carried over, sometimes openly, sometimes in an indirect or subtle way, into the account of all the other impassioned states. In Stoicism the argument against the passions was sealed by means of the invocation of fear as the single central passion. When the Stoics listed the four major categories among the passions, they listed desire and fear, distress and pleasure.[7] The first pair, desire and fear, are positive and negative states of anticipation. The second pair, pleasure and distress, are positive and negative aftermath states, reactions in the present to what has just taken place. Of the four, it is the analysis of fear that provides the larger formula. It was by means of fear that Hellenistic philosophy undermined the passions by pointing out the connections of passions to belief, especially false belief. We readily acknowledge the large part played by exaggerated or mistaken belief in our experiences of fear. Many things we fear turn out to be harmless. Sometimes this is because they do not, in the end, occur. Sometimes it is because we are completely mistaken about the object of our fear. Shadows at night that we interpret as crouching figures turn out to be nothing at all. In other cases of false belief we overestimate the seriousness of the situation. Fear is the best starting point for examining and making central the problem of the part played by belief and false belief in our experiences of the passions.

When fear is taken as the template, it is easy to see that passions like intense and prolonged grief felt for the sudden death of a child, envy, jealousy, and even melancholy conform to the descriptive pattern of fear and seem comfortable together on any list we make. Wonder, anger, and falling in love seem marginalized by any template for the larger idea of an impassioned state that has had its starting point in fear. One effect of each and every template (including the modern template which assumes that the best instance of passion is sexual desire) is to make a small set of passions seem natural and central in importance because they include most of the features present in the template passion that had been subjected to extensive analysis first. At the same time, an equally important set of states, as a result of the same process, come to be brushed aside because they do not fit the details of the formula secured in our minds by that same initial description.

The history of philosophical descriptions of the passions has been strongly dominated by templates of fear and anger. For Plato, for Aristotle, and for Thomas Aquinas the template is anger. In Plato's *Republic* the third part of the soul, distinct from reason and equally from the desires and appetites, is made visible by and defined by anger. The *thumós* is "that with which we feel anger."[8] All passions for Aquinas are divided into the concupiscent (or desire-driven) and the irascible (or anger-driven). For Hellenistic philosophy and, above all, for the Stoics, who did most to shape all later Christian and secular thought about the passions, it was the template of fear that was always in the back of the mind, if not conspicuously onstage. In modern philosophy it is fear that regulates discussion of the passions in Hume or Kant, in Hobbes or Heidegger. Today, the articles on brain localization of emotion that we find in *Nature* or *Scientific American* bring us first to fear and anger, and above all to fear as the defining template.

When David Hume wrote the last groundbreaking work on the passions within philosophy almost three centuries ago, he used anger and fear as instances of what he called the violent passions. His only full and detailed analysis of a state examines fear. Into that analysis he introduced the topic of uncertainty, which would come to be of inestimable value for modern economics, strategy, and game theory, several of the most important recent disciplines engaged with questions of the passions.[9] Modern disciplinary interest is largely an interest in the matter of fear. For Hume it is because uncertainty is a pervasive fact within our experience, and because the mind moves continuously from one thing to another along paths created by the association of ideas, that the ground state, or fallback position, is the state of fear. Fear is not one state among others but a state manifesting the restless action of the mind itself as it moves back and forth among the objects of its attention.[10]

The same primacy of fear can be seen in a very different work. Each of the chapters of Darwin's book on the expression of the emotions traces a family or cluster of emotions, often grouped by common physical manifestations. In his twelfth chapter he begins with surprise, then wonder, astonishment, fear, horror. His assumption is that all of these states are varieties of fear. His summary states it this way: "I have now endeavored to describe the diversified expressions of fear, in its gradations from mere attention to a start of surprise, into extreme terror and horror."[11] By including "mere attention" in this family of states, along with what we now call the "startling reflex," Darwin asserts that the mind's most basic act of awareness is patterned by fear since mere attention has to be one aspect of any focused state. Darwin also links to fear what we would think of ordinarily as those pleasurable forms of attention like surprise, wonder, and astonishment, states for which he usually gives frightening examples. For surprise he recounts the story of an Australian native who saw for the first time a human being on horseback and ran off terrified.[12] Just as with Hume's uncertainty and motion, Darwin has managed to graft a state of passion, in a low-level way, onto the very activity of the mind itself: attention. With Hume and Darwin we can see the deepest possible grounding for the idea that there is, in most complex presentations, one passion offered as the template for the impassioned state itself, because what that template is linked to is the most basic element of experience itself—motion between ideas for Hume, attention for Darwin.

Occasioned and Dispositional Passions

It is the strong, coarse, or violent states, as Hume, Darwin, or William James meant those adjectives, the states of vehemence, as I will call them here, that will be the subject of this book. We need to notice first the difference between the eruptive momentary impassioned state and the more enduring underlying states of which we sometimes speak when thinking of the passions, the difference between occasioned, onetime events and the passions as we experience them in settled, persistent, temperamental facts (or, in Kant's term, inclinations). Grief felt at the unexpected and sudden death of the central person in one's life might be the best example of an occasioned vehement state. We always distinguish a general disposition, like the fear of heights, from a moment of fear when we see a large snake in front of us on a path. Note first of all that strong phobias of which we are conscious are most likely to lead us to avoid any occasion where fear might actually be experienced. The real gauge of a dread of airplane flights is not the passenger trembling at takeoff in the seat beside you but the man who always takes the train from New York to Los Angeles, will not go near an airport, nor take a job requiring any travel, and so, as a result of these and many other arrangements, never has any "episodes" of fear at all because he has eliminated from his life the very things that he can predict would lead to moments of horrible fear.

Ambition and avarice are passions commonly invoked as settled, underlying dispositional facts about a person. Grief and fear are examples, on the other side, of passions that we think of first by means of single, experiential moments. When you hear the word, you think of an occasioned event of grief or fear. In other words, even within any ordinary list of the passions some are likely to seem essentially occasioned, eruptive, and eventlike, even while having also a dispositional form, while others are the opposite, primarily dispositions, and only rarely eventlike. Among the most clearly episodic, it is hard to think of wonder as anything but a momentary event in which we feel surprise and pleasure at something noticed just now.

Passions such as avarice that have both forms display different aspects when we think first of temperament and underlying disposition, and then of those aspects visible in any single moment of impassioned greed as it might be displayed, for example, at the reading of a relative's will. The channels in which the passions habitually run, Hume noted, become what he called "calm passions" like patriotism, love of money and gain, fear of animals, so that the eruptive, unexpected "experience of a moment of passion" is not necessarily a sign of the persistence, importance, or depth of the inclinations at all. Deep, permanent jealousy has often so terrorized the other person in advance with small-scale suspicions, extreme measures of control and observation, that no true episode of full-scale jealousy will ever occur.

Philosophy and literature have always distinguished between these two kinds of states, often by using different terms—like the contrast between anger (eruptive moment) and hatred (abiding state), or between falling in love (eruptive moment) and love (abiding state)—or by having larger distinct categories that put on one side the episodic, vehement, but brief possession by fear or anger or grief that Kant called *Affekte* (in English, emotions) and on the other settled inclinations that guide actions in a permanent way, like the passion for freedom and ambition, which he called *Leidenschaften* (passions). As one of the many puzzles and reversals within language in the long history of the passions, we need to notice that Kant is using the word "passion" to reverse earlier usage because he eliminates brief moments of aroused grief or fear from his concept of the passions. In his *Anthropology* Kant elaborated this difference around the experience of anger: "Emotion is surprise through sensation, whereby the composure of mind (*animus sui compos*) is suspended. Emotion therefore is precipitate, that is, it quickly grows to a degree of feeling which makes reflection impossible (it is thoughtless). . . . What the emotion of anger does not accomplish quickly will not be accomplished at all. The emotion of anger easily forgets. But the passion of hate takes its time to root itself deeply and to associate itself with the energy."[13]

Kant sets up a moment of anger as the example of emotion, anger that is surprising and precipitate, quickly at its peak, then quickly forgotten. He sees the moment of anger as an eruption within our background condition of apathy, composure, and equanimity, with which it is contrasted. But on the other side it is contrasted with the steady, gathering force of what Kant calls a passion: hatred, in this case, or ambition, the love of freedom, or any other enduring inclination of the soul. To establish a similar distinction Hobbes made two lists, calling anger, for example "sudden courage," and in the long list of the "sudden" states he preserved the idea of brief episodes, set off or occasioned by a specific event.[14]

It is the occasioned, momentary episode, located at a specific point in time, that Aristotle always used for anger or fear. He did not use irascibility, an abiding fact of temperament. Hellenistic and later descriptive terms for the passions, like disturbances, perturbations, commotions, were terms for the episodic and intense. The analogy between the passions and an acute illness that is rapid, fully possessing the victim, but quickly fading and returning the victim to health obviously is based on the occasioned, brief episode. Our modern broad use of the idea of crisis would fit both acute illness and the passions. The Greek word for the passions means both passions and experiences, brief eventlike episodes.

My primary concern will be with the occasioned, dramatic, experiential moments of the passions, not with ambition or avarice or love or hatred as underlying dispositional or inclinational facts about a person, facts that shape from below many or most of a person's actions without appearing as surface disturbances. The inclinations that are related to the passions exist alongside many other inclinations that do not have any connection to the passions at all—for example, the preference for calm situations or lively ones, the inclination to maintain high states of order or to tolerate disorder, the inclination to simplify or to complicate as much as possible. The inclinations or dispositions are a far wider category than the passions. They include many things for which Hume invented the special term "calm passions" and that Kant made into the essence of a rational person: one whose actions always reflect the integration of his inclinations, or one whose choices take into account the sum of his or her inclinations rather than allowing any one inclination to dictate a choice or an action. The inclination that was single and therefore tyrannical Kant thought of as a disease.

From the standpoint of philosophy and literature it is important to see why the episodic, incandescent moment of the occasioned passion—falling in love rather than love, the rage of King Lear rather than the deep background love for him that Cordelia's lifetime of everyday actions demonstrated she felt—must be the central matter, while needing to be kept distinct from the inclinations. It is by means of the vehement states and their causal power that we derive one clear model of what "having an experience" looks like. Literature's reliance on moments of experience, rather than summary, generalization, or long perspectives of time, gives to vehement states an important position as one central matter for literature. This includes the fact that the duration of such states and their consequences, the time span of rage and its immediate consequences, the time span of falling in love and its immediate consequences, of grief and its immediate consequences, happens to match the particular kind of timescale on which literature operates best. Episodes have, for literary or narrative use, only a certain scale, which matches, among other things, the scale of an experience of the outburst, consequences, transformations, and settling into calm of a passion.

Even within the episodic or statelike passions, we might choose to use as our examples, as much of modern philosophy has done, amusing, everyday cases. Or we might use the artificial laboratory setups preferred in emotion research in our modern science of psychology.

We might object to the use of vehement examples in two ways. First, that these are not representative cases; second, that they determine in advance anything we might conclude about the passions on the basis of rare moments and overwhelming, but isolated, experiences.

In Western high culture, the important historical fact remains that the topic of the passions (once we split off the medical tradition from Hippocrates to Galen) was the product of the systematic thought of Aristotle and, to a lesser degree, Plato, using extreme cases from the *Iliad* or from Greek tragedy as core instances. Historically, this cultural tradition—through Stoicism, to the Christianity of Augustine, through the medieval Scholasticism that led Aquinas to divide the passions into his categories of the concupiscent and the irascible—holds the residue and consequences of Aristotle's and Plato's pervasive use of Homer's violent and extreme epic poem. The *Iliad* was the book that educated not only Greek civilization.

A second kind of historical reason lies in the fact that fear, anger, grief, and shame have been the states least shaped by the waves of culture and the passage of time since the point of the first recorded analysis that we have of inner states. They are among the least culturally constructed materials we have. Their stability argues for a certain core of what Hume called, in the title of his book, human nature. Every culture and historical moment erects baroque and intricate structures onto these energies, views them ethically or channels them socially or poetically in different ways, but the core recognizable experience of acute fear appears everywhere and at all times. Darwin used anthropological evidence from every major culture known to him to show similar muscular and facial expressions present within these few extreme states. He also used the facial expressions of the blind and of small infants in an attempt to rule out mere learning. Fear and anger are, for just this reason of unmistakable recognizability, the two subjects of modern neurobiological research into the circuits and brain locations of strong feelings, the biochemical research into the area of the brain known as the amygdala.

A third reason for my focus on vehement states of grief, anger, fear, and a small number of other passions follows from the surprising way this subject of the passions was renewed and given its modern form a century ago, at the moment of the separation of the modern discipline of psychology from philosophy. William James in "What Is an Emotion?" (1884) and in his classic textbook, *The Principles of Psychology*, a decade later, along with Charles Darwin in his *Expression of Emotions* (1873), set the new formal term "emotions" in the location where the word "passions" had been found up to the time of Hume's *Treatise*. Darwin and James were looking at the physical, muscular, circulatory, and above all facial expressions of states. This physiological dimension had been a feature of all descriptions of the passions from the time of Aristotle's *On the Soul*, where the racing of the pulse, trembling, clenched muscles, and pallor were singled out as features of the passions and markers of such spirited states.

In William James and Darwin, emphasis on physical expression, which to James constituted the state of fear or grief pure and simple, and for Darwin was his explicit subject (expression), meant that all description had to be done by means of episodic moments of vehement feeling. That is why Darwin begins with what he terms the "stronger sensations and emotions"—rage and terror. James begins with intense grief and considers only what he calls the "coarser" emotions: grief, fear, rage, and love. The list that began Aristotle's work on the passions twenty-five hundred years earlier in his *Rhetoric* is similar: anger, pity, fear.[15]

Both James and Darwin favored states in which a strong bodily component of the emotion made it unmistakable to an observer. This has important consequences for narrative literature, where, in the absence of analytic attempts to register the purely inner life of those moods and feelings that have no outlet in action or expression, the plane of representation requires action, verbal expression, or describable, visible states of the body. This is also the case in opera, in tragedy, and in contemporary film where, in the absence of analytic description, those visible and half-bodily states define for us the very meaning of being in a state through their unmistakable physical aspects. In modern scientific research, just as in Aristotle, Darwin, and James, the pulse, the rate of breathing, muscular contraction, sweating, and other quantifiable bodily symptoms of a strongly felt emotion are favored for the obvious reason that they give evidence distinct from any report by the subject of what he or she was feeling while seeing the photograph in the experiment. There is, in other words, a clear set of reasons why the literary, philosophical, and scientific characterization of the domain of the passions naturally relies on vehement, episodic states for the marking out of the very idea of passion or, in later vocabulary, emotion.

In Darwin we also return to an important secondary advantage of attention to fear and anger. For Darwin just as for Homer, fear and rage permit the study of a shared domain between humans and animals. In Homer the passions of boars, lions, wolves, horses, and other spirited animals occur as the standard metaphor for intense human states, without any intention to denigrate the states by implying that they represent the "animal side of human nature." The passions track and locate a domain of the highest cultural worth, a domain shared with animals, who also, for example, not only fear and panic, or attack with rage, but mourn their losses. It is by means of the vehement states that what we might call the moral life of animals, their relation to power, to their own will, to their losses and pleasures, occurs in ways humans have always felt confident that they can interpret. Once again, in recent research on fear within modern neuroscience, brain locations and neural paths are tested for humans, baboons, dogs, cats, pigeons, rats, and rabbits.[16]

If less vehement or more nuanced states like nostalgia or falling in love were used, both the arguments about the uniqueness of these states in certain cultures or periods of history and the larger distinction between the human and animal worlds would be one of the implied goals of such an initial choice. Darwin, for example, calls blushing the most human of the expressions. His analysis of self-attention, awareness of one's own body as others might be seeing it, shyness, shame, and modesty in the final chapter of his book makes us see at once his own very Victorian interest in shame as a central, because uniquely human, passion, as well as his claim for blushing as an expression not shared with animals. His neutral word "self-attention" is the ground on which the complex state of self-consciousness within a certain moment of someone else's attention to any part of one's body is defined as the core of the shame experience. Mid-Victorian modesty and sexual shame leave their traces on this final chapter in ways never true in the rest of his book.

Darwin had also begun his series of chapters on specific expressions with a chapter on the crying of human infants, which also, he pointed out, has no animal equivalent. It is with these very striking first and last states, from which animals are excluded, that we enter what now seems, a century later, to be a historically and culturally local world where the wailing of the newborn child and the blush of shame at the moment of awareness that another is noticing one's body, two very Victorian choices, make clear the cost of moving away from the core vehement states—fear, grief, anger, and a few others—that will be my subject. A recent French book by Greimas and Fontanille on the semiotics of the passions examines only avarice and jealousy, a modern, very provincial choice on a par with Darwin's blushing maiden and crying child.[17]

To the historical and biological motives that I have mentioned so far for my focus on the vehement states of fear, anger, grief, and shame, I must add as a final argument the deep puzzle of our literary tradition and its long connection to the vehement passions. In a form like tragedy this is obvious, and the elevated position that we assign to tragedy within the many kinds of literature involves an elevation of the extreme passions as features of any important account of human experience.

We need just such passions as the four at the heart of Homer's *Iliad*—anger, fear, mourning, and wonder—to grasp the mechanisms of a significant number of the greatest works of our literary culture. Shakespeare, who writes at a moment of unusually rich reconsideration of the passions in both literature and philosophy, embraces, in many of his plays, a causality dependent on the unfolding of radical and vehement states. These dramas are defined by the ignition, the unfolding, and the consequences of a vehement state like the jealousy of Othello, the murderous ambition of Macbeth, the rage of Lear, the love of Romeo and Juliet, along with the transformations of those initial vehement passions into equally vehement successor states.

King Lear, which is often taken to be the greatest of Shakespeare's works, and one of the greatest works of modernity, unfolds wrath through fear into mourning, and travels the same path among the passions as the *Iliad*. Herman Melville's *Moby Dick*, the only possible candidate for the title of an American epic, pivots on the wrath of Ahab and comes to rest near the end in a choreography of mourning for Pip, for the lost children of the ship named the *Rachel*, and for the entire world of the now vanished *Pequod* aboard which we, as readers, have lived for the many pages of the novel.

It is good to keep in mind that one alternative to choosing instances from Homer, Shakespeare, Aristotle, and Hume of the kind that I will use throughout this book is to follow the whim of contemporary philosophy in using quirky, odd, low-level examples, a procedure I call "science fiction of the inner life." Here are two examples in the amusing style of recent work on the emotions:

I. "Elisabeth Anscombe once toured America with the following story. A man went to sleep while leisurely making love. He dreamt he was shoveling coal and taking great pleasure in that activity. Then he woke up and discovered what he was really doing. 'Good Heavens,' said the man, 'I was mistaken in the object of my pleasure.' "[18]

2. "Wendy despises Bernie, she thinks for his vulgar musical taste. But really his musical taste has nothing to do with her feelings. The truth is that Bernie's voice, though she has never actually noticed it, reminds her of her hated grandmother, and that is what arouses her feelings of contempt."[19]

We note the heavy shadow of Freud in these words, "But really" and "The truth is" and "although she has never actually noticed it," but of course the amateur psychoanalyst, winking at the reader behind Wendy's back, did notice what it was really all about and what it had "nothing to do with." The contamination of the topic of the passions by this kind of strange, everyday, but theory-laden material is one small, further reason to turn back to the anger of Achilles, the grief at the death of Cordelia in *King Lear*, the fear in the moment of threatened death in Tolstoy, and the wonder of Dante in the *Paradiso*, or the state of any reader being told by Homer about the shield of Achilles in the eighteenth book of the *Iliad*.

Paths among
the Passions

Ever since the work of Aristotle, the passions have been arranged and discussed systematically. Let me mention a few important features. First, pairs of passions are regarded as opposites. Aristotle described the passions as "anger, pity, fear and the like with their opposites."[1] Darwin listed opposition as one of the three structural features of emotions. The discovery of opposites is one preoccupation of earlier philosophical work on the passions. Love and hatred form one common pair; distress and pleasure, another. But even though these four terms play an enormous part in the history of the passions, they are not quite what was meant by passions, as Aristotle's list of "anger, pity, fear and the like" makes clear. Around these four terms, love and hatred, pain and pleasure, which are certainly essential terms for experience, a major historical disorder was built into the study of the passions by Stoicism, one that lasted through the seventeenth century, as did the category of desire as a passion. Desire and the appetites had been for Plato a third, distinct part of the soul, not one part of the passions. Neither pain nor pleasure is a passion. Yet it was the pairs love-hatred, pain-pleasure, distress-delight that were the central examples of opposition, leading to the search for and listing of ever less convincing pair relations.

For Descartes, the first of his passions, wonder, has no opposite because it amounts to the energy by which we are interested in something new and attentive to it. Not to feel this pleasurable interest is not to be aware of something as new or surprising, rather than to notice it in some other way, since wonder is the means by which we single out, so to speak, the figure from the ground.[2] Without wonder and attention, we have neither figure nor ground. Disagreeing with Descartes, Spinoza redefined wonder as a kind of stalling of the mind in front of something in which the novelty is so striking that it does not lead to any association that would bring the mind to connect it and move back and forth from one object to the other. Since for Spinoza the mind is defined by its motion from idea to idea or from sensation to sensation, wonder stalls the mind in a defective way. He then claims that there is an opposite passion to wonder, contempt, the state in which we think so little of an object that the mind, in constant motion, races away from it in any possible direction, preferring any association that might capture our attention away from the original contemptible object itself.[3] Wonder and contempt are as a result opposite or paired passions for Spinoza, but not for Descartes.

This example of how the search for opposites works brings out the ingenuity and arbitrariness of much of this work. Love is commonly the opposite of hate, pity of malice, fear of hope. For the Stoics the opposite of fear was not hope but desire. Attraction, we might agree, is the opposite of aversion. But even with these common and central cases it is important to ask whether these states really do have opposites when we examine the experience itself. Is there an opposite state to anger? or to fear? There are certainly states that lead to opposite kinds of actions. If anger is the desire to injure someone, then benevolence might be called the opposite in that it involves the desire to benefit someone. If fear is the expectation of some future harm or injury, then hope, the expectation of some future good, might seem to be its opposite. The Stoic system of the passions made opposites of fear and desire because both attend to a future experience of an object, the one with the expectation of pleasure, the other with the expectation of suffering or distress.

Once outside the frame of these acts of definition, any concrete experience of anger seems to have little to do with concrete experiences of benevolence. Fear, especially in its vehement form, seems to have little similarity to hope as a state or to desire as a state. Pride and shame are commonly called structural opposites, but extreme shame works along many dimensions other than those of pride.

What would it mean to assert that there is an opposite to grief and mourning? The experience of the death of someone loved and central in one's life does not have an opposite situation, unless it would be the advent of a new person into the sphere of best-loved parts of one's life: joy at the birth of a child, or the joy felt when one finds oneself falling in love. Either falling in love or giving birth to a child does more than add just one new fact; it transfigures the whole intimate world in every way. To that extent it can *seem* structurally opposite to the death of a beloved child, of a parent, or of one's lover. It also seems clear to me that in no way should what we feel when we are in the state of mourning or grief be seen as an experience related to, let alone opposite to, the experience of falling in love or feeling delirious joy at the birth of a child. Only my intellectual description made this opposition momentarily plausible. The three intense experiences are just different, unique experiences, and we supply an intellectual relation among them only to create the possibility of calling them opposites. I have invented this instance to point out that even in places where no opposition has been classically asserted, we can generate one, even a superficially convincing one. But, in experience, mourning or grief has no opposite.

Notice that it is in fact the situation that can have an opposite, not the passion itself. Falling in love and mourning are not in their physical or emotional details related to one another at all, any more than wonder and contempt are. Seeing a snarling dog on the path suddenly in front of me and seeing in the same place an old friend I have not seen for years can be called opposite situations because I draw back in aversion and fear from the snarling dog or walk quickly forward smiling toward my friend. But are the states opposite in any way if we strip away these situational features of shrinking back versus moving eagerly forward? Opposites have been designated through the alteration of one feature within the set of features of a situation already carefully designed to be schematic. Altering some other feature while keeping this one unchanged lets us imagine some other opposite. Spinoza's pairing of wonder and contempt reverses one feature; Descartes's claim that there is no opposite to wonder focuses our attention on some other key feature of the overall case.

Anger, pity, fear, grief, and shame, considered in their vehement forms, are best seen as isolated, freestanding states, as are, to take examples from outside the passions, appetite, hunger, and the need for sleep. Anger, fear, or grief does not seem inherently to be half of some imagined pair. In the same way clouds are not opposite to stones, or trees to the sheep beneath the trees. Opposition and contrast are artifacts of our habits of thinking by twos. We might notice here the advantage of classifications with three or more terms, like our common division into animal, vegetable, and mineral. Here we manage to avoid pair relations and the habits that opposition traps us into. If we always grouped by fives or threes, we would force out a set of bad moves that follow from naming only two things in each grouping.

Greed or avarice, we might claim, is situationally opposite to the wasteful spending of money, but the passion of avarice does not actually have some opposite inner state called spendthrift or wastrel. What really could be the opposite of jealousy? or of ambition? It is crucial, I think, to preserve the commonsense idea present in Descartes's point about wonder. The true alternative to jealousy is not to be in any impassioned state; that is, to be without feelings of jealousy. The alternative to fear is not to feel fear in a given situation. The same is true of anger or grief. When we think of a friend consumed with ambition, what we feel is what it is like to be without ambition of that vehement kind, rather than to feel some other passion. That the passions have opposite passions is a different matter from the far more accurate idea that passions have as their opposite not being impassioned while being in the same circumstances, as two men facing a firing squad might be, the one shaking with fear, the other without fear.

Systems of Primary
and Secondary Passions

A list of opposites is one common feature of the many systematic descriptions of the passions from Aristotle to Darwin. A division into primary and secondary, into simple and compounded passions makes up a second feature. There exists almost a chemistry of the passions, where the elements are mixed and blended into compounds. Descartes and Spinoza, Thomas Aquinas, and Hume are profound and brilliant masters of the creation of matrixlike relations among sets and groupings of the passions. Spinoza arranges forty-eight passions, Descartes somewhat fewer; Aquinas arrays thirteen central passions, and for Darwin eight groupings of emotions break down into approximately forty distinct and definable states of arousal. With Hume we feel the background influence of Newtonian thinking. Both the color theory with its blendings and primary colors—blue and red making purple, yellow plus blue making green—and the composition of forces in motion serve as models for how the energies of the inner world are compounded into nuanced and interrelated families of states. The excessive number of these metaphors—families, compounds, colors, vectors of forces in motion—are themselves the sign of improvisation and the absence of a clear causal notion at the heart of such descriptions.

The two features of opposition and large-scale systematic structuring might be thought of as a natural inheritance from Aristotle and his secondary elaboration in Stoicism and Scholasticism, and the fact that modernity in the seventeenth century continued drawing profoundly on these three earlier sources in the subject of the passions. Descartes claimed to break with all earlier writers on this subject, but in his descriptions, definitions, and choices for the forty-four individual passions he drew on the Spanish Scholastic theologians, especially Suarez, who drew on Aquinas, who drew on Aristotle. No topic in our culture shows such persistence and self-identity even in passing through the phase of Christian theology as the account of the passions of the soul from the time of Homer, Plato, and Aristotle to the edge of modernity with Descartes, Spinoza, Hobbes, and Hume, and then continuing in the later reprise of this work in Darwin and modern scientific psychology.

Passions That Block Passions

Aristotle is also the source of the third and most important dynamic feature of systematic work on the passions, because it was Aristotle who first spoke of passions acting to block other passions. An angry man, he pointed out, does not feel fear. Anger blocks fear.[4] We often see in Homer's *Iliad* that the leaders goad, insult, or create anger in the fighters so that something stronger than fear will block fear or make it less likely. This important feature by which the passions can be controlled by preemption has been elaborated in an extraordinary way by Albert Hirschman in his classic study of thirty years ago, *The Passions and the Interests*. Political society, Hirschman observes, has a deep interest in becoming, first and foremost, an economy, because avarice is the single one of the passions that requires conditions that block out the interruptive, short-term episodes of anger, grief, falling in love, or any other disruption of the smooth unfolding of the predictable future. Falling in love, mourning for the death of a loved one, and being enraged by anger to the point of seeking vengeance are vehement, all-engrossing matters that push aside the everyday attention to the present and the future on which our shared world of everyday work and economic life depends. Episodes of passion within the individual resemble the state of war or a natural disaster in public life. Normal life is suspended for a time, and the pursuit of individual and common interests is set aside. Hirschman has described how our modern political life that identifies each person or group with his, her, or their interests, rather than with passions, permits a brushing aside of the passions and their disruptive effect in social life, while ultimately honoring the one remaining passion of avarice with its link to a stable world of effort.[5]

By its orientation to the long- and middle-term future, avarice also blocks structurally the entire set of passions that give priority to the past: anger, shame, regret, and mourning. Hirschman's is the single most important account since that of Hume, who, alone among modern philosophers, pressed forward the analysis of what we might call the metaconditions of the passions, the structural features responsible for the fact that the passions are an energy system in which specific factors enable and shape that dynamic activity.

Preemption or the blocking relation is at the heart of that dynamic. In his short essay "Of Fear," Montaigne tells an anecdote that captures the heart of preemption and delay. "The thing I fear most is fear," Montaigne writes, and then goes on to say,

> Moreover, it exceeds all other disorders in intensity. What anger could be more bitter and more just than that of Pompey's friends, who were in his ship, spectators of ... [the treacherous murder of Pompey by one of his old centurions as he sought refuge in Egypt]? Yet their fear of the Egyptian sails, which were beginning to approach them, stifled this feeling, so that commentators have noted that they did nothing but spur the sailors to make haste and escape by plying their oars; until, having arrived at Tyre, free from fear, they had a chance to turn their thoughts to the loss they had just suffered and to give free rein to the lamentations and tears that this other stronger passion had suspended.[6]

Both their anger at the murderers of Pompey and their mourning for him are preempted by terror of the enemy, until, free of fear, the strong feelings that were not even felt to have been brushed aside now are free to appear. Blocking is the single most important feature of the dynamic of the passions. It alone has survived our suspicions about earlier attempts to order the passions by, first of all, pairing elements of our list as opposites—opposition; second, defining a set of primary passions from which all others are compounded—reduction. The dynamic of preemption survives where enumeration, opposition, and reduction recede from view.

Paths among the Passions

One final ordering within the passions, the dynamic relation between certain states that succeed one another, has had significant importance for narration, for the law, and for aesthetics. I call this the paths among the passions.

One of the great mysteries is that only certain paths link one state of vehemence to another. From fear we often pass to an intense feeling of shame once the fear has been dispelled, but rarely do we pass from shame to fear. Jealousy, reaching a pitch of vehemence, transposes into rage. Ambition, as we see it, for example, in Lady Macbeth, redesigns itself as guilt while carrying over the same murderousness, but now directed at herself. On the other hand, guilt seldom wakes up to find itself ambition. As La Rochefoucauld put it, many pass from love to ambition, but none in the other direction.[7]

Of these trajectories among the passions the most interesting and at the same time most mysterious is the path that leads from wrath to mourning. Homer's *Iliad* and Shakespeare's *King Lear* are both constructed around an armature where anger, shattered by the death of Patroclos or Cordelia, is reassembled into grief with all intensity preserved, but sublimated into sorrow. Vengeance and mourning preserve while redeploying a common sum of inner excitation, solitude, and prolonged focus on a single object that thins out or cancels any diffuse investment in the rest of the world.

To progress from killing to mourning, from rage to grief, is, at first glance, an obvious and humane sequence. The descent from rage to regret and sorrow, from causing death to comprehending—in mourning—the full reality of death, from the most volcanic of states to the most immobilized, all have about them, as a path, a seeming naturalness resembling that linking exertion and exhaustion. But this explanation is wrong (since all intensity is preserved) and misleads us about what is at stake in these fixed passages.

Within literature rooted in the passions such paths from state to state control the unfolding of the work as a whole. Almost alchemical in their suddenness, and motivated from without, the metamorphosis of rage into grief or ambition into guilt lies at the heart of works constructed around the passions. These transformations of energy operate as plot does in the literature of action or as choice and growth do in the literature of character. In Shakespeare's *Winter's Tale* the ever-changing vehemence is located in King Leontes and passes from jealousy to rage, from rage to remorse, from remorse to mourning, and, finally, from mourning to wonder. What we see of the life history of the king records him as the custodian of a fixed quantity of vehemence that he invests and reinvests, now in rage, now in guilt, now in wonder, until he reaches a serenity that coincides with the final phase of his life.

The literature of the passions tells the life history of a quantity of energy that appears first as one state of vehemence, then, redesigned, as another, until a finality is reached that is best summed up by the final line of Milton's *Samson Agonistes*, "Calm of mind, all passion spent." The state of serenity, peaceful even to the point of exhaustion, that ends the *Iliad, Oedipus Rex, King Lear, Moby Dick,* and *Wuthering Heights,* to list just a few of the works of the literature of the passions, is a sign that the inner logic of the work has been constructed around the excitation, transformation, and final exhaustion of a state of vehemence, but one that traverses a complex series of distinct states at the same high level of energy and investment.

We can at once see why the large summarizing episodes of this path—from energy to exhaustion—could not be reversible: no mystery lies here; nothing needs to be explained. But why within the long episode of exertion should some but not other combinations be possible, and possible in one direction only? Why should it be that locally we move only from fear to shame or from anger to mourning and not in the reverse direction? One part of the answer might be that there is some single state toward which all others tend. Hume felt that he could show that many states have a tendency to degenerate into an unsettled state of fear because the nature of the mind involves motion from idea to associated idea, and because it is commonly uncertainty that sets the mind in motion from state to state and from object to object.

With equal plausibility it might be argued that the aftermath of many states of passion is a feeling of embarrassment or shame, once the social world is once again noticed. The general decline into fear or into shame would then be intrinsic to the mechanism of the passions themselves. But it is not any universal mechanism of this kind that leads jealousy to spill over into rage or ambition into guilt. Nonetheless, certain routes of this kind have an almost uncanny predictability within experience.

Paths and Clustered States

There exists a second kind of path among groups of passions, not temporal but spatial. In this case the path traces out a cluster of alternative responses to the same circumstances or events when those events are seen from different perspectives.

Aristotle, as we all know, defined tragedy as uniquely concerned with the passions of fear and pity. Less well known are his keen but laconic remarks about how they are related. We feel pity, he claimed, when some evil happens to another that if it were about to happen to ourselves would cause us to feel fear. But if the evil is about to happen to one we love, someone close to us, we feel fear, just as we would if it were happening to ourselves.[8] Whether we find ourselves feeling fear or pity about an event illuminates or even reveals to us the closeness of the victim, the intimacy of our relation to him or to her. How the passions illuminate or disclose differences within our world that could not be known to us by any other means will be a central concern throughout this book.

Past a certain point of extreme evil we feel more than fear. We feel a shudder of terror, as Aristotle calls it in the *Poetics*.[9] Importantly, we might feel this even about events happening to a stranger. I will discuss this complex of ideas in detail in chapter 8. I want to mention it briefly here only to set up the following larger picture.

Since Aristotle also identified comedy with harmless evil, we can see that he was aware of the following scale of mounting gravity. If I were to see a man, his arms loaded with packages, sliding on an icy street, twisting, squirming, dropping now one, now another of his packages, gliding into poles, losing his hat, tripping over passing dogs, but never injuring himself, I would be laughing at his harmless troubles just as I do, let's say, when I watch the film of a brilliant routine by Charlie Chaplin. If on the same icy street I see my eighty-year-old neighbor fall and break her hip, I feel pity and sympathy for her. If I think of her slim chances of complete recovery, I feel fear for her when I think how she will manage living alone in her apartment. This is no longer a harmless evil.

Now, if I were to read of a man who fell on the ice, broke his hip, went to a hospital, became crippled because of delicate but failed surgery, lost his job, drove his family into destitution, lost his home when the mortgage was foreclosed, and, on the day of foreclosure, barricaded himself and his family in their house and set fire to it, creating a scene in which he and his family died screaming, while police, fire departments, and television crews were kept at bay outside by the bullets he continued firing until his death and the death of all his family, then this cascading and, finally, monstrous story, which also begins with an icy street and a slip on the ice, produces a shudder of terror, not just sympathy, pity, or ordinary concern and fear for the future.

The scale that I have evoked here extends from comedy and laughter at harmless evils, evils without consequence, to evils that have consequences on a familiar scale where we feel pity, sympathy, and fear, to, finally, the shudder of terror we feel at the larger unraveling of the world in cascading consequences, unique in their severity and finality, and so disproportionate to the initial cause that the subsequent events terrify us about causality itself. Causality is not always proportional, predictable, and finite in its unfolding. Comedy, at the other extreme from monstrous, cascading evil consequences, delights us by the fact that causality has exceptions where harms do not happen even where they seemed likely. This problem about causality, its normal workings and the exceptions at either extreme, gives us the deeper sense of Aristotle's linked definitions of comedy and tragedy. Most of the time the drunk driver swerves all over the road but hurts no one.

This scale relating laughter to pity to fear to the shudder of terror is a profound path among the passions, above all for our understanding of a spectator's relation to events seen in daily life, or, more crucially in society, for the experience of a juror in a legal proceeding, or for the aesthetic experience that occurs as we watch or read a work of narrative art.

The paths among the passions and the preemptive relation between certain passions are two permanent dynamic achievements of the fact that the philosophical and literary treatment of the passions did not define or describe passions one at a time in isolation, as is done in the modern treatment of moods. Philosophers and writers searched instead for systematic interconnectedness, oppositions, matrices, transformations, and compoundings that would organize the inner world of the soul in a profound, scientific manner.

THREE

Thoroughness

Wherever we look at the language for our inner states, we find the creation of, first, a central passion that serves as a template for all others; then, second, a surrounding circle of the "normal"; and, finally, a zone of the puzzling, the defective, the excluded. When Hume, for example, dropped the term "the passions," which he had used in the central part of his *Treatise of Human Nature*, and turned to the term "the moral sentiments" for his later essays, he was breaking free of a vocabulary with too many hostages built in. Now that it was a question of the moral sentiments rather than the passions, Hume found himself free to center his account on questions about the sentiment of self-preservation, the limits of egoism, and the moral possibility of sympathy. The core of Hume's new design was the term that Spinoza and, earlier, the Stoics had made the central inner motive of our actions, *perseverare*, or self-preservation. The sentiments, in other words, do not rename the set of problems posed by earlier discussions of the passions; rather, they install an entirely new geography of the self around self-love, sympathy for others, and the motives of the active will in its endeavor to continue existing. The generalized version of Darwinism, the most important scientific orthodoxy at the end of the twentieth century, assigns the drive to preservation to the species or to the genome rather than to the individual. It is no longer self-preservation, since the life or death of one or another individual has little to do with the survival of the species or of the genome, but the central energy driving all action remains the same: preservation through time. With Darwinism the issue of survival has been divorced from any account of the passions because only on an individual, rather than a species, level can there be anything like passions.

The feelings, the affections, the sentiments, and the passions are not alternative ways of talking about the same matters but language used in the service of quite distinct politics of the inner life. They are terms that do not describe what unchangeably is. Instead they participate in the communal act of installing and defending one or another design within psychological life. They are, we might say, legislative vocabularies. Energies are conscripted; free or adjacent states become bound. The two most dramatic of these legislative orderings of the inner life are the traditional heroic life, with its center in courage and honor (or, to return to Plato's vocabulary, spirit and anger), and the post-Rousseau life of the feelings, with its center in romantic love and the experience of nature. Either of these two ethical designs brings about a commandeering of the resources of the inner life around a few experiences, as does the modern Darwinian account.

The most significant historical redesigns of inner life have taken place within modernity around the vocabulary of emotions, feelings, and moods. What Lucretius describes in the famous passage that opens book 2 of *De rerum natura* is a perfect example of a feeling rather than a passion: "It is sweet, when on the great sea the winds trouble its waters, to behold from land another's deep distress; not that it is a pleasure and delight that any should be afflicted, but because it is sweet to see from what evils you are yourself exempt."[1] This is a classic description of the pleasure we sometimes take in spite of the distress of others, a kind of contrary state to pity, in which we feel the fact of our exemption more strongly than we feel the suffering of others.

Lucretius's description leads, naturally, to a celebration of contemplation rather than passion. The mixed nature of the state is implied by the onlooker's participation and exemption. He both is and is not there. He stands both inside and outside the experience. This mixed condition is the basic mark of thought. At the same time, to imagine oneself in another state while enjoying the state that one is in as a result of that act of imagination points to a distinction between the self and its states, even within the moment of emotion. And it is this distinction that is at the heart of the idea of the state that we call "feeling."

Anger and the other vehement passions—fear, shame, grief, and wonder—provide the most telling experiences that we commonly have of self-identical being, of undivided being. In modern culture our paradigmatic character, Shakespeare's Hamlet, is by contrast the best example of the modern inability to be undivided. One meaning of vehemence is the capacity to be thoroughly and completely in a given state, whether that state be fear or grief, anger or love. Hamlet's irony, his layers of feeling, his self-distance, his afterthoughts and reversals are all features of a psychology in which the self is no longer self-identical. It is no longer characterized by what we might call thoroughness. It is angry, but able to see the other side of the matter; in love, but disgusted with love; committed to vengeance, but unable to believe completely in what it is about to do.

The descriptions of the self that we find in the Stoicism of Epictetus and Marcus Aurelius were the first to make certain forms of nonidentity and inner distance, along with the existence of well-defined inner partitions within the self, not only possible but desirable. Even within personal grief the task set by Stoicism is to reflect actively against the grain of one's passion until it is neutralized. What Lucretius has described is a kind of training experience for the feeling of Stoic distance.

A significant and revealing way of speaking, associated with the word "feeling," traps these features of the feelings that Lucretius's example has introduced. When we think in terms of the word "feeling," we find that the content of this general state has moved off center. We speak of an "angry feeling" or of a "feeling of anger." Similarly, we refer to a "feeling of homesickness" or a "sad feeling," "a feeling of loneliness" or "a feeling of guilt." The content of the

state has moved to the adjectival position or into a modifying preposi-
tional phrase signaled by the word "of." The word "feeling," standing
alone, is a blank. Only in combination does it take on content: "a
feeling of pity," "strong feelings," "ambivalent feelings," even "a feeling of indifference." When, in contrast, we use the vocabulary of the
passions, such specific passions as grief, anger, hope, and fear are
states, and they are represented by nouns.

The personality is not extinguished by "ambivalent feelings" or
"jealous feelings." Just the reverse: it is present as any owner is present when surrounded by his varied possessions. The vocabulary of
the feelings creates a grammatical foreground and background by
positioning the actual state as a modifying adjective or as the object
of the preposition "of." In the foreground occurs the psychological
personality—the "self," as we often say—and in the background,
the temporary state of that self. In the vocabulary and grammar of
the "feelings" we see a mechanism for a controlled fading-out of
the passions, a subordination of them to the self that in earlier
vocabularies they had flooded and eclipsed. Still, in the redundant
formula "a feeling of pity" or a "happy feeling" the claim is retained
that the great variety of states are not substantially different from
one another but are variations of a common material. This is a feature
that is grammatically secured or lexically secured. It makes explicit
the common substance that all philosophies of the passions assert
without being able to impose on language itself, because within language the diverse words—anger, fear, hope—insist on absolute
uniqueness.

Unlike the feelings, the affections, or the emotions, the passions
are best described as thorough. They do not make up one part of a
state of mind or a situation. Impassioned states seem to drive out
every other form of attention or state of being. Someone in a rage is
not also at the same time noticing the bright snow outside or aware
that his chair is uncomfortable. The passions are what we could call
monarchical states of being.

It follows from this that the passions are at the farthest remove from irony; they are its diametric opposite. Irony, and all forms of double consciousness, for which a sense of humor about oneself and one's actions would be the most common case, define by way of contrast the single-mindedness of the passions. The passions are humorless.

The passions are thorough in a second way. They involve the most complete identification of the self with its momentary state. The angry man forgets that he has not always been angry with this person, that he will someday be beyond anger, and that there are aspects of himself forgotten by him in the vehemence of his anger. In mourning or fear or wonder the rest of the self seems not only absent but unbelievable. Decisions are made and steps are taken as though this and only this state were the self itself. This aspect of thoroughness opposes the passions to our standard modern idea of the prudential self, which weighs the near and long-term future, balances the full range of desires and obligations, and integrates the many inclinations into the actions of any one moment. The unique grip of the present moment and the present vehement state in its thoroughness also undoes the very meaning of that modern notion of the self first found in Locke, where my integrated memory of my own earlier states makes up my identity in my own reflections.[2] The relation of any present moment to this remembered anthology of past states is, like the prudential relation to the future, a strong anchoring device against any state that could be called thorough.

When we think of Achilles' anger, Othello's jealousy, or the rage of King Lear, we can see that so thoroughly does each of these characters enact the passion he finds himself in that whatever else there is of the self is liquidated. To use a term from the philosophy of Stanley Cavell, we could say that it is in the moment of repudiating the hold of the ordinary and the everyday that an impassioned state begins.[3] Mourning for a loved one begins with the suspension of the ordinary work and activity of individual and family life. Fear stops cold all other everyday concerns. People run from a house on fire without stopping to put on their clothes.

When we move to the other, more modern designs for the inner life, we can see that the emotions and the feelings give an account of our common states that seems, at heart, receptive to ambivalence. I can both like and not like someone at the same time; both respect and not respect someone; both feel sorry and secretly enjoy another's difficulty. The very term "emotions" in its modern usage seems to imply that in their natural state the emotions are moderate, even reasonable, and that extreme examples (vehement feelings) need to be explained as exceptional, even unnatural. Emotions sustain daily life; the passions break it off. A passion works the way wartime does, or a great flood, or a terrible crime in a neighborhood, or a death in the family. Stories like those of Achilles, King Lear, and Othello are initiated by a moment in which anger or jealousy breaks off ordinary life and its variable conditions (the everyday) and makes impossible any later recovery of ordinary life and its multiple interests and relations.

The very essence of the emotions lies in their variability and in their location in daily life. Someone whose emotions are extreme we regard as out of control. He needs to learn to "control" his emotions. Extremity or fixity of emotions suggests to us the need for therapy. Intense, prolonged mourning or a sense of rage over an injury that is all-preoccupying leads us to think in terms of the socialization of the condition. "You need help," we say. By help we mean that you need to learn to hear a dispassionate, external, reasonable account of your condition and then attempt to come to feel that way yourself. In our modern psychology, we also suspect that rage is often displaced from its "true" biographical target. Therapeutic cultures are always cultures of suspicion, because they begin by assuming that we can never be the authoritative tellers of our own life story.

The emotions or feelings are categories for the absolute priority of the everyday world, as all middle-class categories are. That is their strength. Such categories guard the ordinary and preserve its varied claims. They are the democratized, mixed conditions of an inner life that is, at the same time, tolerant of others and their quite different inner lives. To be tolerant of the feelings of others is as essential a feature of what we mean by the feelings or the emotions as is their moderate strength. The passions are, by contrast, at bottom, intolerant of the state of others and even of the consequences for others of the passion felt by the self.

The vehement passions reinstall an absolute priority of the self, with its claim to be different from and prior to others both in the claims of its will and in its account of the world. The passions are the states of a king in a world in which all others are merely subjects. Where we speak of the passions, we are, in political vocabulary, re-creating a monarchical world in which there is only one real self. This is also the world of monotheism. There is only one will, and that is the will of God. Such a God is more commonly a God of wrath than a God of reason. God creates and destroys, because these are, finally, the only two acts of the will.

The emotions or feelings, in their rather natural alliance with moderation and tolerance and in their proximity to ambivalence, irony, and mixed states of many different kinds, picture for us an inner life compatible with the hold of daily or ordinary life within the middle-class world. Extreme and fixed states are one definition, within this middle-class world, of insanity. The mad become, in a secular, nonheroic world, the best image of what it means to live in a world of one and only one person. The mad, we could say from our modern perspective, occupy the place once held by kings and gods. Whether or not Shakespeare's Othello, Macbeth, Lear, and Leontes are mad rather than vehement or impassioned is one of the lines that our new world of emotions and feelings must attempt to draw somewhere, and to think about, but in this question of madness, we define a problem that occurred in a different guise to the Renaissance. To be insane and especially to be formally judged insane is, in the first instance, the judicial category that cancels the legitimacy of all acts of the will, all thoughts, perceptions, and passions. Our modern readiness to use the category of insanity cancels large sections of the territory that used to belong to the passions just as effectively as the modern notion of irony does. The modern reliance on ambivalence and tolerance achieves the same result.

In combination, the political term "insanity," the temperamental stance of irony, the civic virtue of tolerance, and the psychological conviction that most deep feelings are marked by ambivalence act together to police so successfully the borders of ordinary life within modern consciousness that the passions are not merely excluded; they appear quaint and archaic. This combination of features explains one reason why the passions are no longer our vocabulary of inner life. From the opposite direction, these four terms—insanity, irony, tolerance, ambivalence—stake out the deeper meaning of thoroughness as a central feature of the vehement passions, because we can extrapolate from just these four terms exactly what thoroughness must have included.

The passions are located in the space that a civilization leaves open between its concept of insanity and its concept of irony. The passions occupy that space between no state (the condition of insanity) and two or more states (the condition of irony or ambivalence). The passions describe the fact of being in one and only one state: fear, grief, anger, wonder, delight, jealousy, shame. These states occupy the full self as far as the self can see. They install a single reality in its state of highest energy. They single out my own self to me in an absolute way over against all others. There are no other claims: none from the side of other people (the issue of tolerance); none from what the self might remember itself to have been or to have felt previously (the identity of the self as a construct of the memory rather than as an immediate intuition).

Nor is there any future self that is weighed against the present. There is nothing held in reserve. Along with the future, the calculating self that holds as much as possible in reserve, open, uncommitted to the gamble of the moment, vanishes. The concern in Hume with the moral sentiment of prudence installs this cautious self that keeps the future always in mind. Prudence, like Aristotle's moderation, is one of those revealing technologies of the inner life that are the photographic negative of those very passions which they are designed to master. In the case of Hume's prudence what we see, by negation, is the thoroughness, the way of living the present state as if no change could ever take place. We also see a perspective in which no other residue of the self counts.

States and Opposed States

To see the consequences of the idea of thoroughness, we can usefully consider the larger relation between two or more states of any kind, between states and substances, and between two or more substances. Since the clear distinction between passions and states became the turning point for a Stoic definition of character and, collaterally, for the Stoic control over the passions, the best entry point into the distinction between the self and any one state of passion lies in the larger question of substance and states. A burning tree is not a certain kind of tree, like an oak or a pine; rather it is a state of the tree. A dying horse, a collapsing wall, a running deer, an angry man are each momentary states of an underlying substance. Shakespearean tragedy could be described as based on situations within personality in which substance and state are each present to so great an extent that either might seem about to eclipse the other, while, miraculously, the tension between the two is sustained. What Leontes was before his jealousy, or what Lady Macbeth might be outside her states of murderous ambition or self-murdering guilt; how Lear can be distinct from his wrath; or what remains intact, but separate, of the Othello we see possessed by jealousy, or Miranda under the spell of her wonder, we cannot precisely say. The power of states lies in a situational flooding of the entire terrain of the personality in which it is both altered from end to end and, paradoxically, expressed most completely for the first time.

The Stoic assault on the passions served to make it possible to imagine a conception of human nature only partially present in any one of its states, even the state of dying. Stoic character, or the ideal of the Reasonable Man, as Marcus Aurelius described him, displays to us the essence of that new norm of character.[4] The reasonable man of the Stoics holds himself always partly in reserve. Such a self overlaps with its situations while remembering that it is distinct from them. It seeks to return to itself and agrees to participate only grudgingly in its own states. The passions are only one sector of the states of the self. Other states, such as health or the various states of sickness, are distinct from the passions while sharing the thoroughness that is one of the most important features of the passions. The goal of Stoic practice was also to install an independence from each and every state similar to the distinction that even those who are not Stoics commonly maintain in the categories of sickness and health, where we commonly fight to hold on to a sense of ourselves prior to and distinct from the particular sickness we are, for a time, conquered by.

By erecting a notion of character that is mainly violated by states of variability, the Stoics could imagine immunity to situations as one of the highest ethical goals. One empirically accurate claim in Stoicism rests on the fact that in any given situation we can remember our self as something distinct from the particular state. We can wait to regain that self on the other side of this momentary situation. In sickness this is a common thing to do. This remembered self might be called an inexpressible self, since it contains a fullness only one part of which can be realized in any local situation, no matter how complex or intense. Such a full self, which cannot be known by anyone else, implies a radical privacy. Although I cannot realize this self in any one state or at any one time, I can, and only I can, while within whatever partial embodiment of myself that this or that situation makes possible, reserve part of my energy to remember my own full self and maintain an open line of relation to myself through memory and imagination focused away from my current state.

The invisibility of such a self follows automatically. What is enacted about myself in any one situation or elicited by any one set of events, and therefore becomes visible in the world, is not equivalent to this remembered fullness. In fact it is the opposite. The inexpressive Stoic surface denies the bystander the expression of the partial self because under no condition could it make visible the full self. The enraged face, the sobs of grief, the surprise of wonder are deleted from the surface.

What this description of Stoic reserve and privacy makes clear at the same time is the opposite case: the Homeric and Shakespearean relation of states to substances and its relative indifference to the deeper lines of character. A radical priority is assigned to states. When used to define and express the substance of the self, the vehement states—anger, wonder, ambition, jealousy, shame, pity, or fear—draw on an essentially Greek and especially Homeric theory of substance and struggle, or, as the Greeks called it, *agon*.

It is a striking detail of this theory that if there were only one substance in the universe, it could never be known. Substances mutually make each other known, not only because of their differences but because of moments of conflict. It is at the meeting point where combat takes place and mutual destruction is possible that each becomes for the first time visible as what, in itself, it is. A large rock is one substance, the water of the sea another. At the shoreline where the sea pounds against the rock, the rock registers in its shape nothing but the consequences of thousands of years of waves cutting into it, even as each individual wave was, in turn, stopped and broken by the rock's resistance. The sound of their collision makes each substance known, and it does so because each is now set into a state. The shattering wave, the pounded rock make visible on each side the nature of sea and rock, but they do so at the very moment that each of the two is situationally flooded from without by the differences that occur as each limits the other.

By these differences we can see in nature something parallel to the human will, which extends out, appropriates, meets obstacles, and is finally given limits. We might say that the will is a psychological and human version of what is a basic fact of all substances. This would be Spinoza's description of what he called *conatus*—endeavor.[5] The collision of the will with its limits, which lies at the heart of anger and grief, can, in this wider frame, be seen as the situational way that we come to know substances in a world that is not continuous or harmonized; that is, a world that is not, from end to end, the same ordered whole. A substance encounters difference only in being blocked or impeded. Where it is a human being that we are describing, the moment of discovering difference—that the will cannot project out without undergoing change or limitation—is what triggers the condition of becoming an impassioned will.

At the very heart of the possibility of making visible is the act of destruction. A ship at sea, breaking up or not breaking up in a storm, is locked into a limiting state that at once makes its nature apparent while at the same time doing so on the ground of its possible immi-nent destruction. Every physical detail of the ship was designed to survive at sea, to float, to outlast salt and waves of a certain height and intensity. The energies of the storm test on both sides the strength of the sea and the strength of the ship in a situation that had been imagined in advance in the very choice of wood, the thickness of spars, the number of crew members, and the designed relation of length to width to weight in the ship itself. What is designed in the ship when it is first built is nothing other than the imagination of the conditions under which it might be destroyed.

Limitation, or what I will later call the humiliation of the will, can now be stated as the second decisive component of the vehemence of the impassioned states. Along with thoroughness, limitation is a precondition of the passions, distinguishing them from the emotions, feelings, or moods—from, in fact, the entire range of vocabularies favored in modernity.

FOUR

Privacy, Radical
Singularity

Central, incontestable details of vehement states arise from the one fact about the passions that most interested Darwin and William James, the physical component visible to any observer and measurable by scientists in pulse rates; in changes in muscle tension, posture, and gesture; in trembling, blushing, and smiling—or audible in the shouts of rage or the sobbing of sorrow. The passions are deeply physical and deeply mental phenomena. They make it impossible to draw a clear line within experience that would let us place corporeal events on one side and mental events on the other. Aristotle's small book *On the Soul* was the first complex account of this interpenetration of the physical and psychical aspects conspicuous in the passions, but not necessarily in those more subtle domains that we now call the moods, feelings, or emotions.

Those like Plato, Lucretius, or Descartes for whom the unity of the body and the soul must occur *as an experience* find that experience in moments of passion. Lucretius, for example, in the third book of *De rerum natura* writes:

Now I assert that the mind and the soul are kept together in close union and make up a single nature . . . , when some part of us, the head or the eye, suffers from an attack of pain, we do not feel the anguish at the same time over the whole body, thus the mind sometimes suffers pain by itself or is inspirited with joy, when all the rest of the soul throughout the limbs and frame is stirred by no novel sensation. *But when the mind is excited by some more vehement apprehension, we see the whole soul feel in unison*

through all the limbs, sweats and paleness spread over the whole body, the
tongue falter, the voice die away, a mist cover the eyes, the ears ring, the limbs
sink under one; in short we often see men drop down from terror of mind; so
that anybody may easily perceive from this that the soul is closely united with
the mind, and, when it has been smitten by the influence of the mind, forth-
with pushes and strikes the body. (Emphasis mine)[1]

The moment of vehemence is being used by Lucretius to display the unity of mind, body, and soul: the one moment of experience in which we see no part of the totality of the self at rest but all engaged with equal depth. In a moment of extreme fear, the self is completely given and brought to a peak of concentration. No part remains focused in another direction or distracted by its own actions. Even physical pain, Lucretius points out, may be localized in the eye or foot. Mental states like joy might leave the body uninvolved. Only terror and other vehement states saturate the body as a whole and the soul or psyche as a whole.

By way of contrast, consider for a moment a man walking along the street, gazing at the various things that catch his attention for an instant, while within his mind he worries over an appointment later in the day at which he will have to borrow money from a friend who, he worries, may refuse. His body is engaged in the habitual act of walking on a city street, but he is not directly conscious of the act of walking; his sensory life attends here and there to the sounds or sights that happen to be loud or sudden, striking or novel enough to be noticeable. Within his mind a third array of things is going on: worry about his finances, worry about his powers of persuasion, memories of the friend, rehearsal of the words that he will say. His body, senses, thoughts, and feelings are all scattered into quite separate tasks and states.

In the moment of extreme fear that Lucretius describes, full momentary unity of the self is achieved, and it is a unity within which each part is pitched at a peak of activity. Hume, in pointing out that a passion, unlike an idea or a sensation, does not represent anything else, described this unity in a telling set of examples: "When I am angry, I am actually possest with the passion, and in that emotion have no more a reference to any other object, than when I am thirsty, or sick, or more than five foot high."[2] Like Hume's anger, Lucretius's fear is both thorough and vehement. For that reason it becomes for Lucretius a way of pointing out the fact that all of the parts of the self which require separate analysis—the body in medicine, the mind in science, the soul or spirit in psychology—can, in the aftermath of all distinct analyses, be demonstrated in an impassioned state not merely to be connected but to pervade one another so as to be capable of being fully and simultaneously present.

The opposite is the case with thought. The state of keen and concentrated thought, for which we often close our eyes, requires a diminution, even a forgetting, of both body and sensation. To realize that one is hungry, or that a pain is throbbing in one leg, distracts thought, breaks its path rather than deepening it. In the most perfect moments of thought, the fullness of the self is not present. As a result, whenever we locate the core of human worth in thought, a hostility to the body and to sensation follows at once. Where reasoning (the logos) or the act of choice (moral life) is taken to be the highest activity of the self, the inner state of conflict which those activities reveal between the mind and all other features of the self turns out to be a fundamental fact. But equally, of course, it is not in the everyday, scattered state of body, mind, sensation, and memory—as in the worried man walking through the city streets—that the unity or simultaneity of the whole self can be experienced.

To argue, as Lucretius wishes to do, that the mind and soul make up a single nature and, further, that this nature pervades the body, drives him to take his example from among the passions. That his example is a moment of fear locates him on the Stoic and Hellenistic side, where fear rather than anger is used as the template for the passions. But Hume's choice of example reminds us that this source of unity persists when the template of anger is invoked. Whether anger or fear, the example of the moment of vehemence secures the fullest simultaneous and active presence of every detail of the self.

The experience of the unity of the self that takes place within a moment of anger, wonder, grief, or fear—a unity that overrides whatever separation between body and soul we might otherwise take to be the norm—is one primary value of the passions for certain philosophical accounts of the self, and it is equally an embarrassment, on the other side, for other theories of the self. Entailed in this unity is a second crucial feature: the elimination of any boundary between inside and outside. The Lucretian experience concerns only my own experience of myself. There is no social component. It would be equally important if I were alone on a desert island terrified by the sounds at night that I took to be the cries of a ferocious animal drawing ever nearer. The expression of my fear, whether I am alone or among others, takes no account of any outside world. It does not amount to a dramatization, a display, or an appeal to any possible bystanders.

The Publication of States

Once we turn our attention to others in our social world, we might call this physical component of the passions the publication of our inner states. Around this question of publication, accounts of human nature understood as spirit rather than soul, personality, character, or consciousness underwent a profound alteration in the seventeenth century at the hands of a new economic description of man that had at its center the needs and appetites as well as the single act—work— by which those needs might be satisfied. The expression of the self through work, profession, or what Max Weber termed vocation or calling, externalizes the self in a secular, middle-class world just as the passions and those deeds set in motion by the passions had in a world of the spirit.

Along with work, the new seventeenth-century picture of human nature insisted on a rich inwardness of consciousness, self-questioning, and reflection for which one requirement was a realm of privacy that could be created only by the severing of private experience from the public world. A social crux came to surround the passions, one that concerned the negotiation of one's relations to others in important moments of experience. Most strongly put: the passions are a domain in which our important modern notion of a private life is impossible. This compelling notion of a private life depends not only on the location of essential experiences within the home or within one's own room, away from the view of others, but, more important, on a concept of an inner life that is, first and foremost, for one's own consciousness alone. It is then shared with others as a result of acts of choice. The result of this choice defines what we mean by intimacy. We picture ourselves holding our experiences as almost a form of inner property that we can, for example, record daily in a locked diary, and that we can, then, share or even *distribute* to others, as we do in showing photographs that we have taken on a vacation, or in telling someone about a love affair, or in being willing to cry in the presence of this but not that friend. Those few others whom we think of as intimates are those with whom we share feelings, thoughts, and experiences that, first of all, are taken to be uniquely our own.

In the passions, the deepest feelings are expressed immediately, without any caution about just who might be present to observe our transparent expressions. The tears and sobs of grief, the shouts of rage, the blush of embarrassment, and perhaps most of all the bright "Ah!" of wonder are typical of the *publication* of feeling within the passions. Civilizations that begin by erecting a zone of privacy, of inwardness, and, most important of all, of *control over the distribution of the inner states* (sharing them with some but not with others, under this circumstance but not under that, keeping certain feelings so private that they are not shared even with intimates) end by designing out the passions in favor of emotions, moods, and feelings, because the passions are states that in their rashness and self-absorption forget about others entirely and, as a result, fail to control the selective publication of experience. Once the passions are brought under control, we have instead a privatization of feeling made possible by an impassive exterior that only "displays" emotion when we choose to do so. Stoicism is the master philosophy for the training and creation of an unchanging surface for the body. As a first act toward this impassive mien the passions are brought under control. In fact, they are ostracized.

Within the passions there is neither choice nor what is prior to choice, privatization. When Achilles learns of the death of Patroclos, his grief bursts from him and enacts itself at once. Homer's description first notes what might be purely a state of feeling, but paradoxically described as something falling onto him from without: ". . . the black cloud of sorrow enveloped Achilles." To this point the sorrow might remain within. But the description continues: "He took up the sooty dust in both his hands and poured it down over his head, soiling his handsome face: and the black ashes settled all over his sweet-smelling tunic. And he lay there with his whole body sprawling in the dust, huge and hugely fallen, tearing at his hair and defiling it with his own hands ... Achilles gave out a horrible cry."[3] The "black cloud of sorrow" within his feelings seeks its exact externalization in the "sooty dust" that he pours over his head, blackening his face and tunic. Because he feels that he has received a blow, he falls to the ground. Finally, his inner sorrow voices itself in "a horrible cry." The sootlike dust, the collapse, and the cry publish the "dark cloud" within. They do so instantly—rashly—and without a choice of time or place. The passion is not withheld from witnesses. It is not saved until Achilles is secluded within his tent, either alone or with intimates. On the contrary, it has an almost theatrical visibility to any and all who happen to be nearby. These details of grief are not its "signs" but part of its nature. The body and the spirit are equally present in Achilles' grief. And no realm of consciousness or inwardness exists to be the prior—and private—location of experience where it could occur only for Achilles himself, distinct from whatever surrounding world might or might not be present to witness it.

From our modern perspective, one of the most important features of the passions was their capacity to override any division between inner states of feeling and outward expression. The passions make impossible any split between the spirit and the expression of the spirit in the language of the body. The creation of the crucial realm of privacy is partly made possible by an ethos of restraint that severs the surface of the body from the feelings within. In the blush, the shout of rage, the smile of wonder, and the flow of tears, the inner passions of embarrassment, anger, wonder, and grief are displayed in the outer world. The realm of privacy and inwardness can be created only at the cost of redesigning and filtering the passions, creating a new inner world composed of emotions, feelings, moods, and sentiments. This new realm of privacy presupposed a control over the distribution of knowledge about oneself and one's inner states. Some feelings were hidden from everyone; others were shared with only those who made up the sphere of intimacy; still others were displayed or acted out indifferently in public. Each person's unique control over this triple sphere of self-display, with its implication of choice about the distribution of inner life, defined, in part, the autonomy of the self. To share or not to share details of consciousness and feeling became one of the features of the decorum of civil society and of the confessional or reticent self, and it is this sometimes confessional and sometimes reticent self that defines the citizen within the public realm in modernity.

The transparency of the passions and their disregard of observation was incompatible with the creation of a realm of privacy and choice. The very consciousness we might be imagined to have of others who might be observing moments of feeling is incompatible with the passions. The sighs, groans, or tears of mourning take place "as if" one were alone in the world. What seems at first an indifference to the question of who might witness the display of passion is really a proof of the unilateral nature of the passions. The world of others has so completely lost its standing that it is as if no one any longer existed except the self in its incandescent state. The creation of such distinctions as intimacy and privacy reveals an invasion of emotional life by a constant awareness of the reality of others that in and of itself is at odds with the terms of what had earlier been described as the passions.

The Solitude of Impassioned States

Since this power of the passions to extinguish the reality and claims of others while creating, as illness does, an almost painfully pressing awareness of self—to the point that only the self, and, even more, only the self as it is in its current state of panic, or grief, or rage has any reality at all—will be essential for much of my later analysis, I would like to restate it by reconsidering the moment of terror. As in the moment of dying, the essence of the moment of terror is the knowledge that one is completely alone in the world, face-to-face with whatever threat one feels. Even if others are nearby, they fade in importance to such an extent that it is as if they were in, not just another place, but another time. Instead of the consciousness of others, what completely fills up awareness is the beating of the heart, the paralysis of the will that makes it seem impossible to lift a hand or to run, the dryness of the mouth, the stony weight of the heavy body, the dilation of time into an unending set of tenths-of-a-second intervals, each of which lasts for what feels like minutes. Our cries or trembling are not only indifferent to others, but almost unaware that anyone might be there to see. With extreme fear we seem to enter a world where no other person any longer exists. When later we again become aware of others, we feel shame and humiliation once we realize how we must have appeared in the moments of panic, but no one ever feels that shame in the moment of panic itself, because the very premise of shame is the acute feeling of the reality of others and of their opinions.

Within the passions lies the most potent experience of our own individual reality of which we are capable, and at the same time the most uncompromising experience of the present moment of time. That moment of pure present time stands uninflected and uncompromised by any secondary feeling for claims of other times past or future in which, under other circumstances, we might imagine our identity invested. Whether, in these moments when all else that we have been in the past, and all that we variously hope or plan to do in the future, has been erased, we consider ourselves to be in touch with the essence of our own being, or, just the opposite, outside ourselves—"vehe"-mente ("out of the mind")—depends on how the passions are understood. In one long-standing account they are the clearest instances within experience where the self appears unqualified by others, by the world, or even by what it itself might seem to be in other times and circumstances. In the second account, the passions are taken to be, like illness, an interruption of the self, a disturbance, a possession, that, until it passes, provides no account of the self at all. This second description summarizes the Stoic or Hellenistic account of the passions that has been victorious to the point of dominating all later Western culture with only rare but important intervals of exception, like the late-Renaissance moment of Machiavelli and Shakespeare.

The impassioned state of anger gives evidence of a level of self-absorption that not only abolishes decorum but makes one act as though one were alone in the world, entranced by the conditions of one's own spirit, both its stalemate and its angry solution. For the time that this state lasts, the impassioned person reverts to a presocial solitude very little different from that of the moment of dying. The angry man or woman stands in front of others but alone. The same is true of those in deepest melancholy, frozen in fear, rapt in the spell of wonder, or turned inward with the indifference to all surroundings and all others that characterizes intense grief and mourning. The passions require us to invent a term that would be the opposite of "socialization" so as to represent a process that goes in the opposite direction, breaking the hold of the world, including the social world, educating each of us about our extrasocial being, as, in the end, the act of dying emphatically does.

What Wordsworth called the "discipline" of fear is present in each of the passions. Where socialization crystallizes out of the materials of the self a civic and communal being that might, under other conditions, never have appeared at all, the discipline of the passions gives form and then legitimacy to another type of self altogether for whom the existence of others is irrelevant. What Freud described as the key symptom of both mourning and melancholy, "abrogation of interest in the outside world,"[4] corresponds to a barrier that is conspicuous in each of the passions—even those, like fear or wonder, that take their start from a single object in the world whose presence is so powerfully felt that it and it alone seems present opposite the self, the other details of the world having faded out.

Freud's term "abrogation of interest in the outside world" is literally incorrect, except in the case of melancholy. What fear or grief, falling in love, anger, jealousy, shame, and the vehement passions in general make clear is that, by means of the passions, an absorbing concentration on one present-time object in the outer world exists at the expense of any and all other possible attention. Instead of a diversified investment in persons and objects, in events just past or in the near or slightly more remote future, the impassioned state solidifies attention in the direction of one monopolizing fact: the recent death of a parent, the snarling dog on the path in front of me, the contemptuous insult that I have just noticed, the surprising object in the face of which I feel wonder in the moment when first I notice it.

Only the moods of melancholy and boredom are accurately described as states without interest and focus on the outer world. This is why their inclusion among the passions is a mistake. Interest, energy, attention, complete relation are all features of the passions, but at the expense of all other integrated and diverse attention to the world as a complex, many-sided unfolding process. The attention is to a single, all-absorbing, monarchical object like Ahab's focus on the whale, or Achilles' concern with his insult at the hands of Agamemnon or, later, his loss of Patroclos.

The historical dismantling of singularity into privacy means that the authority of each person's state of being, which was once absolute, now reappears as a cautious island within a more and more universalized and pervasive social existence. This change reflects the transformation from a political culture that included a unique example of singularity—king or prince—whose essence might be taken to be the ongoing unimportance of all others by comparison, to a political culture of citizens, each of whose claim to standing required his recognition of the equal standing of all others. In modern democratic society, Melville's story of anger can occur only on board a ship where the captain retains the archaic singularity and dominion over all he sees that was formerly not an exceptional case at all but the ordinary political norm because of tyranny and monarchy. One meaning of kingship can be expressed only by means of a psychology of the passions which makes literal, in the soul, the unilateral relations with all others that is the essence of the political singularity of monarchy.

It might seem at first paradoxical to claim that the absolute value of one individual, as it is politically stated in monarchy, provides a ground for every other individuality, or, more important, for moments of uncompromised individuality that might be experienced on occasion by any person whatsoever. This we could say is one of the paradoxical facts about the appearance of Shakespearean tragedy at the start of modernity. At first sight these plays describe a world governed by the tyranny of one impassioned person. In such a world, by implication, other selves cannot arise. In fact, Shakespearean tragedy models a new world of individualism in which each person has access to a norm of self that had previously been available only to a king, a norm that can be imagined only through stories in which one person is designated as a king. This trick of the imagination to display genuinely new conditions by means of a generalization of the very past overthrown by those new conditions is a common one. The democracy of the ballot box was commonly described as "every man a king."

Within the mutual world of citizenship both the image of individuality and the grounds for the occasional experience of full and unlimited individual being within states of vehemence require another basis. That basis can no longer be modeled on the inner experience of the passions. The crux of many arguments against the passions lies in the recognition of their hostility to any genuinely social world. What any such social world requires is mutuality, bilateral rights, the acknowledgment of others on the basis of their acknowledgment of myself—in other words, a social contract. The premise of a contract of any kind depends on the fundamental acceptance of there being two or more persons, each having legitimate claims to acknowledgment.

The passions assert a world in which there is only a single person over against all others. The first act of the anger of Achilles is his refusal to fight or even to save the lives of his allies. He withdraws into a solitude from which he can watch the destruction of his own social world. It is clear that anger, like the radical mourning described by Freud in "Mourning and Melancholia," involves a "loss of interest in the outside world, loss of capacity to adopt any new object of love."[5] Jealousy, as we see it in *Othello*, or ambition as Shakespeare described it in *Macbeth* or *Julius Caesar*, leads to the displacement of a social world by one passion and the will of the one impassioned man. In *Moby Dick* the entire world of the ship goes down after Captain Ahab has turned it into a mere arm of his anger.

Is the situation of Macbeth or Achilles or Captain Ahab or of Kleist's Michael Kohlhaus archaic and prior to any social world? Or is the opposite the case? Do these extreme experiences of a world with only one will make clear a revolt of the self against its own earlier concessions that made possible the grounding of a public world? The essence of any such public world is reciprocity and the acknowledgment of the interdependence of wills. Homer begins the *Iliad* with the act of withdrawal from a joint enterprise that makes explicit the revolt of individuality against its own implicit earlier concessions to a common world. One version of such a concession would be agreeing to form part of a wartime coalition.

The Retreat Made Clear by Shame

I want now to suggest a limit to the extreme and extrasocial individualism characteristic of the passions, by concluding this chapter with a consideration of shame as a state that often follows other passions— an aftermath state, we might call it. Shame rebuilds the reality of other persons, not by means of reasoned reflection, but through the agency of a successor passion. Greed, envy, jealousy, and fear might often, and for everyone, be passions that (once we became aware of others noticing our passion) we might feel shame about, but this would not explain the very similar feelings of shame about grief or wonder. Even for correctly judged fear, we often feel a later shame simply because those around us witnessed the symptoms of our terror. The logic of this experience of shame in the aftermath of an impassioned state can be seen best if we first consider the link between shame and the act of apology.

We often apologize later for our outbursts of anger or grief. In apology an act of retraction, or even what we could call a denial of our own will, occurs. The act of apology is similar to the moment when a criminal confesses, because confession involves a moment of self-disowning. In confessing, I distinguish the person speaking now from the one who did the act, even though both are myself, and I agree to side with those who have accused me, siding against that earlier self by testifying against him, just as a former accomplice in a joint endeavor might do.

Since the passions, and anger in particular, display a militant sense of self-assertion and uniqueness, the act of apology as a counterpart is an especially revealing one. The link is less odd when we think of the fact that an act of formal apology is sometimes needed to forestall revenge. Often in a fight, the only way to avoid a beating is to say "I'm sorry." On the other side, a child who refuses to apologize is often punished mercilessly because the refusal to say "I'm sorry" is taken to be one of the most stubborn acts of self-assertion. The act of refusing to apologize makes clear the antagonistic relation between the structure of apology and the unilateral self-importance of the passions. An apology assumes that I have given another person cause for anger. As I will describe in detail later, anger is closely related to informal moments of seeking justice because it is in the everyday actions of noticing offense, requiring apology, and making or receiving apology that a banal but conspicuous policing of the borders of self-worth takes place. In the absence of an apology or freely offered compensation, retaliation sets in motion the escalation of acts that will restate our insistence that an injury or offense has taken place that must be noticed and acknowledged by others. A fundamental definition of the perimeter of the will is implied by this sequence of acts. The details of this complex process will be the subject of chapters 9 and 10. It is easy to see that impetuous people end up apologizing more often than deliberate or prudent people. Rashness and apology, or rashness and restitution, seem inevitably linked. With anger and fear the links to shame, apology, and rashness might seem to reveal a deep problem about anger and fear as well as about impassioned states in general, since anger and fear had so commonly provided the templates for the description of all other states.

With vehement states other than anger or fear what is revealed by the aftermath of shame is more important to what we understand to be the nature of the passions themselves, because it does not concern the content of the state, as was true with fear or anger, but concerns instead the structural features of the impassioned states themselves. We feel ashamed when we think that others have witnessed our jealous obsessions or the evidence of our greed. We sometimes speak of extreme passions as "shameless lust" or "shameless fear."

The feeling of shame occurs in the moment of becoming aware of others, the moment of a return to social consciousness in which, after a time in which it was forgotten, we remember how we look at this moment to those around us who are observers of our condition. It is common, for example, to apologize for tears, angry shouts, or fear, once social awareness and calm return. "I'm sorry, I don't know what came over me" is a common formula of apology and shame. Is this an apology for the anger or grief, or is it an apology for the moments of acting as if the others did not exist? Is it the content that is shameful or the structural fact of indifference to others and our conspicuous withdrawal into a closed world of self-concern?

Certain features of the general case can best be seen in the phenomenon of grief. One component of vehement, all-absorbing mourning is what we could call a certain insult to the living. While we mourn, we remain absorbed in our own loss and in the person whose absence is more important to us than any other present and living person. Those around us cannot relieve or even distract us from our grief, nor can they entice us back into the resumption of everyday life with its pleasures, concerns, and subdivisions of interest and feeling. For as long as mourning continues, our absorbing grief implies a devaluation of them in the face of the one person lost, but also a secondary devaluation in the face of the reality and claim of our own inner state, which we are protecting from interruption by other moods or other claims.

At the point where mourning ends, there is a reentry into the larger social web of relations that begins to repair those relations which had been devalued during the time of mourning. The slight or insult to the importance of all others has to be reversed. What the evidence of mourning makes clear is not only the real importance of the one lost but also the absorbing reality of our own states, our own world over any shared world. Anger, jealousy, fear, and wonder have a hold on the self in its entirety. They have a fixed or immobile quality, a stubborn undiscussable intensity that is one of the strongest proofs in daily life—along with the eight daily hours of sleep—of the minimal or fragile connectedness, in the final analysis, of our own inner life to the fact and reality of the lives and claims of others.

Others who might watch us sleep or watch us enraged or watch us terrified witness the priority of an extrasocial self, of a withdrawn self for whom others do not exist and cannot press their claims at any level of importance that can be compared to the claims from within. Sleep always needs to be included in our minds as a radical fact about our lives that limits any merely social account of existence. In setting such a limit, sleep makes clear the similar radical denial of the social that occurs within the passions.

If we take reciprocity to be one of the most fundamental conditions for any social world, then we require that the sufferings of another count just as much in my eyes as my own, or that the elation or pleasure of another, the comfort or security or expense of effort, the work of another, counts just as much to me as my own. In moments of vehement fear—which we describe in the revealing phrase "Every man for himself!"—we suspend reciprocity and suddenly value only our own survival. The essence of extreme fear is to return us, as sleep does, to an extrasocial condition where I am the only one in my world. In fear we frequently act in testimony to this loss of reality of others by trampling on them to get to the one exit of a burning room or jumping first into the lifeboat of a burning ship.

The later feeling of shame is not different from the much less prominent apology or embarrassment after anger or mourning or jealousy. It is a shame directed at the evidence we come to remember later as a telling revelation to others that reciprocity had ceased to exist in our eyes. For the time of our fear, anger, grief, or jealousy, all others were, in the Kantian sense, not just reduced from ends to means, but unimportant even as means.

Within literature or narrative the formal way to assert this singularity of passion is to begin from a symbolic difference that in advance locates the impassioned man or woman outside the normal fact of reciprocity. In *King Lear*, for example, the rage of King Lear is already, in advance, possible because in a social realm of a king and his subjects there is already one person who does not have to suspend a world of mutual importance and concern, because he already, as king, stands outside it. Each of Shakespeare's kings, by being designated the one and only king in a world of subjects, is already marked socially as within a world in which there is only one center and all others exist as circumference. Similarly, the God of the Pentateuch, in his wrath and jealousy, is, as God, already singular because he is the one creator in a universe where all else is created. Achilles, in his anger, stops and breaks off a social world of reciprocity to set in place a kinglike or godlike world where only the reality of his anger and then, later, of his mourning for Patroclos has any importance. The equation made between Achilles' anger over the injury done to him by Agamemnon and his mourning for his closest friend, Patroclos, makes clear, from the point of view of the passions, the deep subject of Homer's *Iliad*. The second blow—the death of his dearest friend—reveals what was at stake in the earlier loss with which Homer's tale begins.

In other words, the fact that in narrative the passions are embodied in just those figures who, in advance, are excused from reciprocity reveals the understanding of the passions as premised on just this suspension of a mutual world. Unlike a king or a God who remains permanently or ontologically outside reciprocity—and for whom, therefore, the state of thoroughness or vehemence represented by a passion such as wrath, jealousy, fear, or wonder is the normative, the ordinary state of being—the situation of a man or woman who is temporarily in wrath, grief, or fear involves a dissolving of reciprocity, a time spent outside reciprocity, and, finally, a return to a reciprocal world, a repairing of reciprocity. It is this repair and return that the moment of shame or the act of apology reveals. Such apology or shame we might call democratic because it acknowledges the very reciprocity that had been suspended.

Nonetheless in the example of a royal or a divine agent of passions, resting permanently outside reciprocity and entailing no aftermath of shame or apology, we can see clearly one of the fundamental inconveniences of the passions for any account of human nature that wishes to be a democratic account: that is, one in which the power to will is reciprocal and distributed to all who are citizens, and not to one who is a God or a king surrounded by creatures or subjects.

Time

The art of life, Marcus Aurelius said, is more like the wrestler's art than the dancer's.[1] The wrestler stands ready and poised to meet thrusts that are sudden and unexpected. The dancer wills the steps she will take, and if we are our will, then Yeats is correct and we cannot know the dancer from the dance, because the dance is the visible will of the dancer projected through the body in motion. The wrestler positions every muscle of his body to adjust to changing conditions in the few feet of space around him and the few seconds of time in which his opponent might try some new move in the hope of destabilizing him. The word "unexpected" implies that everything he faces next will not be the product of his own will even insofar as his own will is ready for a range of moves he imagines the other will make next. There is always one dancer; there are always two wrestlers.

The sudden and the unexpected are two domains of the passions, as are the nearby time and space that constitute the wrestler's only world for the time of the match. Fear and anger alert us to something in the near zone of time. Hume reminds us that we feel our strongest response to events contiguous in time.[2] Anger notices and then reacts to a slight or insult that has just happened. We burst into grief and mourning for a death that we learn has just taken place. What has just happened makes up what we call the immediate past, or the contiguous past, to use Hume's word.

Imagine that this were not the case. Let us say that we knew someone who, in our opinion, had undergone a serious insult or injury but showed no response until six months later or seven years later, when he, for the first time, grew suddenly enraged about the insult that by then we have forgotten had ever taken place. We would find this gap between injury and the responding anger peculiar. To use a modern vocabulary, we would speak of it as an example of repression.

It is of the essence of anger to occur right away, and it is equally of its essence to reach a maximum or near maximum of heat and intensity right away. Moreover, it is of anger's essence that it fades over time. One week later the insult still burns, but we rage and storm less. We think of it intermittently. A year later it is fainter still and comes into mind only on rare occasions. Similarly, the grief and mourning that we feel at the death of our teenage daughter in an auto accident is most intense, complete, and preoccupying near the moment when we first hear that she is dead. A week later, a month later, a year later, twenty years later, the curve of diminution and the medicine of intermittence have worked their effects.

So, too, with a feeling of shame about a disgraceful act just done. The essence of the shame lies in its occurring at once. Anger, grief, and shame isolate for us the unique importance of this narrow zone of time: the immediate past. They also make us familiar with the track from greatest intensity to slow but progressive reduction, to intermittence, and, finally, to vanishing.

In the other direction, that of the future, we feel fear in the face of what is just about to happen. Our strange use of this word "just" in speaking of what has just happened or what is just about to happen marks the zone of excitation of the passions. The creaking door or floorboards terrify us because they mean that the intruder is already in the house. Whatever will happen will take place in the next minutes. When we see the ship listing and water pouring into the rip in the hull, we jump in panic because the ship's sinking is imminent. We freeze at the snarling dog across our path because in the next few seconds he will or will not attack.

These examples describe extreme fear exactly because they describe a narrow zone of nearby future time—contiguous future time—that defines the imminent future. The imminent future is the symmetrical partner to the immediate past. Between the two rests the thin, near-zero duration of the present moment.

All of us fear dying of cancer in some vague way, but a man pointing a gun at my chest invents for me a short-term future in which my own death is possible, or even likely, so that I become nothing but my fear. All the varied facts, details, plans, and memories that used to make up myself are canceled by the loaded pistol, not by the bullet fired from it, if one ever is. A new self made up of nothing but pure fear and completely defined by the narrow situation of the next few seconds seems to replace the everyday self, with its personality, diversified interests, its long future of varied intentions and scheduled events, and its complex past. If we ask for an exact measure of the vehemence of this state of fear, we could say only that it is equal to the full larger self that this intense state has displaced.

What consequences are there if we think of the time scheme of the passions rather than that of prudential reason or the time scheme of the desires and appetites to give us our central template for experience and our decisive model for time and temporal experience in general?

The most important consequence is that we give an increased weight to the sudden and the unexpected, because these are characteristic of experiences in the nearby zone of future time. What has been anticipated from afar gives us time to prepare a strategy for dealing with it. We compose ourselves; we think; we choose how to face it; and then we execute our plan. We are, in other words, more and more able to be thoughtful and to act deliberately if and only if there is uncrowded time. There has to be enough time for rationality to dominate: time for choice, time for strategy, and time for resolve.

Aristotle claimed that the best proof of courage was how a man or woman reacted to sudden danger, because in the case of quick, reflexive response, the ethic or character of the person, along with the habits that define settled, courageous character, had to be revealed. Shameless panic, flight, and all that these implied about settled character might also, in other cases, turn out to be what was revealed. The sudden, unforeseen death of a friend has the same effect for the passions of grief and mourning that Aristotle's battlefield example of sudden danger has for courage and fear. Where we expect death, as in the case of an eighty-year-old, long-hospitalized parent, the response is prepared and already partly used up as we grew used to thinking of him as dying.

The temporal mechanisms of surprise and suddenness, especially in their deep relation to the will—that is, to the future as we have planned it, expected it, or even caused it—constitute the first of the consequences for experience of the location of the passions in this zone of the immediate past and the imminent future.

Insofar as we think of ethical life as structured by that careful weighing of alternatives that we call premeditation, we commit ourselves to giving salience especially to cases in which there is time for balanced thought, reflection, and choice. Our entire notion of freedom of the will and of responsibility for our lives requires that acts be, as we say in the law court, premeditated. This is just what is ruled out when we deal with the imminent future and the immediate past and consider our acts and responses in these zones to be essential to how we think of ourselves as human beings. In the face of the sudden and the imminent, we act rashly, and rashness is a crucial ethical word for the passions. Our very idea of choice depends on time for the complex meaning of that choice to be worked out in the mind. Instinctive or automatic responses, rash acts, like those done in a rage, are particularly troubling for our time scheme of choice and free will and our notion of a rational act, an act for which we are then applauded or held responsible. The phrase "crimes of passion" exactly describes our legal system's problems with sudden response, particularly killings done in rage or in jealous rage, acts done on the spot and in response to an immediate fact.

On many occasions in the chapters that follow I will describe the features of ethical intelligibility made possible uniquely by the passions. It is wrong to assume that only cautious and prudential choice based on deliberation can enable ethical life. Rashness, or impulsiveness, as it was understood by Aristotle, for example, while only partly describable as choice, rested at the center of the idea of justice. This I will try to show in detail in chapters 9 and 10.

The Imminent Future, the Immediate Past

The passions insert the self into a highly differentiated time in which the past and the future are more like two different mediums—for example, life lived as a fish in the sea and life lived as a bird in the air—than like two different segments of a line we call time, with its arrow sign at one end, pointing us into the future. In particular, the passions give constant clues to the scale and importance of an immediate past and an imminent future. So important a part do the passions play in identifying a "near" or imminent future and a "near" or immediate past that we could say that without the passions these concepts could not exist at all.

Literary modernism and romanticism with, for example, Wordsworth's notion of "spots of time" created a cult of present moments. In Proust, Rousseau, Joyce, or Woolf we find revelatory, spiritually charged moments of time that eclipse the longer temporal perspectives of traditional narrative. Those longer perspectives typically involved the will and its projects, like Odysseus's year-long project to return home, or the project of falling in love and getting married that defined so many nineteenth-century novels, or the detective's project to notice and then patiently solve a crime. But the imminent future and the immediate past are quite different from either the pure present moments known as spots of time or, on the other side, the longer purposiveness of human projects like courtship and marriage, solving a crime, or the long journey home from a war.

Hume made himself the chief modern philosopher of temporal aspects of the passions. He followed Aristotle in pointing out that

75

the passions are felt only for things contiguous or proximate in time. He noted that "the same good, when near, will cause a violent passion, which, when remote, produces only a calm one."[3] In the direction of the past, "[a]ny satisfaction, which we lately enjoy'd, and of which the memory is fresh and recent, operates on the will with more violence, than another of which the traces are decay'd, and almost obliterated."[4] Since Hume means by the violent passions just those states that I am interested in as the passions, per se, as opposed to the feelings or emotions, this demarcation of a neighborhood of time surrounding the present within which the passions operate is one of the key identifying features of his account of the passions. It is a feature of the passions that the experience of fear brings out most sharply.

By means of the passions, time undergoes granulation and is given units other than the mechanical and identical units of seconds, minutes, hours, days, and years. Because of this, the passions set a stubborn obstacle in the path of any theory that insists we treat any equal span of time as having the same worth, no matter how close to or distant from the present it is. This is an important requirement within modern rational choice theory and of John Rawls's concept of a Rational Life Plan in his book *A Theory of Justice*.[5]

The passions turn our experience of time into something like a double landscape of foreground (both into the past and the future), middle distance, and background, all surrounding a standing point that is the emotionally centered and urgent present. The foreground, but not the middle distance or remote background of the past, is the location of rage, guilt, gratitude, grief, and delight, passions that we can feel only for something that has already taken place. I can be angry only about something that has already occurred. I can mourn only over a death that has already happened. Guilt or shame can occur only over something that I have already done. These are, therefore, passions that are directed uniquely at the past. We could say that they make us know the past as the past. The gradations within the past are structured or measured by the intensity and then by the fading of these passions uniquely directed at the past. I usually feel less shame the second day, much less in four days, little or none in two months or twelve years.

In the other direction, the foreground, middle distance, and remote terrain of the future are, in the same way, given gradation by hope, fear, greed, despair, or courage, which are, along with other future-designating passions, our optics onto a personal future. Desire and the forward-looking time span of desire also gives, independent of the passions, an optics onto a personal future. In the direction of the future the passions have a rival in desire for a temporal account of experience. In the direction of the past they have no rival, because desire has no backward-looking partner.

It is the fading intensity of anger or gratitude or grief, their openness to interruption by other passions, and, at last, their relaxation into everyday calm that decide the border between the immediate past and the middle or remote past, one characteristic of which is that things are no longer continuous with the present but have to be remembered. No one needs to remember that his friend has just betrayed him or that his child has just died. But after a certain passage of time a moment will occur, one that is experienced almost with surprise, when, because for a moment it has been forgotten, it can then for the first time be said that it is remembered. The process of the lifting of the passion is marked by that point at which something can for the first time be forgotten and then, in turn, be at some later moment remembered. This we call intermittence.

Once again, literature since romanticism has given nuanced accounts of the later moments of remembering that complement the investment in spots of present time. Proust and Wordsworth are the two masters of this temporality. Any temporal specialization in the present instant and in the much later instant of memory brackets and excludes interest in the band of time in which the passions rule, just as it excludes interest in what we might call the adult time of purposiveness and desire, the world of plans and agency. The very young and the very old are Wordsworth's (and, to a lesser extent, Proust's) natural characters. Wordsworth skips over all that lies between, the lifetime of the will and its projects, but he also, and in a very different way, skips over the two zones of time before and behind the present where the passions occur.

Just as with the past, the line between an abstract future and the imminent future is drawn by the moment at which fear or yearning, hope or dread engages. It is a common experience to feel that it is too early to hope yet about the details of outcomes far in the future. A possible harm located in the indefinite future cannot be the subject of fear, but it is precisely fear (or hope) that tells us where the indefinite future leaves off and the imminent, or definite, future begins. As Hume said: "Talk to a man of his condition thirty years hence, and he will not regard you. Speak of what is happening tomorrow, and he will lend you attention."[6] This zone or neighborhood within which his concern is engaged is the region where the passions are active.

This essential feature of the passions we could call the articulation of time. The passions convert pure, featureless, everywhere-the-same stretches of time into something like a temporal landscape, building an architecture into time. It is by the difference between fear and anger that we know that the future and the past are lived by us in entirely different ways. That we cannot fear the past, or feel hope about something past, that we cannot feel anger or shame about what is in the future, makes up one important aspect of the real existence of a past, a present, and a future. The strongest claim that can be made is that the passions do not mark or give evidence about the structure of time, but that they are that structure insofar as it can enter our personal experience.

The architecture of the temporal past is, in essence, produced for us by our knowing which among our concerns are still within the active sphere of the passions (delight, shame, anger, grief), and which, having left that realm, are now primarily within the domain of memory, forgetfulness, and recall. For the future the same line is marked

PAST		PRESENT	FUTURE	
Abstract Past	Immediate Past		Imminent Future	Abstract Future
MEMORY	PASSIONS		PASSIONS	IMAGINATION
	Anger *Shame* *Grief* *Delight*	*Wonder*	*Fear* *Hope* *Jealousy* *Greed*	

out between the now-active sphere of the passions and the domain of not-yet-imminent concerns that, because they have not yet incited the passions, are the concern only of the imagination. The imagination is to the not-yet-imminent future what the memory is to the no-longer-immediate past. In between lies the temporal territory of the passions: the imminent, the present, and the immediate past. Aristotle defines this territory as anything that has just happened or is going to happen soon. Obviously, we can still feel anger or mourning for things that have moved far enough into the past to have been, at least for a time, forgotten or even intermittently forgotten, but these are already in the process of vanishing.

Summary: Zones of Time

The chart above pictures the characterization just given and sums up the temporal claims made to this point. To sum up the main point, we can say that the philosophical and cultural argument about the passions is a debate about a certain band of time, a debate about what part the imminent future and the immediate past play in our action, our choices, and ultimately in our conception of the self. As a result, the debate between the passions and, for example, prudential rationality, makes prominent certain temporal features within action: the part played by suddenness and unexpectedness, on the one hand, and by rashness, on the other. What part do sudden and unexpected events play in the larger realm of events? What part do our rash acts or responses play in the wider set of our actions? Above all, what do this band of time and the features of rashness and suddenness do to make difficult or even impossible our concept of reason and the deliberative will? It is our notion of the deliberative will, with its acts of choice, its later responsibility for its choices, and its need for and use of an ample amount of time in which to deliberate, to weigh the alternatives and consequences—it is on this temporal and rational account of the deliberative will that our entire notion of ethical life and moral action, including legal responsibility, depends. The premeditated act is our very model for a moral act, perhaps even for a fully human act.

The Imminent Future, Acting, Deciding

The nearby future as a zone of time preoccupies sectors of economics and modern rational choice thinking in ways that show the background activity of the passions. Risk analysis, decision making, along with Aristotle's earlier description of deliberation and choice, presume the unique importance of a certain limited stretch of future time.

Decision making concerns only a sector of future time. We do not make decisions about the past. Nor do we make decisions about the remote future, because we know so little about events twenty or a hundred years from now that we cannot think of ourselves as acting reasonably if we make decisions about them. It also lies outside what we know to be our human powers to make decisions about the permanent underlying conditions of life. About the present it is too late to make any decisions. Even about events in the next few seconds our ability to make decisions is extremely reduced. We deliberate and then decide, for example, about what treatment to try when we have a headache or what route to drive for a long trip we plan to take in the coming winter. We deliberate and decide between two job offers. We deliberate about the set of movies we might go to this evening.

Most of our planning concerns proximate events, imminent choices, events or opportunities within the nearby future. Even though we do make major decisions about events in the far distant future when, for example, we choose among retirement plans and options twenty years before the date of our retirement, it is still true that because the bulk of our choices involve a nearby time horizon, the very qualities of decision making are shaped by that fact. We are simply more familiar with the look and feel of decisions and planning directed to proximate times. The increasing uncertainty as we move out months, years, decades, or centuries presents us with what we might call a higher and higher ratio of noise to signal until what is intended to be, in structure, a rational process (choice or decision making) seems to us more and more irrational, chance-driven, unclear in both details and fundamentals. More and more assumptions enter in; fewer and fewer outlines or conditions can be safely extrapolated from the present, until we find ourselves contemplating a kind of fiction or imaginary statement of the very alternatives among which this rational process is supposed to take place.

There is, in short, a rational motive to our sharper concern with the imminent future. Psychological and economic writing thinks of this as "myopia," as though our vision blurs and our concern fades as things stand farther and farther out from the nearby world.[7] We should, according to this idea of rationality, view events one hour from now or a few days from now within the same categories as one year from now or ten years from now, with only an appropriate discount taken for the increasing uncertainty. We could do so only if past experience had shown us that underlying conditions were constant in a way that would make the extrapolation from the present to a remote future no more difficult than from that same present to the nearby future. Nothing could be less rational. For the imminent or proximate future, barring sudden change, the underlying conditions both of the external world and of our own desires and goals will stay the same. But once longer time units are included, we find that the eight-year-old who plans to earn a lot of money someday to be able to buy as much candy and as many comic books as he now wishes he had will find that at thirty, earning a large salary, he has no interest in the thousands of candy bars and hundreds of comic books he once thought would fulfill his wildest dreams of happiness.[8] In his book *Reasons and Persons* Derek Parfit has given an impressive account of this problem of human choice and desire over longer spans of time, including future time longer than one generation's lifetime.

Decision making also has, like the passions, the consequence of overvaluing events within this nearby band of experience over against remote or nonproximate events or considerations. Economics, game theory, and rational choice create theories about the future just because they are about choices and how we make choices. For that reason the anomaly of what is called future myopia has to be understood in a precise way. Future myopia describes our preference for rewards that are immediate over greater rewards that would be given at a slightly more distant future. Even when we discount the future gains, future myopia leads to choices that need to be explained within any theory of rationality requiring us to treat equal units of time equally, a difference of ten days starting tomorrow and the same amount of time, ten days, starting two months from now. The imminent future, as many experiments in economic psychology have shown, exists almost as a distinct kind of time. The choice between an immediate payment of $100 cash put in my hands now and a deferred payment on the first of next month of $125 is treated differently from an offer of $100 next year on this day or $125 thirteen rather than twelve months from today, preserving the same $25 bonus for a one-month deferral.[9]

These preferences about future gains are considered irrationalities within rational choice theory. They seem to rule out the idea that equal amounts of time will be treated similarly no matter where they occur. John Rawls's treatment of rational life plans in *A Theory of Justice* begins by insisting that any rational life plan will treat all parts of the future as equal in importance without favoring the nearby.[10] It is almost a cliché to classify people socially by their tolerance for what is called deferred gratification over immediate tempting pleasures, no matter how inferior the latter are to the former.

Time is not mistreated in general. Most sectors a certain distance from the present are, in these experiments, treated equally within the limits of human lifetimes. Only the way the imminent future is valued plus the problem of where exactly the line between the imminent future and the abstract future lies seem to be in question.

Economists do not ask, but we might, whether there is a similar anomaly about the parts of the past, a difference between the immediate past and the past as a whole that turns up as a problem for rationality just as it did as a result of the passions of grief, anger, shame, delight, and other passions that mark out the immediate past. Economists are interested only in action and choice. This limits their attention to the future. Since we cannot change the past, we cannot make choices about our actions in the past. For that reason, the question I now want to pose cannot occur as a question within economics or rational choice theory, but it is of significant interest when we consider the much more important and encompassing question of the passions.

We can say that there is just such a signal in our thinking, as well as in our experience of the passions, that the immediate past must also be separated off from the past as a whole. One clue to this anomaly is the commonly noticed mistake that is described by the statement: military planners are always trying to win the last war. Our problem-solving mind is always trying to solve the last problem, not the one in front of us now. People in the generation devastated by the stock market crash of 1929 and the depression that followed were well prepared all their lives to handle the next crash or depression if it came, but it never did. The German central bank was always accused of extreme caution in its attempt to prevent the repetition of the runaway inflation of 1923.

If the past taken as a whole comprehends an almost infinitely varied domain of experiences, it is irrational not to draw on and think equally about the likelihood of any of the solutions or catastrophes that happened as we make a plan in the present. What we actually do is quite different from this fair and equitable treatment of the examples of the past. The effect of any striking recent experience is to blot out or overshadow the full domain of possibilities. This myopia within past experiences overcounts in a major way the most damaging event in any series of recent past events. After a once-in-a-hundred-years flood, everyone prepares for the next one at great cost, even though, by definition, it was a once-in-a-hundred-years event. Past myopia also leads to the conviction that any wildly successful recent strategy should be tried again if current circumstances can be even remotely aligned with those where the hot strategy worked.

Just as with future myopia, the grip on thought of recent examples that structure the larger domain of past experience argues for a category difference between the zone of time that makes up the immediate past within the past, parallel to the widely accepted category of the immediate future within the abstract future.

Here rational choice theory reiterates—but, more accurately put, is explained by—that part of any theory of the passions insisting that the zones of time on either side of the present are actively structured by fear, anger, regret, hope, and grief in ways that are not true of the distant future and past. Hume, who thought most carefully about time and the passions in the context of uncertainty, called these zones proximate, meaning by proximity a loose form of contiguity. To illuminate the claim over us of proximity, I want to introduce what will at first seem only a loose analogy, but as I explain it, I hope that it will seem far more than an analogy.

All that is near or nearby in space is epistemologically different from the rest of space, because the curvature of the earth limits our eyesight, creating a horizon line and a limit to the field of vision. Because we see only so far, space or the world per se is always divided for us into an active domain of our attention, the nearby, and an abstract, much larger domain of things and places that we can think about and imagine. I can see this room or this field ending in that line of hills several miles away, but London and the sea just beyond those hills are not proximate to my vision. There is a natural priority in space given to the nearby, because it is the only domain of my sight and hearing and, more important, of my acts. It is also the domain of those things that can happen to me soon, because I can see them coming toward me. This is the analogy I want to propose to the operation of the passions in time, even though in the case of the passions there is no equivalent to the absolute experiential barrier between the seen and heard nearby world and the world beyond, which is only imagined. The small percentage of the space of the earth that we can see, touch, smell at any moment as the landscape in front of us marks out the relative overweighting of the nearby over the equally important rest of the space of the earth.

Hume devoted a series of rich speculative thoughts to why distance in space counted more or less to the passions than distance in time, why looking far down from the top of a building to the street below seems a greater distance than looking up, when we stand on that same street, to the top of the building.[11] He asked why events at a certain distance in the past seem more remote than events at an equal distance in the future. Hume created what we might think of as a full theory of the effort or work we must undertake to reach and think of events or experiences at different distances from that image of ourselves from which all measurement starts. Why does the metric for the past seem to have different-size units from the metric for the future? Why is lateral space felt to have a different metric from ascending or descending space? Why are there inconsistencies within same-size intervals? These different scale intervals were Hume's schema for the analysis of the inflection given to all measurement by the passions.

The term used in modern rational choice theory—future myopia—implies a defect. Myopia is a flaw compared to normal vision. As a treatable divergence from the normal, myopia presumes the familiar Stoic account of the passions as perturbations altering some presumed normal state, as high fever and hallucinations in an illness are temporary perturbations of normal bodily temperature and sight, or as blindness is a defect in a world arranged for vision.

When we replace the covertly Stoic alternatives of myopia and clear sight with the correct distinction between sighted space (the landscape in front of my eyes as far as sight extends) and space imagined to lie beyond that landscape which I am confident that I could see if I moved forward ten miles or two thousand miles, then we have a more exact account of how the proximate or nearby world, the here of space and the now of time, stands to the imaginable world of remote but equally real space and time.

The passions operate in time just as the senses do in space to give an absolute meaning to the nearby or proximate world, because beyond that unique local domain brought forward by the senses and felt to surround us, or brought forward to us by the passions and felt to surround us, there is, in both cases, a far larger domain of which we can think or within which we can imagine events, but without the structuring of that world that the senses and the passions give to the nearby world. The proximate world is the domain of what we speak of as my own world, just as what I can see, but only this, amounts to my landscape or visual field, bounded by a horizon, beyond which no sensory information at all comes to me.

As agents, or insofar as we think of ourselves as agents, it is the nearby future along with what is spatially or geographically proximate that concerns us most, because this is the only sphere of our effective activity, the only domain in which what we do is likely to matter. If we want to view human nature as purely contemplative, then the past is a field that is even richer than the future, and all that is unchanging might be more profitable to think about than those few things that can be altered by human action. The necessary might be more intriguing to pure contemplation than the possible, or the impossible more interesting than the contingent and everyday. What is imaginable, but unreal, might attract us as contemplative beings more than what is actual. But once we turn away from contemplation to regard human life as action, as choice, as filled with planning and the bringing about of plans, as expectation and decision making, then one and only one domain of time becomes the essential focus of our interest: the proximate, immediate future. In economics the paradox of nearby rewards' being chosen over larger, more remote future rewards confirms the same fact. A unique alertness governs our confidence and attention to a nearby band of imminent future events. They make up our temporal neighborhood because we are human agents. It is not myopia but a fundamental fact about eyesight and vision that the nearby is the domain of our endeavors, our passions, and our responses.

The Duration of a Passion

The passions design time, but they are also themselves temporal. They unfold in time and, as we could say, they take time. In their occupation of the self, a characteristic that I have called thoroughness, they take up time the way a large object takes up space. Achilles cannot do anything else while in the grip of his preoccupying wrath. Later he once again can do nothing when that wrath has been displaced by grief for his close friend Patroclos. After that death his every act is an instrument or display of mourning.

The passions are strongly marked by an appropriate duration. In *Hamlet* the prince's sullen gloominess protests against the casual brevity of the period of mourning allowed for his father. How could the joys and passions of his mother's new marriage take place so quickly after the sudden death of his father? What is mourning if it is too quickly ended? Finding in your own heart that it takes time to mourn, you realize that there is a duration of mourning, and that duration, in each case, is of its essence. Too-quickly-ended mourning is not mourning at all but perfunctory gestures of mourning. This is Hamlet's accusation against his mother and her new husband. How quickly after the unexpected death of a beloved husband could the widow enjoy the sexual pleasures of the first days of a new marriage? This would be one intimate detail of the question of the duration of mourning. You can see that duration involves only superficially the sense of propriety in a culture's requirement that we mourn for just so many weeks or months. How soon can another passion, another interest, a new delight, displace what we might call the preoccupation of mourning? The first day that a widow might enjoy sexual pleasure with a new partner would be one exact mark of the domination of new interests over recent losses. Hamlet's challenge to his mother and her new husband implicitly states this point.

Similarly, too-long-delayed revenge is not revenge at all. Its essence depends on its sudden, driven rage. What Hamlet causes us to notice in his protests against the too-quickly-ended mourning is a temporal quality to all passion that ends up accusing most powerfully his own too-slowly-ignited revenge. A symmetry of too-quickly-ended mourning and too-long-delayed revenge is one of the means within the play to pose the close relations of anger and mourning, relations that had also been at the heart of the *Iliad* and would later in Shakespeare's career be posed once again in *King Lear*.

But at the other extreme, too lengthy mourning is also not mourning but acedia, despondency, depression, or obsessive fixation. This is the new king's, Claudius's, accusation against Hamlet. That mourning must be of a certain length and intensity is part of its essence. Otherwise, whatever it is, it is not mourning. The same is true for anger or shame. In the case of the imminent future, intense, preoccupying fear about events many years away is as much a violation of appropriate duration as is many-years-long mourning that cannot return to ordinary life.

The time in which each passion unfolds and then exhausts itself poses a different question about the nature of the passions from our earlier concern with the insertion of experience into time, in which the imminent future is cut off from the abstract future and the immediate past from the past that is the territory of memory.

One of the best-known modern analyses of a single passion hinges on the puzzle of the duration of the passions. In his essay "Mourning and Melancholy" Freud answers in a curiously mechanical way the question of why grieving takes time. He invents the concept of *Trauerarbeit* or "the work of mourning." In the work of mourning, Freud claimed, every single memory or detail of the lost love object is brought up, bit by bit, hypercathected, and then discharged. In Freud's description of the work of mourning there is almost a pedantry to grief. The loss is atomized into its details; the lifetime of experiences is taken up in some sequence so that each and every part can be gone through separately. The literalism of Freud's description is quite clear in his summary: "Reality passes its verdict—that the object no longer exists—upon each single one of the memories and hopes...."[12] Freud's is, as he himself describes it, an economic theory and therefore quantitative. The self's "investment" in the love object must be "disinvested" coin by coin before mourning is over.

What Freud notices in his concept of *Trauerarbeit*, despite the literalism of his economic picture of the soul, is that the duration of the passions is of their essence. Just how long the passions endure remains unexplained. The timescale of the passions controls the fact that a literature structured by the passions works out brief episodes of time. That Homer's *Iliad* tells in microscopic detail the events of four days within a ten-year war follows from the fact that its subject is the anger of Achilles and not the action (in Aristotle's sense of a complete action) of the war itself. The time scheme of the passions requires brief, close-up episodes. Where longer time schemes are used, they often break up, as Emily Brontë's *Wuthering Heights* does, into dozens of two- or three-page scenes, each of which tracks the explosion, enactment, and dissipation of a passion.

The duration of the passions cannot be reduced, as Freud did with mourning, to the mechanical labor of turning over the photographs within the memory one by one to place them all face down upon the table of the mind. And yet his use of the term "the work of mourning" is an important one because it suggests that we do not simply wait for the passions to fade of their own accord.

The feverish activity of Achilles exhausts his mourning for Patroclos. Whether rolling in the dust, pacing the shore, weeping, arranging and carrying out the elaborate funeral and funeral games, caring for the body, or slaughtering the enemy to take revenge, and, finally, in the act of hunting down and killing Hector, Patroclos's killer, Achilles is engaged in "working out" his passion. He fatigues it instead of waiting for it to fade. He uses it up in a set of actions some of which are ceremonial and customary, others personal, and yet others violently murderous in their search for revenge and satisfaction. The final quarter of the *Iliad* is, in Freud's term but not in Freud's meaning, a *Trauerarbeit*. So is Faulkner's entire novel *The Sound and the Fury* or the final third of Proust's masterpiece after the death of Marcel's grandmother and the loss of Albertine.

What Freud has described in this concept of *Trauerarbeit* is one of the ways in which passions enter into or, we might say, become narrative. Grief works itself out in time. It dissipates or exhausts itself. Revenge we could also speak of as a "work of anger," flight as the "work of fear." The narrative of working out describes one, but only one, narrative formula within the literature of the passions. Mourning is incited, then enacted, then dissipates until it passes into memory. What was lost is, at a later time, "commemorated" but not any longer mourned. The energy of grief, of anger, of shame, or of fear is invested, spent, exhausted.

The temporal narrative implied in "working out" or exhausting the passion in step-by-step negation has in the literature of the passions two important alternatives. The first is a narrative made up of the sudden displacement of one passion by another: anger is replaced by mourning in *King Lear* or the *Iliad*; ambition by guilt in *Macbeth*, at least in the case of Lady Macbeth. These cases of displacement preserve the quantity of passion but not its theme or character. Fear is often replaced by shame, once the fear has passed and we say to ourselves, it was really nothing.

In his book *On the Soul* Aristotle noted that we often feel an intensity of fear unrelated to the situation of fear, if in the moments just before the onset of fear we felt intense anger or some other state whose vehemence can be carried over into the new passion.[13] Two independent explanations are possible for the intensity of what we feel: (1) the seriousness of the occasion; or (2) the vehemence of the state we were in, for other reasons, just before the occasion. The second explanation is the more interesting one for a narrative aesthetics of the passions. It is the vehemence of Othello's jealousy that slips over into murderous rage in his conversation with Desdemona. It is this process that I described in an earlier chapter when I delineated the paths among the passions. Here I want to recall only that the preservation of a fixed quantity of vehemence, while it is reassigned to a new state, as happens in the important passage from rage to mourning, does not depend at all on the fading out of one state and the arousal of another. What takes place is the redistribution of vehemence from one location to another.

What we could call the narrative of displacement or sideways substitution makes up the first, and most important, alternative to the narrative of "working out" that exhausts, reduces, empties, and outwaits the vehement state, as in Freud's term the "work of mourning." But a further alternative also exists, one that is far more pervasive and decisive in the literature of the passions. This alternative depends on the temporal importance of rashness and the narrative importance of acts of killing in the literature of the passions.

The alternative to the inner pedantry of mourning described by Freud is the instantaneous discharge, the rash explosion of the will, and the location of single acts that can measure the full extent of anger, grief, jealousy, in one episode of the will. The most compressed narrative discharge is the act that in Shakespeare's many narratives of the passions, or Homer's *Iliad*, or Melville's *Moby Dick*, occurs with—as Simone Weil pointed out in her essay "The Iliad as a Poem of Force"—a numbing reiteration: the act of killing.

Killing poses, traditionally, one crux of arguments against anger and against the passions per se. If killing, as in crimes of passion, is structurally prominent within the passions, then every argument against impetuous, rash, and unmeasured response, against immediate response, against actions based on the immediate past and the imminent future, will find wide and immediate acceptance. All of this has to be granted. Killing is very central to any literature of the passions. What I wish to do is to locate this fact within the larger issue of rashness, which we might think of as the suddenness of the will in its response to sudden and unexpected situations in the world as they elicit passion.

Rashness

Rashness, commonly understood, is the defective, minor partner term to our central notion of the deliberate pace of reasonable action. Rashness stands in even stronger contrast to hesitation, Hamlet-like doubt, or to prudence that slows down the will, allowing time for careful thought before action begins, or even, in extreme cases, paralyzing the will and making action impossible. Only by taking time can we weigh the consequences and enable a choice of the best possible next-on action before we turn to execute that action itself. When Adam Smith set up his central principle of prudence within the moral sentiments, he used caution as a chain to restrain the actions of the passions as a whole.[1] "Prudential rationality" is now so basic a phrase that it might seem impossible to describe any other kind of rationality that gives us an acceptable relation of the intellect to moral action. Throughout my argument I claim that by means of the passions a kind of revealed, instantaneous understanding is discovered by anyone in a state of vehemence at the same moment that it is revealed to others observing that state. The sudden external event and the rash response or reaction are bound together and mirror one another in actions dependent on an impassioned state. Suddenness and rashness in combination define a quite different kind of rational action.

Later, in chapter 10, I will make an argument for the unmistakable way in which rash response, whether made up simply of the display of anger itself or the actions that might follow that display, plays a fundamental role in a wider notion of justice within which the formal legal system's concentration on a certain small set of acts and harms regulates only a small part. What is rational and defining about the passions is also the subject of my arguments about grief, wonder, and fear where, once again, a disclosure to others, and often to ourselves, happens as a result of the occurrence of the vehement state, and not because of that state's relation to some later action. The difference between a rational state and its content for recognition and thought, and a rational action must be kept clear. But in the case of rashness, it is precisely to the question of the rationality of action and response that we must turn.

In those of Shakespeare's plays designed around the passions the essential trait of the will of Lear, Macbeth, Othello, Romeo, or Juliet is that the will is rash. King Lear listens for only a moment to Cordelia's stubborn refusal to pledge her love before he passes into rage and disowns her. Cordelia passes in a few moments from being "our joy," as Lear addresses her first, or his "best object, / The argument of [his] praise, balm of [his] age, / The best, the dearest,"[2] as France reminds him later, to a discarded daughter who is as disgusting to Lear as a cannibal who feeds on its own offspring. Kent interrupts Lear, asking him to delay, to use "consideration." Kent calls what has just taken place "this hideous rashness."[3]

Lear's rashness is not more precipitous than Leontes' in *The Winter's Tale* when he rages at his loving wife and at his oldest friend and seeks their deaths. The resoluteness of Macbeth, who never turns aside from murder even when the killings have become monstrous, is the stubbornness that prolongs through time the rash initial momentum of his will. The mechanism of tragedy is more often rooted in the dogged persistence of the will, its world-annihilating lack of compromise—as we see it, for example, in Captain Ahab in *Moby Dick*—than in its vacillation or *akrasia* (weakness of the will). Rashness and stubbornness are aspects of the inflamed will. Both reveal, by being opposite to it, a norm of the will in caution and deliberation, a deliberation that also allows for reconsideration and later adjustment. These normal features of the reasonable will are precisely spelled out by means of their absence in the rashness and stubbornness of passion.

For Aristotle rashness was one of the extremes that defined the virtue of courage; inaction or cowardice defined the other extreme.[4] The close links interconnecting rashness, courage, anger, and the will can best be seen, before Shakespeare, in Sophocles' *Oedipus Rex*. The rage of Oedipus at Tiresias, at Creon, and at the shepherd from whom he forces the final evidence defines him as a rash, headstrong man. The warnings of those, including his queen, Jocasta, who plead with him to delay or call off his search only make clear to us his own angry, impetuous progress. In the present time of the play his rashness is an aspect of his courage, which supports his determination to know the truth no matter what the cost. But in the past it was his rashness that led him to run away in an attempt to escape his fate, and then, at the crossroads, to slay his father. The killing was an angry impulse within a trivial dispute with those he took to be strangers sharing the same road.

One part of the mystery of knowledge in *Oedipus Rex* lies in the interdependence of, on the one hand, the courage that alone suffices to enable Oedipus to press on to complete knowledge, the courage that had in the past saved society from the monstrous, when he solved the riddle of the Sphinx by finding the identity of man in general, and now impels him on to the personal solution—Who am I, really?—and, on the other hand, the rashness that produced the monstrous murder of the father and the incestuous marriage and children. Rashness and courage are interwoven, primary aspects of the vehement self, which we should see as the self considered purely as will.

To look at rashness as it intersects with each and every passion in a complex array of passions, I want to pass quickly in review the carefully designed array of rash actions and passions in Shakespeare's *Romeo and Juliet*, because, by means of this well-known story, a full account of rashness can be compressed and quickly explored.

In *Romeo and Juliet* the very overheated pace of the play itself is grounded in rashness. It is not just the ardor of the two very young lovers that we could call rash as they fall in love at first sight. First sight could be one dreamy synonym for rashness.

When Juliet's father, for example, hears that she wants no part of his suddenly announced plan to marry her in one week to Paris, he sputters with rage, denounces her, and claims that if she disobeys him, he will never speak to her again and will have no further concern for her welfare or even her life. He calls her "green-sickness carrion!," "Wretched puling fool, / A whining mammett," and then invites her to "hang, beg, starve, die in the streets."[5]

His rage reacts suddenly to an insult to his will—his plan for the marriage, a plan that had been itself a rash, disturbing plan, coming as it does in a family still mourning a recent, unexpected death. One of Shakespeare's many raging fathers, Capulet fumes and raves when his plan is frustrated. His will is injured, and his behavior has the full spirit of impetuous rashness. First of all, it is instantaneous. In strength, it is at once at its maximum. We expect his passion to fade rather than build because in its temporal scheme it begins at its peak.

The rash fury of Juliet's father also acts as though time itself were abolished. No past history of his fondness and pleasure in his only child any longer exists. In front of the father and his now despised daughter stretches a future than can be imagined only as a simple extension of this moment of hatred. He imagines her starving, begging, hanged, dying in the streets, and promises to pass by with indifference. Like Lear cursing Cordelia, Capulet will "never" speak to her again, "never" acknowledge her again. In this threat or curse the clear connection of stubbornness to rashness is clear. It is as though rash action, knowing itself to be sudden and extreme, has to be aware that some other sudden and extreme state is likely soon to displace it. To block in advance what it knows must happen, the rash state couples itself to stubbornness and utters curses to destroy in advance the very future in which its own displacement might take place.

Rashness makes the single present moment into the final moment of time. Naturally, all those around the father beg him to restrain himself. They try to rein in his anger but only incite him to turn that rage on themselves. The anger, because it is rash, insists on projecting a never-ending continuation of itself that seems unbelievable even to those standing in the angry man's presence, might seem unique among the passions of the play. In fact, this small event of the father's vehement cursing of his daughter gives us a model for the rashness that drives the play as a whole. The relations between the passions and permanent conditions—ever, never, forever—lie at the heart of rashness as a temporal scheme.

Within twenty-four hours of their first meeting, Romeo and Juliet agree to marry one day later. What does this rash decision mean? It sets up the same relation between "ever-after" (marriage) and the first moment of feeling as we found between the father's wrath and his vow that he will see his daughter die in the streets. The "at once" of rash, forward-speeding love to install itself as a permanent condition of reality, by means of a hasty marriage, confronts, in the larger plot of the play, the slower-moving background of arrangements, prudence, courtship, and familial schemes, not to mention the still deeper background of permanent family hatreds and the cycle of revenge. But the structure of love, as a passion, does not take its shape by opposition to the mercenary or familial schemes.

Where this rashness of love, as it speeds forward to convert itself into marriage, finds its complement throughout the play is in the many acts of killing. We see this above all in the custom of dueling. With a duel in the streets, a momentary state of passion caused by a passing insult has, in the sword fight that follows, a means to fix itself in a permanent result. It is only the state of death that lasts forever. If Mercutio and Tybalt annoy one another today in the street, the honor system and the swordplay that follows will convert that accidental moment of pique into the death of Mercutio. The rash moment of passion will be translated into a permanent fact more certainly than marriage will freeze at its highest peak the sudden falling in love of Romeo and Juliet. When Romeo later kills Tybalt, this second act of killing freezes the conditions of the moment of quarreling into an enduring permanent state both for Tybalt, who is now dead, and for

Romeo himself, since he must now be sentenced to die, or, if the sentence be mitigated, banished forever and separated from Juliet. In other words it is in the act of killing that the rash, absolute, and forever-after structures of the passions reach their literal embodiment. The father's angry vows and curses might later be retracted, but killing is the one certain translation of the instant into forever.

In passionate love with Juliet, Romeo marries her in a day. But in despair over the news of her supposed death, he drinks poison, also in a day. The passion of despair, with its rash consequences, leads to the impetuous suicide that blocks the few hours of necessary delay that would have permitted the real situation to become clear. Juliet is not dead at all. Despair, with its crystallization into the permanence of suicide, acts out the time scheme of the passions in a way that the father's rage, or Romeo's love for Juliet, or Juliet's mourning for her cousin could not.

The suicides of Romeo and Juliet are temporally different. Romeo's is a classic argument against haste, against impetuous final actions, and against rashness. It could be a classic Hellenistic instance of the idea that all passions are based on beliefs, commonly false beliefs. Had he waited an hour, his happiness might have been possible; at least he would have learned that the news of Juliet's death was false, a staged death to bring the two lovers together. Juliet's suicide, on the other hand, at the sight of the now dead Romeo, is based on accurate, full knowledge. Her act makes permanent the condition of loss and despair of the first moment of her grief. By means of suicide the fading of the passion, its distraction over time by other scenes, or by other lovers, is made impossible. Death at first sight is in this case more accurate than love at first sight, and suicide more certainly succeeds in converting a first moment of a state of passion (grief and despair) into a fixed, vehement effigy of itself than does sudden marriage in the instance of passionate love.

The mechanism by which passion denies its own temporal course, and therefore its own diminution and disappearance at some point in the future, drives the passions to block future time and the possibility of change by means of absolute acts. Although the marriage that one-day-old love uses and the suicide that one-minute-old despair uses are primary examples of this, we must also include the more everyday instances of the oath that the angry man takes, or the curses that he utters, curses that will scar the innocence of the future in a way that can never be undone, even if the oath or curse is later retracted. Capulet's cursing of his daughter is a weak example of the curses of King Lear, the curses of Leontes in *A Winter's Tale*, or the curses within *Cymbeline* or *Timon of Athens*. It is when these less murderous acts like the curses of humans and the wrath of God are taken into account that the full impact of rashness is felt. The curse or the vow is the rash act alternative to killing within either religious literature, where the central instance is the wrath of God, or the tragic literature that amounts to one key territory of the literature of the passions.

A curse, for many of Shakespeare's fathers, is the final imaginable human act of damage. It is the absolute of vehemence, the unretract-able, formal display of the white heat of a moment of anger extended out into time without limit. A curse takes what is a momentary peak of vehemence and, instead of spilling it out at once in an equally momentary act like a blow, even a murderous blow, freezes it like a law into an abstract punishment. The morally central part played by promises and contracts in the life of reason, binding oneself in the future to the state of mind and understanding of the present moment, is played within the passions by the curse or the vow. Out of a state that could not be prolonged, the curse builds a residence of suffering and confines its victim to it without hope of release.

For most of us today execution or murder would be a stronger act of vengeance, displaying anger in a way that makes an unalterable new state of affairs in which the other no longer exists. It may seem ingenuous to claim to find any mitigating value in homicide, but both execution and murder permit the victim to die after a short episode of violence. A curse deliberately condemns its object to live, deprived of all escape, even death, and deprived of all capacity to renew or become another self through change that would itself diminish the curse. Cain is cursed rather than executed because a sentence of death would be the lighter punishment. A curse makes the rest of time an aftermath to the one act for which vengeance is taken. Oedipus does not kill himself; he curses himself and his eyes.

The human race itself stands defined, after expulsion from the Garden of Eden, as cursed to give birth in pain, to labor for its food, and to die. In Genesis it is an ontological description of human life to say it is accursed. That is its fundamental nature: first created, then accursed.

As revenge is the personal form of law between equals, prior to the law and banned by the inauguration of impersonal legality, so too the curse is the prior form of law between fathers and children. But unlike revenge, the curse is only partly brought under control by justice and the impersonality of the law. The father's curse as we see it in Shakespeare's *King Lear* or *Romeo and Juliet* amounts to an extreme act of will that strips away the will of the other. It also reaches without limit of time. The curse outlasts the promise or the contract, those central binding acts of the reason. Contracts and promises commonly link only a certain limited future moment or set of moments to the present, freezing them into adjacency or proximity. Rashness finds an ultimate and lasting problem in the unretractable curse or vow, which destroys the open future while compelling us to live out its sterilized days one after another.

To sum up the importance of rashness, we might note that rashness lies at the heart of the puzzle for philosophers of the will. Since free will is based on the picture of deliberation and responsibility, the threat posed by any mechanism that is inherently rash is a very serious one. If the will is in some of its moments instantaneous or mechanical, or, to put it in biological terms, instinctual, then the recoil of fear or the vehemence of anger calls into question the wider picture of a will that chooses, one key element of which is the span of time for choice to take place and, then, the time for assent on which any later responsibility will depend. This is what "premeditation" sets up as a criterion for responsibility. The premeditated act and the rash act are nearly antipodal.

Philosophers have been intrigued for two thousand years by the topic of weakness of the will, or *akrasia*. How is it that we can choose to do something and then fail to carry out our choice? For Aristotle, *akrasia* was composed of two defective positions of the rational will. Only one of them could be called weakness of the will. The other was impetuousness or rashness. "But there are two forms of [*akrasia*], Impetuousness and Weakness. The weak deliberate, but then are prevented by passion from keeping to their resolution; the impetuous are led by passion because they do not stop to deliberate. . . . It is the quick and the excitable who are most liable to the impetuous form of [*akrasia*], because the former are too hasty and the latter too vehement to wait for reason, being prone to follow their imagination [*phantasia*]."[6]

The removal of the passions from philosophy has meant that only the one half of Aristotle's *akrasia* is mentioned, and the concept itself is frequently translated so as to reflect that one half: weakness of the will. In seeing that the two defective possibilities of the rational will are both caused, in his description, by the passions and are differentiated only by whether the passions act first or second, we can see that it is in fact rashness that is the true alternative to the rational will. We see, moreover, that the Christian and, at a later point, modern interest, primarily within ethics, in the minor problem of weakness of the will strips the deep problem of its essential feature, the temporal intervention of the passions at either the first (and, in this case, final) stage or at a second stage where once again the passions determine the outcome. Both cases reveal that the rational will is only a component of a more encompassing notion of the will that must include rashness, prudential behavior, and the failure to act after deliberation as three distinct but equally important unfoldings of the will into action. We could say, in fact, that the third case, the so-called weakness of the will, could in Aristotle's description equally be understood as stubbornness of the passions, since they endure the deliberation of the rational will, wait for their turn, and then define the outcome in spite of the part of the will that pretended temporary loyalty to prudential reason.

Temporal Alternatives to Rashness within the Passions

What this characterization of the temporality of rashness makes clear is the simultaneous interdependence of the will and the passions and, on the other side, the impediment that the existence of the passions offers to a certain type of reasoned and morally responsible picture of the will, of the kind that we associate with Stoicism and Christianity. Rashness occurs within the narrow time frame of the immediate past and the imminent future. It translates into action the thoroughness and presentness of vehement states. Closely linked, as a response, to the sudden and the unexpected as they come at us from without, rashness has that unique relation to the passions which deliberation has to the rational will. At the same time, rashness or quickness marks out only one of the possible time schemes for action within the vehement passions.

To conclude this chapter, I want to use the full range of time schemes of retaliation to fill in a wider cultural description of the operation of time within the experience of the passions. In doing this, I will be looking forward to chapters 9 and 10 on anger and everyday justice. At the same time, I do not want to limit the categories of time to the single passion of anger. The imminent future and the immediate past have deep connections to each and every one of the passions. Rashness is a mechanism within the will itself and touches fear, grief, hope, anger, shame, and most other vehement states. In this final section, too, the variations surrounding rashness, while presented through the single question of justice and retaliation, are meant to stand for the wider tracking of vehemence and action.

As we see from the street encounters in *Romeo and Juliet*, retaliation that follows from aroused anger must be sudden. Rashness implies suddenness. We act without hesitation or deliberation. Anger and vengeance as forms of justice depend on rashness. The longer the time between the outrage and its punishment, the more we transfer legitimacy from vengeance to impersonal justice. The key lies in the duration, first, between the outrage and the onset of the passion, and, second, between that onset and the act of retaliation which brings the anger to an end. Both durations are carefully built into our formal system of justice with its vocabulary, and into our everyday reactions, as onlookers, to the impassioned acts of others.

A man who comes upon a murderer just finishing the grisly slaughter of the man's child appears justified in our eyes if, on the spot, in his rage, he strikes the murderer dead. King Lear hangs the killer of Cordelia on the spot. But should that same father do so just one day later, our doubts about vengeance and revenge would begin to come into play. If he takes revenge a month later, we feel that he is at fault, because now the matter should be in the hands of the state, transferred to the realm of objective justice. Should the father take his revenge twenty years later, we would pity him but think him mad.

When Lear acts on the spot, having discovered the killer just finished with his work, the immediacy of grief and rage gives to the revenge the feel of rightness as if it were little more than the defensive blows he would have struck had he arrived just a few minutes earlier, in time to defend his child rather than avenge it. Ten minutes earlier, the father would willingly have killed his child's assailant to prevent the child's death. Since he arrives a few moments too late, his murderous stroke has the effect of being "as if" in defense, "as if" to prevent, although slightly too late.

Here vengeance and prevention, revenge and defense seem so near as to be inextricable. So Lear says, "I might have sav'd her, now she's gone for ever! / Cordelia, Cordelia, stay a little. Ha! / What is't thou say'st? Her voice was ever soft, / Gentle and low, an excellent thing in a woman. / I kill'd the slave that was a-hanging thee."[7] This is the purest case of vengeance, mourning and grief threaded together. Cordelia seems still alive, and Lear's moment of imagining that she is still speaking, but in her customary soft voice, disguises the line between life and death. This, in turn, erases the line between prevention and revenge: by killing the one who was *about to hang her but had not yet completely done so*, he acts to save her life and prevent the act that, once complete, makes his killing into vengeance.

One aspect of vengeance is this prolonged, "as-if"-but-too-late prevention. That is the innocence at the heart of revenge. It serves to show just what would have been done to prevent the act and defend the victim if these acts had been, as they were not, in time. There are no stronger words than the words "in time." The contraction or expansion of the time in which revenge is tolerable—or the temporal lines demarcating an act as one of determined prevention, furious personal revenge, or impersonal justice—creates the key borderlines that define the sphere of the passions in their duration.

Even without the fiction of prevention that blurs the line between defense and vengeance, the location of justice along a scale of anger that requires the precise awareness of duration and separation in time is built into the legal system itself, and into the range of later satisfactions that our systems of religion, culture, and informally sanctioned private justice entail.

Within Judeo-Christianity it is because God administers justice that he is, then, in the face of transgression, a God of wrath. What the concept of Hell measures is not the level of warning needed to make humans lawful, but rather the spirit of wrath and rage within infuriated divine justice. The Christian Hell of the Middle Ages is God's anger in embodied form. It is the materialization of divine wrath in the same way that the Creation is the materialization of divine love.

For every outrage, God in his Last Judgment is in the position of Lear holding the just-murdered Cordelia and knowing that he has slain the man that was "a-hanging thee." The participial "a-hanging" exactly marks the timeless present of God's point of view in the Last Judgment; for God every theft goes on "a-thieving" throughout all of what to human beings is the duration of time. The fading and final indifference that constitute an essential feature of the human experience of the passions in time is nonexistent within timeless eternity.

The meaning of a Last Judgment within a philosophy of the passions lies in the fact that each and every act has to be seen to lie adjacent to the final moment of time, and to face judgment as though the "work of time" would never take place. Nothing makes clearer the human connection of justice to time as measured by the passions than the concept of a Last Judgment in which those very actions of duration are neatly set aside, and each act finds itself unprotected by the length of time between its horror and the response of its judge. It is in Dante's *Inferno* that we can see the consequences of this collapse of duration. Dante sets out to display the exhaustive material forms of God's anger in the same way that the entire range of species on the earth, from insects to fish to birds to mammals in their tens of thousands of forms, exhaustively embody the energy of divine love. In his notebook Kafka wrote, "It is only our conception of time that makes us call the Last Judgment by this name. It is in fact a kind of martial law."[8]

By contrast to the durationless relation between act and punishment, and then to the permanence of punishment within the concept of a Last Judgment, we can see that everyday social justice amounts to a process of setting limits to anger in order to refine the distinction between justice and revenge.

Historically, it is precisely this setting of limits to private vengeance that creates the transition from systems of revenge to an impersonal system of justice. One essential feature of the control of anger is the element of temporal delay within the process of justice. To our intuition, the punishment that feels "just" or "deserved" is very much dependent on how near in time to the crime itself the punishment can be administered. In the hours or first days after a gruesome and brutal crime no punishment, however cruel, seems even adequate. If we imagine every murderer, rapist, or torturer caught, tried, convicted, and prepared for punishment within forty-eight hours of his crime, the sentences that we could imagine society imposing would be so severe that they might match or exceed the cruelty of the crimes themselves. While still in the shock of the crime, the imagination returns again and again to the possibility that this did not have to happen to the victim, who still, for a time, retains the full human reality that he or she had prior to the crime. The punishment, at first, is related in intensity to the imaginary possibility that we are undoing the damage to the victim as if by magic. Punishment in the immediate aftermath of the act, as in King Lear, has still the aspect of prevention.

On the other hand, if we imagine discovering about an eighty-year-old man, because of evidence that has only now come to light, that sixty years ago he committed a crime equal in horror and cruelty to those mentioned above, it is often felt to be hard, now that sixty years have passed, to imagine any severe sentence's being imposed at all. In the immediate aftermath of the crime, so centrally is anger a feature of what we are calling justice that it is hard to think of any punishment as strong enough. But once we move to the opposite extreme and picture a full lifetime between the crime and its moment of punishment, it is often hard to imagine a punishment lenient enough.

Our lenience has in part to do with the ebbing of outrage, but also with deep features of justice. The element of prevention is removed when we look at the eighty-year-old man. So is the motive of rehabilitation as a justification for punishment. If he has lived sixty years without committing another crime, he does not require "rehabilitation." Many crimes—an obvious example of which are the Nazi war crimes, for which eighty-year-old men are still being sought and tried—are perceived by many as events unlikely to recur because they are products of unique sets of larger, unrepeatable circumstances.

What we mean by justice in its temporal relation to the passions, as these examples make clear, includes the question of the distance in time from the original act within which a trial and sentencing must take place. Neither a time too immediate nor one too distant will constrain the passions in the way that justice requires. The one year between crime and trial typical of American justice outwaits communal anger and yet takes place before indifference is complete. It is along a scale of fading anger that we can place legal systems, from the lynch mob (close to the crime) to the Last Judgment (as far from the crime as human time allows, but from God's point of view timelessly adjacent to the deed—and this is the meaning of God's "patience").

Delay creates a significant gap between crime and justice for two distinct reasons. First, with time the fact of even the most heinous of acts becomes familiar through repetition. We become used to its having taken place. It is no longer possible in the imagination to picture its not having taken place. The essence of revenge lies in this image of still possible reversibility. Second, as the act no longer seems reversible, so too does the condition of the person hurt. With time the victim can no longer be remembered as undamaged. Now, instead of seeming to our minds like someone who will return or get better, the person seems like someone (with full personhood) whom we have seen for many years blind or in a wheelchair. The mind does not instinctively undo the new state—as it tends to do at first—to replace it with memories of the person before the event.

In the case of a murder victim this is especially true. Someone who died yesterday is thought of as someone alive about whom we keep having to remind ourselves that he or she is alive no more. But those who have been dead for a year, three years, ten years, have had for a long time their primary image in our memory as people about whom it is the first and most prominent fact that they are dead. Their death no longer feels like a contingency, a horrible accident, because it has been for so long their very nature, their substance.

The aspect of rage within justice and the fading of anger over time mark out the path along which our mind is forced to reimagine someone, and in so doing to convert the unthinkable into the contingent and, finally, into the necessary. This particular rage is the sign of the work of the imagination struggling with that opposite of prevention: irreversibility. Once the irreversible fact of the crime has been memorized, what the mind is forced to picture as contingent is no longer the victim but the criminal, who, now on trial, might or might not be executed, jailed, and so forth. He absorbs the contingency that in the first moments after the crime (the essential moment of outrage and revenge) was the primary attribute of the victim, about whom we feel that his or her death did not have to happen. It might have been otherwise. The slightest change of timing or intervention would have prevented the death.

These temporal features of the relation of anger to justice are the signs of the temporal work of the imagination: its protest against what has taken place, its futility in unimagining the act, and, finally, its surrender to what did take place. In this last step, there occurs the resigned transfer of contingency from the person hurt to the perpetrator. Within our systems of justice, whether human or religious, as in a Last Judgment, we trace out techniques for using, but then defeating, the temporal features of the passion of anger, a passion that is both necessary and inconvenient to the idea of justice that both society and religion, in their different ways, require. Anger testifies to an injury to the worth of the self, as any visible wound notifies us of an injury to the body. And yet in all systems of religious or civil justice the time scheme of anger is overridden in ways that trace out by negation the essential features of time within anger itself. In justice we find a template through which we can see clearly the temporal features that we know to be intrinsic, because we can locate the path by which they are placed in suspension.

SEVEN

Mutual Fear

Thirty years ago Robert Nozick imagined one of the most extreme extensions of freedom in his book *Anarchy, State, and Utopia*. Why not, he asked, permit all actions, even violence to others, if compensation be paid later? If someone breaks my arm, he must pay compensation: not just my medical costs, of course, but full restitution for my suffering, loss of work, and so on. Why have laws against anything if we could establish, so to speak, a market for damage?[1] Nozick saw that there is an unexpected answer to this wild proposal. Only the suffering of those actually injured by others would be compensated, but if we knew ourselves to be living in a world where our arms might be broken by anyone willing to pay the price, there would be what Nozick calls "general anticipatory fear," a fear that would damage every life but could not be compensated. This is a flaw that we find in even our current laws of compensation. If a hundred men are sent to work in a dangerous coal mine and one of them is crippled by the fall of badly arranged timbering, he will be compensated, but the other ninety-nine miners whose days are shadowed by fear of just such an accident receive nothing.

Nozick's concept of general anticipatory fear, separated from the context in which he discusses it, is an important political notion in modernity. It describes, for example, one of the least discussed true costs of crime in a neighborhood, the cost for those who are not robbed but seldom walk at night, are never raped but always adjust detail after detail of daily life because of the ambience of rape.

It is important to notice what Nozick is not concerned with in his example. He does not ask us to picture the moment when, on a street at night, alone, I see coming toward me a man who will in the next few moments break my arm. This final moment preceding certain harm, along with the inner state of the victim who knows what will soon happen to him, makes up what I will be calling the classic model for the description of fear. Instead, Nozick lets us imagine a model where the state of fear of those in no imminent danger at all is placed at the center. This fear is general rather than individual, and its object is any possible other person, not one specific man facing me on the street at night. It is also any possible time, not a specific now moment, which after all is an exceptional moment, one that will come to an end. This fear never ends, never starts, is always present like gravity.

Nor is the general anticipatory fear only a fear of someone's breaking my arm. In such a society a whole menu of harm—someone's setting fire to my car, but compensating me; firing bullets through the windows of my house, but compensating me; slashing my new coat, then buying me a replacement; kidnapping my children, returning them unharmed a few days later, and paying me rent and damages for my suffering; taking over my house and locking me out, and happily paying compensation two months later after vacating. General anticipatory fear is fear of everyone, at every minute, and across the full range of imaginable damaging acts.

Nozick's replacement of the legal system with a market system for harms has one further important component. Each citizen of this rather brutal community will find in her own mind that she has a specific cluster of dangers of which she is constantly or intermittently in fear. Each person will localize the general anticipatory fear in a personal geography of fear, and that act of localization will require the work of my own projective imagination and will, in an important way, amount to self-disclosure, self-discovery, self-revelation. Each would, somewhere in his heart, have an image of "the worst that might happen," and this would differ from person to person, as would the many other harms felt to be "not so bad."

Nozick has, in this section of *Anarchy, State, and Utopia,* suggested a model for fear profoundly influenced by economics and game theory. He, along with Derek Parfit in his book *Reasons and Persons,* has been instrumental in exploiting elements and practices of modern economic theory for a metaphysics of social subjectivity.[2] If we consider the characteristics of Nozick's market for harms, we can see at once that it shares many features with markets in general. The one difference is that there is no chance of profits in this market, only losses.

All economics, as Frank Knight wrote in his classic book of the 1920s *Risk, Uncertainty and Profit,* is about "acting [and] competing on the basis of what [we] *think* of the *future.*" "We live," Knight wrote, "only by knowing *something* about the future; while the problems of life, or of conduct at least, arise from the fact that we know so little" (Knight's emphasis).[3] This imbalance is a structural fact about the future.

The term "anticipations" as it is used in economics includes anticipated profits, anticipated markets, anticipated costs, and even anticipated frequency of unforeseen breakdowns of machinery, loss of workers, or strikes. From a cultural point of view, the overall weight of economic facts and energies in our daily lives implies the growing importance of anticipations over memories, habits, customs, and, most important, the increased weight of the future as opposed to the past. To speak psychologically and ethically, the increased weight of the economic sphere enlarges the social value of optimism, confidence, of courageous and shrewd anticipation, over memory, knowledge of the past, and the ability to execute customs or rituals, or even to learn from experience.

The Nozick model, by contrast to the classic image of a man in the street facing imminent harm, asks us to discount (in the economist's meaning of the term) or to evaluate an open but not an imminent future, and this is, so to speak, the essential future time used in economics, what Alfred Marshall called the "long run" or long-term future.[4] The elements within experience that are forced to the surface when we face the open-ended, long-term future are uncertainty and, so to speak, the cost of uncertainty in inner life. It was Hume who first added uncertainty to the topic of the passions. He argued that because of uncertainty, the mind jumps from option to option and turns a wide range of states into fearlike states. Hume's example is perverse but brilliant: a man learns that one of his sons has been killed in a battle, but he does not learn which son. We can see that he would fall into profound grief if he knew that John had been killed, or that Will had been killed, but not knowing which one, his mind jumps back and forth between the two possible losses and falls into a state of fear.[5] I will say more about this example later.

Uncertainty became, after Hume and Adam Smith, the proxy for fear, but this is only to state that in these two authors we see for the first time the growing importance of the future over the past, of economic life over political or legal frames for the general conditions of life.

When I face a man in the street at night, uncertainty plays little part in the experience, but in general anticipatory fear, uncertainty about who, what, or when can be taken as the Humean proxy for fear itself. Frank Knight wrote eighty years ago about the growing importance of systemic uncertainty in modern life brought about by, among other things, "changes in technological methods which ... increase the time length of the production process and correspondingly increase the uncertainty involved."[6]

Because of these longer units of time, most of our anticipations take on the quality that was once associated with merchants whose ships departed from Venice for lengthy voyages. The opening of Shakespeare's *Merchant of Venice* speculates that the melancholy of the merchant, Antonio, follows from general anticipatory fear. His friends propose that once he has sunk his wealth into the voyage and the ship disappears from sight, the wind cooling his soup makes his mind picture what harm a wind might do at sea. When he looks at the sands running through his hourglass, he is forcibly reminded of sandbars, shallows, and flats and imagines his ship wrecked and sunk in sand. Even if, in desperation or anxiety, he goes to church to pray for the ship, the stone walls of the church make him think of rocks onto which his ship might be driven by a storm and sunk to "scatter all her spices on the stream, / Enrobe the roaring waters with my silks."[7] Antonio answers that he thinks no such things, since he has, as we would say, diversified his risks: his wealth is not all invested in one ship, nor in several ships going to the same place, nor is his total wealth all in play in any one year. Ships, destinations, and time are all diversified to reduce merchant anxiety or, as Nozick calls it, general anticipatory fear.

General anticipatory fear differs from what Judith Shklar in a well-known essay defined as the liberalism of fear.[8] Shklar insisted that we agree on a kind of minimal liberal agenda based on opposition to cruelty, and on the universal validity of human rights and the politics of suffering. Such a liberalism would concern itself with no wider range of issues than that demanded by the agenda of fear. Modern political thought like that of Shklar and Nozick, from two opposite directions, shows the imprint of one of the deepest currents within modernity, the political aspect of what I call the spiritualization of fear. The ultimate usefulness of fear for a theory of political life increases within modernity.

Mutual Fear and Surrogates for Fear

In Thomas Hobbes's unforgettable phrase, all society is constructed by men because of "mutual fear."[9] It is not the advantages of cooperation, nor some innately social and communal feeling of the kind Aristotle spoke of in his book on politics, but mutual fear that leads men out of solitude and self-sufficiency into society. Hobbes is eloquent in showing that the evidence of our fear is visible everywhere in the physical facts of our lives.

Relevant here is a point I made earlier that the real evidence of a terror of flying is not the passenger in the seat beside you trembling at takeoff and landing but your friend who never flies and last year took a train from New York to California. Where fear is too strong, it never, in fact, occurs as an experience because we sidestep or design out the occasions we know would trigger fear. Hobbes wrote: "I comprehend in this word *fear*, a certain foresight of future evil; neither do I conceive flight the sole property of fear, but to distrust, suspect, take heed, provide so that they may not fear, is also incident to the fearful. They who go to sleep, shut their doors; they who travel, carry their swords with them, because they fear thieves. Kingdoms guard their coasts and frontiers with forts and castles; cities are compact with walls; and all for fear of neighbouring kingdoms and towns."[10]

Looked at closely, every lock and every high window is a trace of fear anticipated and forestalled. Every gun is a surrogate for fear, but so are psychological facts like mistrust, prudence, and caution. Every town built at the top of a hill, or at the bend of a river, betrays a geographical provision against fear. We live inside an architecture that displays our fear, and we have an architecture inside ourselves—including fainting, not remembering, and, most important of all, not being able clearly to imagine or to concentrate on the distant future—installed by fear in our innermost beings.

Why does Hobbes concentrate not on fear but on "mutual fear"? The simple answer is important in the long history of the analysis of fear. When we speak of mutual fear rather than fear, we are forced to realize that not only do I fear others, they, in turn, fear me. My consciousness is forced to imagine and take account of the inner life of others whose acts and arrangements result in part from the exact shape their fear of me takes. I am both fearful and feared at the same time, and my bond to all other humans is forged from this double fact. This exercise of consciousness—imagining the state of the other in a circumstance in which I am locked into attention to my own state—has important aesthetic implications beyond the political use

Hobbes makes of the idea in founding political life and society on the fact of mutual fear.

It was also Hobbes who made the simple admission "[T]he strongest emotion I ever felt was fear."[11] As the translator of Homer's *Iliad*, our culture's single greatest poem of fear, Hobbes lived through the English Civil War within the century of European religious wars, the most brutal wars in Europe until they were matched and exceeded in the twentieth century.

No list of strong, violent, or primary passions ever omits fear, although there is striking variation among such lists as to which other passions they contain. Stoic philosophy listed four primary passions: pleasure, distress, desire, and fear.[12] Stoicism grappled with preparing the mind by careful training to face moments that would ordinarily call up anger, grief, or fear, but where it failed entirely was with extreme and sudden fear, which required Stoicism to invent the sophistic notion of uncontrollable, instinctive "preliminary passions"[13] that even training could not touch. Stoicism had its triumphs with anger but fell before the facts of fear and grief.

Extreme fear is the very state that makes plausible the division that we find in so much writing on the passions between everyday emotions and violent, primary, or strong passions. Sometimes we use the word "terror" for this extreme, all-pervading fear, but as Aristotle's classic analysis of fear depended on the fear of death of a soldier on the battlefield, it was always extreme fear that was meant by fear itself. Many of us never experience rage, but every person alive has at some time experienced extreme fear. It is the case of extreme fear that makes believable the characterization of the passions on the whole as perturbations, diseases, and merely negative disturbances of the mind and body.

"No passion," Burke noted, "so effectually robs the mind of all its powers of acting and reasoning as fear."[14] When fear is taken to be typical of the passions or the template for all other passions, then the long history of therapies against all passions would seem wise, even necessary. Who would not choose to reduce or eliminate fear if that were possible? Hasn't one of the central accomplishments of modern civilization been the overall reduction of fear, by nighttime electrical lighting, insurance policies, police forces, standing armies, the destruction of predatory animals, lightning rods on churches, solid locked doors on all buildings, and thousands of other small designs?

What we call the increasing security provided by civilization as it eliminates war, bandits, pirates, predatory animals, and plagues, brings flooding rivers under control, builds larger and more solid ships for voyages at sea, increases communications from sea to shore, sets up a coast guard rescue system, issues insurance, creates financial instruments to protect farmers from crop failure—all of this amounts to a net reduction of local experiential fear. But the very acts that remove short-term experiences like the wolf outside the door or the bandit met by earlier travelers open up, for the first time in history, the possibility, as a result of our new confidence and security, of longer-term planning, investments sunk into long projects, and what we might call the exposure of the human community to a partly predictable but ultimately uncertain longer-term future. More and more of our hopes and expectations thus come to be located in this distant future, exposing us to new sources of fear, which in the past might have been taken on by a whaling ship setting out in the nineteenth century on a two-year voyage or a businessman building a factory in China in anticipation of a market for toothpaste three years in the future. Only a civilization that has partly tamed or thinned out the traditional objects of fear—constant war, predatory animals, the variations of nature—can then, as a result, begin to expose itself to a long-term future as part of its daily imagination and give hostages to fortune that never existed before. Only in a very secure state could anyone encounter the fear that retirement funds will run out in the year 2040. As a society that has successfully conquered or reduced imminent fear, we live more and more in an extended future, and therefore we expose ourselves, as no earlier human group had, to the unmanageable uncertainties that long future units of time impose on us.

We now live in a new geography of fear that plays no part whatsoever in the lives of those living one season at a time, a few days at a time, or a few minutes at a time like a soldier on a battlefield in Homer's *Iliad*.

The Traditional Model

The classic model of fear examines a single person's state of mind and resulting acts, the state and acts, for example, of a man out for a walk who sees a snarling dog facing him on a path, or the condemned man who knows he will be executed in the morning. I call this the classic model because from Aristotle to Kant to Darwin to William James to Heidegger to modern psychology and neurobiology it is this model of a single person facing a threat to his life—a snake, a soldier about to fire, a ship about to sink—that generated our root idea of the salient elements of an experience of fear. One important use of the traditional model of the state of fear lies in the fact that it is with fear that the clear connection between the passions and the wider idea of "having an experience" can be seen.

At a certain instant it begins—when I first see the snarling dog; then it lasts for seconds or minutes and, finally, ends. For the duration of the state of fear nothing else seems to exist, neither the long-term future, nor whatever happened minutes or weeks ago. Brief in duration, compelling, thorough, begun and ended: surely the clarity of these features makes the episode into what we mean by an experience. We often, for example, relate later just such moments as "what happened to me today," or we remember them later as "one of the most terrifying things that ever happened to me." Matching what we mean by a story and later by a memory, the fear experience can stand as surrogate for "having an experience" per se. Of course, moments of wonder or sexual pleasure must also be counted as templates for having an experience, but in fear something must be done. I must act. There is a plot to fear, and there are choices within the plot, flight being the first of those choices. With choice there is self-revelation: cowardice or everyday bravery, heroic, almost superhuman calm, or disastrous collapse. Finally, there is one outcome or another: the defeated dog slinking away, driven off by rocks I threw at him; or the night I spent in the tree with the dog snarling below. How did it end? we ask.

These narrative features of the fear experience—inner state and consequent actions, the link to what we mean by a story and a memory, the short but complete time unit, a closed and complete action with both choice and self-revelation at the moral level—will lead at a later point of my argument to an account of the aesthetics of fear. Because experiences of fear prominently display the features of having an experience per se, and those of remembering per se, and those of a story per se, the strongest claim would be to say that narration and narratability have their background sponsor, among the passions, in fear. They have a second sponsor in desire and its narrative possibilities, but among the passions, as opposed to the appetites, it is the model of fear that sponsors narration.

The classic model for which my snarling dog is a low-level modern instance was stabilized by Aristotle in his analysis of courage. Aristotle's definition of courage is a virtuous comportment in the face of fear—of all that is fearful, but above all in the face of death. Aristotle quickly lists three kinds of death: at sea, by disease, or in battle. Only in battle is a noble and ultimately courageous death possible—first of all because in battle there is the alternative of flight, which there is not at sea or in disease. Second, in battle we must act. At sea or in fever we can only wait passively. The sailors (as opposed to the passengers) can act to try to save the ship, but it is of passengers that Aristotle, Epictetus, and Augustine are thinking in their analyses of fear on board a sinking ship.[15]

Finally, for Aristotle, the battle is an opportunity for the display of prowess. It is where men will arrange themselves in an order of greater or lesser by their deeds, as well as by their skills, leadership, and simple energy. It is not a blank universal fate like the sinking ship on which all will drown equally. The possibility of flight—and with it the choice to flee or to stand one's ground, and with that choice our ability later to judge the act, applauding those who did not flee, condemning those who did—lies at the heart of the classic model. The Greek and Latin terms for fear are not distinct from the word for flight: both *phobos* and *fuga* automatically speak of flight in speaking of fear, insisting on just those strongest states of fear in which flight is natural and impulsive—but, when resisted, courageous.

From the start this ethical model looks forward to the later moment of judgment or, in legal terms, to a verdict. We acted courageous or cowardly, slightly or supremely courageous. These verdicts are Aristotle's goal as he defines the features of experiences of fear. Of course, the term "verdict" includes our silent judgments of others and our judgments on our own acts. Because even the description of the experience looks backward from the verdict—ethical or legal—it is in essence a narrative of a legal structure. Both legal and ethical judgments look backward in time to resolve or conclude, in the present moment, a case that can now be told as leading up to this moment of judgment.

The economic model behind general anticipatory fear or behind the strategic games of Thomas Schelling's game theory depends on a relation to the future and sees the present as a moment of decision about strategy—a choice among alternative actions—whose only interest looks forward. By contrast the Aristotelian model looks back to a past, just as any legal system does in concerning itself only with complete actions done at a certain moment of the past—actions that will be brought to an end point now in the present moment by means of a sentence or ethical judgment, which might include praise, a reward, or an honor just as much as a punishment. The difference between verdicts and strategic decisions is one key feature of these two models of fear, models that are deeply legal and past-action-centered, on the one hand, and deeply economic and future-action-centered, on the other.[16]

In Aristotle, the essence of courage lies in the occasion that requires choice followed by a revealing action (to fight or not, to flee or stand one's ground). Battlefield courage requires brave actions as opposed to a merely brave inner state. Aristotle quickly adds that the highest form of courage has to be distinguished from five conditions or motives whereby men appear to be courageous but act from fear of punishment or hope of honor, from anger or pain, from sanguine temperament, or, finally, from ignorance of the reality of the danger.[17] This precision serves to create a pyramid of behavior at the peak of which is the highest courage in the face of what is most fearful—death. In these subtle differences we can see the goal of a precise verdict.

A final detail that Aristotle adds at the end draws his analysis into the problem of time. It is more a mark of a truly brave man to be "fearless and undisturbed in sudden alarms than to be so in those that are foreseen; for it must have proceeded more from a state of character, because less from preparation; acts that are foreseen may be chosen by calculation and rule, but sudden actions must be in accordance with one's state of character."[18]

It is the passion of fear, above all, that isolates this element of suddenness and the part it plays within the passions. The template of fear, where suddenness and unexpectedness make up so decisive an element of what creates extreme fear, leads us to think of the part of suddenness in all other passions, but it is because we think of fear first that suddenness becomes prominent as a feature. Such directed attention is one meaning of a template and one outcome, historically, of the prominence of the template of fear within the passions.

If we consider the other two of Aristotle's three examples, we can see what his cunning set of cases is designed to bring out. On a sinking ship we cannot flee, except by jumping into the very water that is destroying the ship. If the sea or nature is threatening to take us back into itself, we cannot run out of nature. All will drown equally, the brave and the cowardly, the skilled mariner and the passenger, the sleeping man in his cabin and the frantic sailors working to the last moment to save the ship and themselves. On the ship there can be no profound climactic moment like that when Hector has run three times around the walls of Troy chased by Achilles but then turns to face his death. From a sinking ship there will often be no survivors left to tell just who was courageous and who shameful and cowardly. No verdicts and no fame or infamy will last through time after an event of this kind.[19]

Disease is similar to the ship in ruling out the question of flight. For that reason disease draws a modern distinction between inner state and action. Disease is inside us, and there is nowhere to run from ourselves, a different problem from the Stoic fact that we cannot run out of nature. Disease is also structurally unlike a lion that we see on our path. The lion is out there, fifty yards away, moving at thirty miles an hour. We can run right or left, climb a tree, turn our back on him and run. He is a specific external point of danger in a world of imagined paths to safety or to a possible postponement of death. The disease is in my body, everywhere.

Once we consider the disease example, we can see what Aristotle's example of the ship, so prominently used by Stoicism, preserves: an aristocratic image of the world of death. On the ship there are passengers and sailors; the latter's skills let them act to save themselves as well as the set of passengers whose lives depend on the sailors' skills, but only if those skills and courage are adequate and the danger not overwhelming.[20]

Disease is the democratic image of fear in Aristotle. It strikes at random: there is no skill involved, nor is there any display of courage except in the modern passive meaning of courage, which certainly was not what courage meant outside the walls of Troy. On the battlefield there are no passengers; on the sinking ship there are both passengers and fighters (the crew); but in the hospital there are only passengers. On the battlefield we meet death at the hands of a brave man, on the ship at the hand of nature, but in the hospital it is simply time and the fact that we wear out and decline. Disease is on Aristotle's list because it names what we all do in fact die of, the using up of our own time. The greatest modern story of dying, Tolstoy's *The Death of Ivan Ilyich*, has as its subject Aristotle's third category of death, death by disease.

To look more closely at the legal, verdict-based model of fear and at its modern alternative—the economic, future-directed account of uncertainty—I want to consider two moments of fear. The first comes from Homer's *Iliad*.

In the tenth book of the *Iliad* two Greek leaders, Diomedes and Odysseus, are hiding at night in ambush among corpses on the battlefield, halfway between the walls of Troy and the Grecian ships. They watch as a spy from the Trojan camp passes by them in the darkness. Springing from ambush, they trap the panicked and fleeing Trojan by aiming a spear just over his shoulder, fixing it in the ground just in front of him.

"He stood still and fell into a gibbering terror—his teeth began to chatter in his mouth and he went white with fear. . . . He burst into tears. . . . His body was trembling."[21] Fallen into the hands of two enemies covered in animal skins who have leaped from among the corpses in pitch darkness, Dolan, the Trojan spy, pleads for his life; he then quickly betrays the secrets of the layout of his own army's camp, revealing where guards are posted and where kings and troops can be found sleeping apart, unguarded and ripe for the massacre that the two Greeks will soon carry out, thanks to his treachery. The slaughter of the sleeping men is one of the most brutal episodes in the *Iliad*, at least in part because the normal warfare of Homer's epic involves combatants who face one another on the field of battle, fully conscious that they might gain victory or die in the next few moments.

Dolan's trembling, tears, pallor, flight, surrender, and craven pleas for his life, along with his desperate but false hope that he will be able to avoid death by a treason that betrays a dozen others: these external details of body and action make unnecessary any elaboration of inner consciousness.

Unlike his Greek captors, Dolan had set out alone. Now, in the state of terror only his own survival any longer matters to him. His sleeping friends and allies he now eagerly bargains away in hope of saving his own skin. He has become individualized, we could say, by terror. The two Greeks were more clear-sighted. When Diomedes volunteered for this mission, he insisted on a companion.[22] Two men have four eyes, but even if captured they would remain a small society where many shameful acts would be unthinkable because each of the two men stands next to the other as a witness. Two men are also less easily terrified than one man alone in the dark, sneaking across a field littered with dead bodies into the enemy's camp. It is easier for two men to propose to one another that they hide among a scattered bunch of corpses. Could a man alone make this choice?

Note the instant on which Homer focuses our attention. Dolan, already captured, pleading for his life, betraying his allies to slaughter: this is the very moment that a later judicial inquiry would examine most attentively. Here the choice is made. A heinous crime is committed under the extenuating circumstances of duress; that is, fear for his own life. Of course, there will be no trial. Dolan is executed by Odysseus and Diomedes with a single sword stroke that severs his head. He will never be brought to trial and executed for treason by his own army. Nevertheless, the angle of vision is that of an imagined later trial. The interest is in the evidence, in his choice and his responsibility, in the gravity of the crime and the extenuating circumstances. Even in the present, long before any possible trial, the shadow of a legal proceeding falls across the incident and guides the eye of narration.

After betraying everything, Dolan is executed by his captors as if such a trial had happened. His cowardice was futile. These were the last seconds of his life: flight, trembling, pallor, cowardice, betrayal, futile and desperate bargaining, when all had already been lost. The state of fear that we see here is physical, spiritual, and ultimately ethical. The frozen body, petrified by fear, as we would say, has already surrendered. The will is now enslaved. Dolan makes himself the instrument and ally of his enemies, spying for them better than they could have done themselves. He reminds us of Hegel's famous parable of the master and the slave, a parable of fear in which, to save his life, one combatant surrenders and becomes the slave of another, constituting the other as master. With this act begins all of human culture and history. Hegel's account of how consciousness arises—for it arises in the slave, not the master—proposes that consciousness arises as a by-product of a surrender in the face of fear.[23] Just as in Hobbes, Hegel traces the entire later history of civilization to an originating moment of fear. Dolan does not get a Hegelian reprieve to live on as a slave. He is used as a two-minute slave, then executed. In his initial fear he does not turn to face and fight his enemies.

As we pass judgment on Dolan, and surely this is precisely what Homer intends, we might ask what is missing from this legal or ethical model that looks back at his completed acts, at his crimes or his cowardice. What is missing is any consciousness or estimate on Dolan's part of the minds of his captors. He gives them at once the information that makes them no longer interested in keeping him alive. He offers this information in wild irrational hope that if he gives them something, they will, in gratitude, give something in return, his life. But he would then be a burden to them, as prisoners always are to armies. We can fault Dolan for never having learned even the first elements of modern game theory. Odysseus, had he been captured, would have given out only enough information to make his captors interested in keeping him alive, or might even have lured them, with him as guide, closer to his own army, where they in turn might have been captured. Dolan lacks, in his terror, that most elementary strategy: to play for time. Each of these moves would have required him to be able to think two or three moves ahead and to imagine the minds of his captors, especially the circumstances under which they might have a motive for keeping him alive. Homer shows us a case where, in terror, there is no such imagination of the future or concern with the mind of the opponent.

Creeping out from their respective camps at night, Homer's three spies are engaged in what could have been a moment of mutual fear. Odysseus quickly transforms the case to the one-sided fear of a prisoner and his two captors, and it is only this later moment of the one-sided fear of the already captured spy Dolan that interests Homer.

Forty years ago, at the height of the Cold War, the economist Thomas Schelling, in the ninth chapter of his book *The Strategy of Conflict*, asked his reader to imagine the following situation. "If I go downstairs to investigate a noise at night, with a gun in my hand, and find myself face to face with a burglar who has a gun in his hand, there is danger of an outcome that neither of us desires. Even if he prefers just to leave quietly, and I wish him to, there is danger that he may *think* I want to shoot, and shoot first. Worse, there is danger that he may think *that I* think he wants to shoot. Or he may think that *I* think *he* thinks *I* want to shoot. And so on. . . . This is the problem of surprise attack" (Schelling's emphasis).[24] Schelling's scenario of mutual fear opens his chapter called "The Reciprocal Fear of Surprise Attack," and its connection to the global politics of the Cold War period is obvious. Schelling's modern armed suburbanite and armed burglar reenact the mutual fear of Homer's nighttime spies who meet on a battlefield of corpses, except that, in Schelling's case, neither has as yet made a move to take the other prisoner. Schelling, unlike Homer, invites us to examine the situation at an instant once the basic facts are established, but where time stands still. The future is still open. The next move will decide everything. This temporal slice— open to the future—is one essential feature of economic or game theoretical thought about interdependent action. The legal model that we sense within Homer observes the present from the point of view of some future moment when we return to judge this instant of the past. Within models of fear, everything turns on this contrast between the backward-looking legal model and the open future of the modern, forward-looking strategic alternative.

Schelling at once surprises us with the reminder that what he has described in the armed burglar face-to-face in the dark with an armed householder is "logically equivalent to the problem of two or more partners who lack confidence in each other."[25] With this brilliant move, fear and the temptation to strike first no longer define merely the problem of enemies but the everyday problem of the fearful cooperation of business partners who mistrust one another. It also describes those living together in any society, or married couples, each of whom is tempted to act injuriously so as to damage the other out of fear that the other might do so first. Each knows the other has what Shakespeare called "the power to hurt." By noticing the logical identity of his case with "partners who lack confidence in each other," Schelling sets in front of us by means of his interrupted burglary every important social and intimate strategic situation imaginable under the auspices of fear: the agony of Marcel's fear of Albertine in Proust's novel, for example. By this means Schelling defines the important category of games midway between zero-sum games (where one person's gain requires the other's loss) and cooperative games. Schelling calls these situations games "where conflict is mixed with mutual dependence."

"These are the 'games' in which, though the element of conflict provides the dramatic interest, mutual dependence is part of the logical structure and demands some kind of collaboration or mutual accommodation—tacit, if not explicit—even if only in the avoidance of mutual disaster. These are also games in which, though secrecy may play a strategic role, there is some essential need for the signaling of intentions and the meeting of minds."[26] Such games involve what Schelling refers to as interdependence of expectations.

Schelling's model of burglar and homeowner, part of his wide-ranging contribution to game theory, has an important variant in the type of game that has perhaps become the single most discussed modern social allegory—the prisoner's dilemma—a crystallization into one simple narrative of complex rational questions about self-interest and cooperation, betrayal and defection. The prisoner's dilemma is a way to contemplate society by means of fear. Only punishments are at stake, and some level of punishment is certain for the two prisoners under any outcome. Each in his cell, alone, schemes only for the least possible damage. Will he serve a shorter sentence by turning on and betraying his accomplice, or will he, if he remains silent and the other betrays him, get the most severe punishment possible while the other walks out in a year or two? Defect, cooperate, stand silent in the hope of the other's cooperation, then be betrayed by his defection? This lens of fear and suffering as the means to think through the larger social questions of self-interest, individual choice, cooperative behavior, and defection should make us aware that the same issues could have been focused through an example of rewards rather than punishments, hopes rather than fears.[27]

The politics of fear—in the prisoner's dilemma, or in Schelling's reciprocal fear of surprise attack, or in Shklar's minimal liberalism of fear (which puts aside the Benthamite "greatest happiness of the greatest number")—illuminates the remarkable hold of the template of fear over the background structure of thought ever since the time of Hobbes's mutual fear and the rise of the modern state.

Hobbes's contemporary Pascal, in one of his best-known images, created the spiritual dimension of this same template, an image or model that can bring into focus just how much has been revealed by the prisoner's dilemma or by Schelling's armed homeowner and armed burglar. Pascal wrote, "When I see the blind and wretched state of man, when I survey the whole universe in its dumbness and man left to himself with no light, as though lost in this corner of the universe, without knowing who put him there, what he has come to do, what will become of him when he dies, incapable of knowing anything, I am moved to terror, like a man transported in his sleep to some terrifying desert island, who wakes up quite lost and with no means of escape."[28]

Pascal's is also an image of a prisoner with no means of escape. But, as fits his theology, it is a single man alone with his will, as Dolan was in Homer's tenth book in the episode with which I began this section. The richness of the prisoner's dilemma and of Schelling's armed pair is that they face us with the interpenetration of wills, the modeling of fear in a world in which it is no longer possible to act by consulting only your own reading of the situation. What has been added in this new situation is the key role of my consciousness of another's consciousness of me, along with a deeper speculative identification with the other in the hope of guessing what he is thinking, and, as Schelling adds, what I imagine he might be speculating that I am thinking.

Reciprocal fear, at first, seems to present a problem of simple epistemological regress of the form "I think that he thinks that I think that he thinks . . . , or it might be that he thinks that I think that he thinks that . . .," and so on. But this state of fear of the other also makes us do more than think about what the other thinks. It requires us to enter the question of what his fear is like, how extreme, how impulsive or rash or nervous his split-second surprise, when he sees I have a gun, makes him. I mention this fact here only as what we might consider a strange example of sympathy—simultaneous passion, mutually interdependent, rising and falling as each person observes the other's pallor, jumpiness, trembling, bluffing, and so on. Later I will talk about the important aesthetic consequences of a slightly different condition that I will call shared fear. We cannot think of the homeowner and the burglar as having shared fear, because that involves fear of the same thing. What the homeowner and the burglar fear, or what the two former accomplices in the prisoner's dilemma now fear, is *each other*, but let us note how carefully each has to be able to grasp empathetically what it might be like to fear *me*, just how frightening I am even in the moment when I am in fear myself. Each has to know how terrified the other is, and to know that he has himself caused the very state he is now trying to grasp.

Let me now return to Hume's example of a father who learns of the battlefield death of one of his sons, but not which one. Now we can see several ingenious features of this example. Although it is designed to isolate the part played by uncertainty, Hume has constructed his model so that in a very unusual way the uncertainty is about the past, not about the future. The son is already dead. For that reason, there is nothing the father can do. His uncertainty requires him to wait, nothing more. He can have no strategy or forward-looking choice of plans. Hume fastens on his state of mind, and his state of mind is circular, self-employed.[29] He has no reason to reach out, as in a game, to the consciousness of others, to enter the dynamic of "I think that he thinks that I think," the primary step to a socialization of affect by means of the imagination of another person. Instead Hume's father is like a man confronting a completed act for which the verdict is not yet in. The verdict, in this case, will be his own state of grief once he knows which son to mourn.

We see Hume stretching the outer limits of the older judicial, past-looking model, twisting that model to build in uncertainty and fear, while retaining the terms of a model never meant to include such features, features that would find their natural location once it was the future rather than the past on which the template of fear was built. Of course, Hume's father, like Pascal's man taken to an island, stands alone. He lacks, we could say, the modern problem of reciprocal consciousness found in Schelling's armed homeowner and armed burglar.

Mixed Games

Schelling uses his example to introduce and define what he calls a "mixed game." Mixed games involve two or more persons whose wills are interdependent, like drivers in a dangerous traffic jam who will survive undamaged and reach their destinations most quickly only by a combination of advantage seeking and cooperation.

With mixed games, as Schelling pointed out, we have no common term for the other player or other players when there are more than one—as in a traffic jam. In games of cooperation, the other player is my partner; in games of pure conflict, the other player is the adversary. But what do we call something that lies midway between partner and adversary and includes elements of both, sometimes more of one, at other times more of the other?

Why are these mixed games of special importance to the aesthetics of fear where fear is a proxy for uncertainty, as it is after Hume and Adam Smith?

First: Mixed games depend on a unique form of uncertainty—two-person (or more) uncertainty, where each person's focus is on what the other will do, and, behind this question, a second question about what the other's strategies are, his limits, his state of mind, and, behind these questions, who the other is, what he is like that might make his actions predictable. At the same time the other is speculating in just this same way about me. Each of us knows, at the second level, that the other is engaged in this exercise of imagination and consciousness of the other person's inner world. Reciprocal uncertainty differs from the kind of uncertainty when I bet heads or tails and then flip a coin. The objective uncertainty present in all games of chance tells us nothing about reciprocal uncertainty, the basic condition of all markets, all marriages, all strategic relations—including the principal-agent relation examined by Kenneth Arrow in his famous essay "The Economics of Agency," where the term "agent" is broadened to include, for example, my relation to the other driver in a traffic accident who damages my car.[30]

The eloquent models provided by economists are not limited to economics. Henry James's *The Wings of the Dove* is one of the greatest modern works of art based on interdependent wills, reciprocal uncertainty, incomplete information, principal-agent relations, moral hazard, hidden actions and information, with one disastrous outcome holding in its net five persons whose wills have become interdependent in this game.

Second: A mixed game is a game of consciousness, of speculation about the likely next move of another person, about what compromises and risks he or she will accept. It is therefore a game of *moves* and of the hermeneutics of moves—reading each move for its disclosure about the strategy or state of the other player. It is an important fact about the prisoner's dilemma that no moves are possible, only a single decision taken by each player, of which the other knows nothing. The prisoner's dilemma is a game of one isolated moment of choice.

Third: Mixed games focus our attention on the middle of an unfolding action. The basic conditions are set, sunk costs and engagements, alliances and oppositions are already clear, but decisive acts to resolve the game still lie in the future, the pressing future. It is always the late middle (we could say) in such games.

Fourth: Mixed games are not onetime events like the prisoner's dilemma, nor are they repeating events, like successive tosses of a coin, that have no memory. Instead, they concern ongoing relations between rival countries, investors in a market, producers of computers, husbands and wives, a parent and a child, a labor union and management where it is *equilibrium* that is sought, rather than victory or defeat.

With the economic and the legal perspective we now have before us the two models of fear. It is important to underline all that we gain by the modern consideration of two or more persons when thinking out the conditions of fear. Once the aesthetics of fear tries to model mutual, reciprocal, or general fear, or any condition involving more than one person's state, and once it is uncertainty and a long, open future rather than a onetime episode that we are interested in, and, finally, once conditions rather than events become our concern, then it is the economic model rather than the legal-ethical model that proves rich, suggestive, and, in the end, necessary to aesthetics. I will now turn to the aesthetic payoff of these two models of fear.

EIGHT

The Aesthetics of Fear

The classical model of fear arises out of what we would today call interdisciplinary work. To grasp Aristotle on fear we would begin with his discussion of courage in the *Nicomachean Ethics*: courage in situations of a fear of imminent death, and above all on the battlefield where the option of flight and cowardice exists, where skill matters, and where the soldier must act, must face and go toward the very thing feared—the enemy soldier. To this profound argument must be joined the analysis of legal cases in the *Rhetoric* where the assessment of a crime's severity and the appropriate punishment follow from whether the crime inspires fear rather than pity. At the same time, any classical model based on Aristotle must draw on literary works like tragedy, where the exact relations among pity, fear, and the final extreme state—called a shudder of fear or terror—define the essence of certain stories and literary experiences. These three domains—ethics, law, and literary mimesis—are not simply added together. In fact, it is the legal trial and, above all, the moment of verdict or judgment, along with the relation to an experience already past but now placed fully before us once again for reflection, impassioned response, and verdict, that lies at the center of all three domains. Acts judged to be courageous or cowardly (with all gradations) in ethics; defendants deemed guilty or innocent in the court of law; spectators experiencing fear or pity or the shudder of fear in the case of literary representations: the real model in each case is the court of law, its decisive moment of the verdict, and its adjustment of every prior detail toward a moment of verdict.

The aesthetics of fear, in the classical instances, relies on the legal system, with its structuring of already concluded, discrete episodic events. The theft, the beating, the murder, the treason must have already happened and must have the completeness of a specific act, like the fire set by the arsonist that began at two o'clock and was finally extinguished sixteen hours later. The arsonist's trial that ended with a verdict and sentence occurred ten months after the event. The same is true for the courageous action on board a ship that took place in the night of August 14, for which the sailor was awarded a Medal of Honor two years later, or for Sophocles' play based on the actions of Antigone who buried her brother, which we see two thousand years later, like a trial made up of accusations, opposed summaries, evidence, testimony, and punishment.

Aristotle worked out his aesthetics of fear by considering three kinds of experience: first, a man in battle; second, a spectator in a theater viewing a tragedy; third, an extreme crime and the later framing of laws that sometimes follows, along with the legal cases that brought those extreme crimes prominence and attention.

Since aesthetics is, in part, the question of aesthetic pleasure, it might seem surprising that Aristotle spoke of the pleasure of fear and pity in the spectator's experience of a tragedy.[1] How can such dire passions be sources of pleasure? Homer had referred to the pleasure of Achilles' anger as "far sweeter ... than trickling honey."[2] When, in the final book of the *Iliad*, Priam and Achilles sit together and weep, the one for his son, the other for his friend and for his father, of whom Priam reminds him, Homer speaks of Achilles as taking "his pleasure in mourning."[3] In our own time the category of the sublime defines a kind of pleasure in fear that, to us, makes clear that the earlier aesthetic pleasures in mourning, in anger, in fear, and in pity are not far from our own way of thinking.

The pity and fear that Aristotle assigned to tragedy are not in fact two completely distinct passions. The relation between them is as important as their separate conditions. From the start they require us to think not only of tragedies but of courtroom trials and the criminal law. Pity is, so to speak, a secondary, derivative, product of fear.

We feel pity for another facing just those things that would cause us fear if they were occurring to ourselves, Aristotle pointed out.[4] Because of my fear of having my arm broken, I feel pity for someone whose arm is being broken in front of my eyes, or even when I hear about it later as a story or report, or even if I see a representation—mimesis—of arm breaking in a play or film where I can assume that the actor's arm is not really being broken. My own fear when I am or might be the victim produces a concern when I see someone else the victim of the same harm. On this fact Rousseau built his notion of species-preserving feelings by contrast to ordinary, self-preserving sentiments like fear, anger, curiosity, shame.[5]

But the situation is more complicated. Aristotle noted that "the people we pity are: those whom we know, if only they are not very closely related to us—in that case we feel about them as if we were in danger ourselves."[6] The line between feeling pity and feeling fear is one of the many lines of intelligibility within the passions. That is: something is revealed or disclosed to us and to others observing us. At times what is disclosed is something surprising or even disconcerting. No other means except passing through the experience could disclose these particular facts. Such lines of intelligibility are basic features of the passions, playing the same role that "revealed preferences" do in economic theory. Within a game, what we call a "move" discloses or reveals the thinking and strategy of an opponent in an irreversible way.

"Amasis did not weep," Aristotle tells us, "at the sight of his son being led to death, but did weep when he saw his friend begging; the latter sight was pitiful, the former terrible, and the terrible is different from the pitiful; it tends to cast out pity, and often helps to produce the opposite of pity."[7] One implication is that we would feel pity for a young soldier being led out to be shot for desertion, but not if the soldier were our brother. Then fear would be felt. And when we found ourselves feeling either one of the two—pity or fear—in less predictable cases, the actual closeness of our relation to another person would be, only in this way, disclosed and revealed to us and to others observing us.

In discussing crimes, Aristotle says the crime is worse "the more brutal it is, or when it has been for a long time premeditated; or when the recital of it inspires terror rather than pity."[8] This distinction implies that we normally think of the victim when we hear of a robbery, a beating, a neighbor murdered, and as a result we feel pity. But with crimes of shocking brutality and horror we no longer think primarily of the victim but of the crime itself, of nature or of whatever it is in human nature in general that makes such acts possible. Now we feel terror.

Aristotle added that "[a] man's crime is worse if he has been the first man, or the only man, or almost the only man, to commit it: or if it is by no means the first time he has gone seriously wrong in the same way: or if his crime has led to the thinking out and invention of measures to prevent and punish similar crimes...."[9] In these categories for crimes we can begin to see most of our own categories for legal gravity: premeditation, long planning, repeat offender, unusual brutality, even the case, as in the recent example of what we call "Megan's Law," of instances where a crime leads to new laws' being passed. In contrast, modern legal thinking has no formal place for Aristotle's aesthetic distinction between cases that, when we hear about them on the evening news, cause fear (or terror) rather than pity. But we can see at once what he means.

In speaking of plot within tragedy, Aristotle made a parallel point of great importance. He claimed that something is more dire when we feel a shudder of fear (terror) from the mere account of the events as opposed to the spectacle of those same events.[10] If we are present at the actual spectacle of an execution, a guillotining, as Albert Camus was, for example, we would expect strong passions of fear and disgust to be aroused. The gouging out of Gloucester's eyes in Shakespeare's *King Lear* occurs in front of our eyes as a spectacle on the stage. We are forced to witness all the moments of the event: about to happen, now happening, having just happened. But in *Oedipus Rex* we do not witness the spectacle of Jocasta's hanging, or the subsequent moment of Oedipus's self-blinding. Instead, we hear the report of these dire events, and we might think of this as one of the reports that produce the shudder of terror that was Aristotle's test. But the report of an isolated act or moment is not, in fact, what Aristotle means at all. In the *Poetics*, these terrible or shocking instants are separated off and called the "suffering" of the plot.[11] Suffering, recognition, and reversal are the three elements of an Aristotelian plot. The shudder of terror is not elicited by a scene of suffering, or even a report of suffering, however cruel or unprecedented. It is a response to the whole.

Aristotle's test for the small number of most terrible plots is that the mere summary of the whole causes a shudder of terror. Far less severe, isolated events will cause fear if seen directly as spectacles. This is a profound aesthetic fact about narration and spectacle, what we call showing versus telling, and about the difference between response to a part and a unified response to the whole.

The example Aristotle uses is the outline story of King Oedipus: to hear the simple facts of the case causes a shudder of fear. Parents warned about their newborn child send it to be killed; the infant is exposed on a hillside, crippled, rescued, raised elsewhere, warned; the young man flees, kills a man (his own father), saves a society, marries the widowed queen(his own mother), fathers children, brings plagues to the society, learns of his guilt, blinds himself on seeing his mother (his wife) hanged in their shared bedroom, a suicide.

Surely Oedipus is the only man in all history to whom this has happened, and that singularity is part of the horror. We would not even be tempted to pass a special law setting out a punishment for cases like this, once Oedipus's guilt became clear, because we would never imagine such a thing would happen again. One implication of terror like this would be that to pity someone, we have to be able to imagine that something like what happened to him or to her could have happened to us. We cannot literally imagine this in Oedipus's case. Shakespeare's *Romeo and Juliet*, because we can imagine it happening to us or to someone close to us, is a perfect example of a quickly summarized story that arouses pity. How sad, we say, how unfortunate. Because of their youth, their innocence, and their bungling arrangements, it is easier to pity them. But where the events seem uniquely grave, as in Oedipus's case, we no longer feel pity, and we are strangely freed of self-reference.

Only a very few stories could have this effect. Most grave plots, if staged as spectacles, or if we ourselves had witnessed the events as they happened, would cause fear but not the *shudder of fear* or terror that Aristotle uses as a term only once, and only for this case, amid the other ordinary uses of the word *phobos*, fear. Most gothic novels or modern fright movies of the Stephen King variety would seem banal if reduced to the simple report of what happened. It is only in turning the page or watching the unfolding spectacle of the film that we experience fear.

One feature of narration, especially the bare outline of the case, is a compression that forces us to take in the entire story almost instantaneously. A painting, for example, confronts us with an all-at-once first glimpse of a situation, before we enter its details. A rapid summary of horrid events can approach the suddenness of the visual. Suddenness is, as I noted earlier, a crucial feature within the passion of fear.

If we turn back to the criminal justice system, we notice that in a murder trial the jury hears narration; that is, they hear reports. Jurors are not set down in front of spectacles—a reenactment of the crime as the prosecutor claims it happened, plus another spectacle or reenactment as the defense claims. Law cases are about narratives. Telling not showing. The defense presents one narrative, the prosecution another. Each witness is asked to tell a story. Tell us what you saw on the night in question. In her or his opening argument, the prosecutor gives a quick summary of the case aiming to elicit the shudder of terror.

Since the report or summary tells the entire action in compressed form, we are able to have a complete action experienced in the way that only a moment within the action usually is. The whole is made nearly instantaneous. Because the action is the most important feature of a tragedy, this shudder of terror, usually aroused only for an unanticipated local detail like the gouging of Gloucester's eyes, has materialized as our relation to the whole. Aristotle's larger point is that if the report causes a shudder of terror, the gravity depends on a kind of horrible unity and order of the whole, rather than on an unexpected or startling part or a local detail, as happens in spectacle. What is implied is a universe where things hold together in some frightening way, and it is this that has the most profound aesthetic effect.

One last difference between story and spectacle is the fact that a report has the same effect no matter when it is told: thirty minutes after the events, thirty years, or three thousand years—our distance from Oedipus. The effect of spectacle wears down because at any remove of time, it too becomes a report, a memory. Gloucester's eyes were torn out on the stage last week. In the moment after a terrifying or disgusting film, the events convert to reports in memory or in our conversation where we describe to a friend what happened. At that point a stronger test is being applied. Extreme events, summarized, often seem ridiculous in the absence of the present-time spectacle.

In modern legal systems a trial takes place roughly a year after the events. The facts have sunk in. We have reported and repeated the Oklahoma City bombing to ourselves many times. Only those stories whose gravity and monstrosity have survived the conversion from present-time spectacle, or our first violent assimilation of the fact that something like that has taken place, can, after a year, create the shudder of terror in the once-again-repeated report of the mere facts that Aristotle brilliantly saw was the key test for what we call "the worst." This effect of the report is a classic fact about those short, interpolated stories told within the wider plot of such novels as Stowe's *Uncle Tom's Cabin* and Morrison's *Beloved*, both of which aim for the shudder of fear about the order and unity of a certain life that can be told in half a page. By means of that first shudder a second shudder of fear occurs, addressed to the system of slavery behind the quickly summarized life.

Aristotle's point about the unique gravity of those histories where the report produces a shudder of fear is one of the most important aesthetic discoveries ever made about the ethical difference between narration and drama, the report and the enactment. This discovery is the major aesthetic payoff of the classic model's choice of past-looking experiences, and of the legal system (along with its informal partner, the ethical system) as the locus within which fear experiences are set before us for our attention, an attention that is locked irreversibly to the moment of judgment or verdict. Narration and the spectacle of tragedy, news reports, and stories we tell one another are subtly defined by this priority of the legal system.

Finally, Aristotle opened up the nuanced relation between fear and pity that marks the path along which I move in consciousness, from my own full experience—my fear, here and now—to a civic interest and full experience of the states and harms of others, whether in pity, in fear, or in the shudder of fear that we call terror.

If we now return to the distinction presented in the previous chapter between the backward-looking legal model of fear and the forward-looking economic model of fear, we might ask whether the second, or strategic, model of fear offers any similar benefit for consciousness, for aesthetics, and for the necessary links outward from solitary experiences to the civic space where we live joined to the lives of others. What do we gain once the economic system, with its future orientation, replaces the legal system, with its orientation to the past, as our instinctive pole of reference? The aesthetic payoff would have to involve uncertainty, the consciousness of another's consciousness, and the interdependence of wills.

Shared Fear

In a wide range of aesthetic and legal experiences we have, to this point, considered fear in its relation to sympathy or pity, and then the difference that the shudder of fear at a report makes between narration and enactment, both in legal and aesthetic situations. Now I want to add a final refinement within the ordinary meaning of sympathy or pity.

We can begin by noticing this fact: we need not use the spectatorial model of an observer seeing and responding to someone else's state of mind in a theater or a courtroom to grasp the relations of pity to fear in consciousness. A number of false conclusions follow from an insistence on the image of a spectator or juror not himself or herself in any danger.

Fear often befalls several people at once. The ten soldiers on a night patrol in the jungle with its unknown landscape are all simultaneously afraid of the dangers around them, and each person knows that fate alone determines which ones among them will be killed and which will survive. When the soldier next to me is hit, my pity for him is strongly marked by my own intense fear and now my relief that it was not me killed this time. My ability to imagine his injury or death slides over from and absorbs the fact that my every thought had been about my own possible injury or death just in the moments before I saw him go down. In this case my pity taps into the already intense passion about imminent death that I feel. I almost see myself dead, but I am alive to bend over the body that did actually fall: his body, not mine.

Pity, I am suggesting, has its roots in the fact that fear is often felt in groups where each person is in the identical, imminent danger of death, but where some will die and others survive. Shared fear, like that of the passengers in a plane making a crash landing, or of those in a car as it crashes, or of those villagers taken out to be shot where every tenth man will be executed, leaves survivors who profoundly pity those who had been, a few minutes earlier, fused with them in the solidarity of terror in the moments of being about to die. Shared fear creates a model of pity far more important and empirically accurate than such traditional examples as the pity of a calm member of a theater audience watching Gloucester's eyes pulled out on the stage, or Lucretius's image of a man safe on the shore watching a ship founder in a storm, or Rousseau's man in a prison cell watching through the bars as a wild animal tears apart a child snatched from the arms of its weeping and frantic mother in the street below his cell.[12]

Pity should not, first of all, be modeled on experiences where a mere observer, as in Rousseau or Lucretius, safe from any personal threat, manages to shed tears or feel sorrow for the sufferings of another. Of course, the moral and aesthetic importance of the fact that, safe as we are, we can experience this form of pity and sympathy is one foundation for part of our idea of narrative in reading a novel or watching an opera. In spite of this aesthetic fact, the background template on the basis of which we think through pity should not be that of examples like these but instances of the shared danger of imminent death, where some in the end survive and carry over into the pity they feel for their unlucky fellow passengers the full weight of their own recent terror and encounter with their own mortality.

The shared fear of those about to drown together in a sinking boat is clearly different from the simultaneous fear of one another that Schelling's armed burglar and armed homeowner experience. Mutual fear or reciprocal fear is not shared fear, but each of these three conditions overrides the singularity, the radical individualism, of the passions that has been at the heart of our classic account. Mutual fear, even more than shared fear, forces us to imagine and contemplate the other to learn exactly what he or she is thinking and feeling. That is one source of the richness of the prisoner's dilemma.

Sympathy and Volunteering
to Feel What the Other
Does Not Feel

By sympathy we usually mean that I feel what the other is feeling. Rousseau's terrible example is of a man in prison who sees through the bars an infant torn from the arms of its mother and mauled to death by a wild beast. The man behind the bars is in effect identical with the reader of Rousseau's story. He can respond, but he cannot act to change what occurs in front of him. He feels the terror of the mother. He sympathizes with her fear and then with her grief, but hers is the primary feeling, his the secondary replication. He grieves because she grieves. The two states run parallel to one another, as the word "sympathy" explains.

What Hume points out in his famous chapter on sympathy in his *Treatise of Human Nature* is that there are many cases where we feel something exactly because the other does not. If we see a man asleep in a field endangered by a horse running in his direction, we feel the fear of imminent death that, asleep, he can not feel.[13] Hume also speaks of someone who is too modest but deserves honor for something done, for whom we feel the pride his modesty does not permit him to feel. If someone acts shamelessly, we feel the shame for the action that the other seems unaware of, a situation commonly found in a Jane Austen novel. When out of bravery or stoicism someone seems not to express or perhaps even to feel a terrible loss, we supply, as we watch the situation, the grief or sorrow not present in the agent.

People strongly under the influence of religious belief sometimes present a different but important kind of example. Take the case of a mother watching with bright-eyed fanaticism in the Roman period of Christian martyrdom the terrible death of her child. Convinced that this child will be at once a saint in Heaven, she seems thrilled with the death. If we imagine watching her as she sees the child suffer and die, we supply the missing grief and horror that her beliefs about martyrdom cause her not to feel or to feel as only a smaller detail within a larger radiant joy.

These examples that I have invented in the spirit of Hume are profoundly important for aesthetics because they describe the channels of emotion one experiences in watching a tragedy or reading a novel.

In the fact that we step in to feel what the man sleeping in the field cannot feel as the running horse approaches him, we can see the explanation for a number of devices or configurations in the wider process of narration. First, the power of using naive central figures such as a child. All that the child cannot understand or know to feel has to be supplied by the reader, who becomes, so to speak, a second central character responsible for the absent emotional register on every occasion. Not only do we fill in an alternative understanding of each event by knowing what the child cannot know; we also fill in the completely unsuspected emotional states that such understanding would normally require. Hume's argument leads to the conclusion for aesthetics that art makes in some ways a more powerful demand when we are forced to supply unfelt passions than when we simply replicate what we see being felt by a person within the scene. The naive or uncomprehending child or childlike character imposes this demand on us structurally and from beginning to end in a work of art. The use of such central persons is rare. It is revealing, but not essential to how we think passion functions between persons in works of art.

A more important, because more common, aesthetic case is the ignorant or mistaken figure, otherwise equal to us, who in this moment does not know what is happening, or misreads it, while we, knowing better, must supply the passion that his mistake or un-awareness rules out. Dramatic irony is one familiar version of this case. The audience knows more than Oedipus does in Sophocles' tragedy, and for that reason any member of the audience fills in the fear or the shame that, because of his false assumptions, Oedipus does not feel.

Traditional literary thinking about naïveté, dramatic irony, moments where a figure is mistaken, along with wider, more structural kinds of ignorance, illusion, unawareness, or self-deception—and all other gaps between the frame of the central person and that of the reader or spectator—has concentrated on the epistemological question, on what is known or not known, on blindness and seeing, and on frames of knowledge under conditions of rapid change by what Aristotle called recognition and reversal. We have rich accounts in a book like Wayne Booth's *The Rhetoric of Fiction* of how moral knowledge works under these gaps. But from the side of the passions a very different aspect of these same situations forces itself on our attention. What happens in these cases is a blank spot where the reader or spectator *volunteers* passion, stepping in to supply the missing fear, grief, shame, or anger. Volunteered passion is a stronger demand on the spectator and a more perfect aesthetic strategy for the eliciting of passion than sympathy, understood in the narrow sense of feeling alongside another's explicit emotional state, can ever be.

We can see that this is true in the common situation that does not depend at all on exceptional cases—like that of Hume's man asleep in a field, or the naïveté of a child—on dramatic irony, mistaken reading of a situation, or unawareness. We often find in a novel, a play, or a film that the author has set up the unfolding sequence so that the reader or audience will know that a disturbing event has happened before the central person concerned does. We often know in a frightening film that the killer has already broken into the house before the one upstairs who will be his victim does. Or we witness a scene in which a lover has been betrayed, while he will learn about it only later in an angry confession by the one he loves. Even when we see it happen, we think of him and respond as he will respond once he knows. We see the soldier die and then watch as the messenger travels to tell the wife of the death. In these three cases we are, I am assuming, aligned with the victim, the lover, the wife, and we fill in the emotions by anticipation. We often speak hypothetically about situations like these: If only she were here seeing this! If only he could hear the glass break! Only later do we witness their reactions and, finally, in the normal meaning of the term, sympathize with their fear, anger, or grief as we see them feel it. In the second phase we feel what they feel, as they are feeling it, and in the terms they feel it. Ours is now a pale copy of how much and in what way they grieve or fear, now that they are present to do so.

This common aesthetic fact of anticipatory feeling—what we could call our state before we have in front of us the enacted state on which to model our more colorless, secondary version of a character's feeling—allows us to see that the anticipatory state is not a question of mimesis or reproduction at all. It is one where we have been deliberately left alone, without a model. We are forced by the blank space in front of us to volunteer in our own terms, and with our own discretion about intensity, the not-yet-present state of vehemence.

Volunteered fear reminds us of one important feature of Aristotle's shudder of fear. We feel the shudder of fear in relation to a summary, a report, or an outline of the case. It is a feature of summary in narrative that it leaves out the analysis of feeling or the notation of response. Scenic moments in real time or moments of analysis give us the inner account to empathize with, but a summary or report leaves just this set of layers out. My earlier summary of the story of King Oedipus's life omitted every detail of what he felt or thought. We learn nothing of what his passions were at the different stages of his life. Reports force us, just as does Hume's sleeping man in a field, to volunteer and fill in the states ourselves without a represented model for us to copy.

To supply this missing emotional layer, an author often sets between us and a report a figure we can call the "register," whose response models our response. This is what Rousseau's man in prison watching the horrible scene outside the bars of his cell does: he registers for us the "correct" response. Aristotle, with his notion of a shudder of pity, and Hume, with his idea that we often provide what cannot be provided in experience, underline the stronger case where we face alone, anticipate, and volunteer passions, rather than echo what we find in front of our eyes.

The Modern Spiritualization
of Fear in the Sublime

If we think of Aristotle's shudder of fear in its profound legal and aesthetic use as what we might call a signal of gravity, then nothing could be more surprising than the dilettantism of the aesthetic path that our thinking about fear has taken in the two hundred years since Edmund Burke wrote on the sublime. Burke and Kant produced their work on the sublime in the half-century after Hume had opened up the new territory of uncertainty and consciousness in his analysis of fear. Hume's breakthrough would find its natural elaboration in economics and later in strategic thinking. The aesthetic counterpart to Hume's new territory of interest appears first as a current within the novel of strategy and consciousness, and above all in the novels of Trollope, Henry James, and Proust. Modern aesthetic interest was enchanted by the spiritualization of fear in the sublime, an episode to which I will now briefly turn.

The spiritualization of fear within modernity in the form of the sublime occurred side by side with the rise of boredom as an inner state of deep interest, and with the new category of mood, of which boredom and angst became the characteristic instances. Boredom, even when spiritualized, as both Baudelaire and T. S. Eliot succeeded in doing, remains an example not of a new passion but of a certain antivehement state: a position outside the passions altogether, but not outside the newly popular category for inner life, the moods.

Within aesthetics, the romantic notion of the sublime spiritualized fear by removing from it personal interest and danger and then imagining conditions within experience that blend fear and wonder. The storm at sea (witnessed from afar), the innumerable stars of the night sky, the mathematical infinite, the wildness of fire and waterfalls—here incomparable power displays itself before an unthreatened observer who need take no step to save himself or flee. It is from this side that fear was spiritualized in romantic aesthetics.

Kant's theory of the sublime merges experiences of wonder—especially in the case of the mathematical sublime—with the more traditional, Lucretian experience of the forces of nature that so outweigh the tiny human force that the imagination feels its own annihilation in standing in their presence. The imagination then experiences the expansion of the human reason, which can encompass even this scale of power. Kant's is ultimately a theory of moral feeling. The starry sky at night, the boundless ocean, whether calm or turbulent, are magnitudes against which the puny scale of human force in nature is measured, followed by the measurement of that part of human reality not in nature, the moral reason, which Kant claims dwarfs natural force or violence just as that force had dwarfed any human ability to resist it on its own terms.

Kant's actual examples are all in the spirit of Burke, whose details he follows while providing a profoundly new interpretation of those experiences and details:

> [A] any spectator who beholds massive mountains climbing skyward, deep gorges with raging streams in them, wastelands lying in deep shadow and inviting melancholy meditation, and so on is indeed seized by *amazement* bordering on terror, by horror and a sacred thrill; but, since he knows he is safe, this is not actual fear; it is merely our attempt to incur it with our imagination, in order that we may feel that very power's might and connect the mental agitation this arouses with the mind's state of rest. In this way we [feel] our superiority to nature within ourselves, and hence also to nature outside us in so far as it can influence our feeling of well-being.[14]

The mind, Kant says, has a "vocation that wholly transcends the realm of nature (namely, moral feeling),"[15] and it is in the face of the fearful that this exemption of a part of the self from nature can be made concrete in an experience. We have to see here the profound Stoic experience of nature of which humans are only a part, but now transcended with Kantian devices unknown to the Stoics. In the fear of a man on a boat in a storm we see the Stoic theory of death. In drowning we are reabsorbed by that totality of which we have always been a part. The sea stands for this totality, for nature as a whole pictured as a mere, featureless, extended domain of matter. Kant and Burke, along with romanticism in general, use nature and its force but presuppose a final safety of the human from nature, a superiority to nature that is a residue of otherworldly Christianity.

> [C]onsider bold, overhanging and, as it were, threatening rocks, thunderclouds piling up in the sky and moving about accompa-nied by lightning and thunderclaps, volcanoes with all their de-structive power, hurricanes with all the devastation they leave be-hind, the boundless ocean heaved up, the high waterfall of a mighty river, and so on. Compared to the might of any of these, our ability to resist becomes an insignificant trifle. Yet the sight of them becomes all the more attractive the more fearful it is, provided we are in a safe place. And we like to call these objects sublime because they raise the soul's fortitude above its usual middle range and allow us to discover in ourselves an ability to resist which is of a quite different kind, and which gives us the courage [to believe] that we could be a match for nature's seem-ing omnipotence.[16]

Standing back from Kant as he claims to stand back, finally, from nature, we have to recognize the sophistry involved in his interpreta-tion. Where all earlier writers about the scenes described emphasize the words "provided we are in a safe place" that Kant uses in passing, and see in this safety the difference between terror and pleasure, Kant—while never denying that a safe place is a precondition of the feeling of the sublime rather than the raw terror of those in the volcano's path as the river of molten lava races toward their homes—nonetheless requires us to believe that it is not this safe place but a subtle belief in our reason's location outside nature and encompassing nature that generates the feeling of the sublime. Fascinating as this subtle possibility might be, it is important to notice that Kant never leaves out the words "provided we are in a safe place."

The sublime occurs in response to deism, to an Enlightenment celebration of the watchmaker deity whose rational precision could be decoded by the human powers of reason that ran in the same purposive directions as the Creator's own. With the sublime it is the force rather than the order of the universe that is remembered, and the fear of God that religion had always recommended as the correct response to that force is secularized in a pleasing way.

In the long history of fear it might be best to see this moment of Burke and Kant, the moment of the human pleasure in the Alps and in mountain climbing, as a new taming or domestication of Stoicism in which the extraordinary accomplishment of Stoic physics and philosophy in imagining human life within the long rhythms and laws of nature—an accomplishment still present in Spinoza—is stripped of its force and reduced to a certain kind of sensation from "a safe place" unimaginable to the hardheaded Stoics.

In the past two hundred years the absence of an aesthetics of wonder, along with our fascination with this spiritualized aesthetics of fear, our conviction of the philosophical profundity of both fear and the revelation of the self that occurs within the experience of fear—the psychologically important dimension of the sublime—reveals an unconsciously Stoic and Pietistic account of the passions within modernity.

Where the sublime returns to dominate aesthetics, it is frequently found to share the aesthetic terrain with elegy. The elegiac is, of course, the aesthetics of grief, as the sublime is the aesthetics of fear.

In the ancient four-part Stoic division, distress (grief) and fear stand against pleasure and desire, both of which would be the ordinary objects of aesthetics.

In Wordsworth we can readily see the division of art between a poetry of elegiac loss, only in part recovered in memory, and a poetry of the sublime, with its center in experiences of fear. Wordsworth would, I think, stand here for romanticism as a whole. Its elegiac and sublime aspects locked in place a configuration of the passions around fear and mourning.

Fear and Boredom:
From Emotions to Moods

Starting from the romantic description of the experience of the sublime, fear has been within modernity a fundamental route of access to the most highly spiritualized remnant of inner life. No longer religious, but reflecting the truth of the famous description of all romanticism as "spilt religion," the fear present in the aesthetic experience of the sublime discovers, that is, *makes visible,* both the self and nature in the visceral and usually visual encounter with power. In the aftermath of romanticism, Kierkegaard and then Heidegger domesticated what had been the one experience in which anyone might feel (in the grandeur of sublime fear, as, for example, in looking over the edge of a cliff during a thunderstorm) that scale of feeling which a genius or great poet (to use romantic language) might be capable of in many different moods, converting it into the everyday, nonheroic, and nonaesthetic experiences of dread and anguish (*Angst*). For Kierkegaard, the experience of dread lies at the heart of how, in a Christian sense, we discover and continue to experience sinfulness, and this makes of dread the route by which we remain in touch most convincingly with what we ultimately are.

Kierkegaard's well-known analysis of fear occurs in his reading of the biblical story of Abraham, commanded by God to sacrifice his son Isaac. *Fear and Trembling* and *The Concept of Dread* are Kierkegaard's most analytically rich, detailed explorations of a single state. Along with Burke's analysis of the sublime, they make up the most significant markers on the path to the modern analysis of states.

In dread we have the undisguised experience of what our human essence consists in. For Kierkegaard that essence consists in sin. For Heidegger, discarding the frame of religious language while holding onto all of its inner life, angst and dread are the fundamental moods or states around which the very fact of human nature (*Dasein*) is displayed. For both philosophers the romantic exhilaration of fear, in which the magnificence and scale of nature and its forces are directly experienced by the mind, has vanished. Fear has been, as we might say, remoralized. It has been recaptured by the religious tradition of thought from which romanticism had made an attempt to spill it over into the aesthetic. The remoralization of fear as dread (in Kierkegaard), and then, in the 1920s and beyond, as *Angst* in Heidegger and his successors, did, nonetheless, have the effect of assembling human experience around a single central passion much as Plato had done around anger.

Unlike anger, fear carries with it an argument against the passions as a whole. From the Stoics to Hobbes, to their modern inheritors of a psychology centered in fear rather than wonder, to propose the passion of fear is always the preface to a solution to fear. Sometimes that solution is faith, at other times self-control, enlightenment, or apathy. To think of fear is immediately to imagine relief from fear. Fear made the gods, as the saying goes, but philosophy begins in wonder. The Enlightenment was not alone in seeing the entire life of reason as a triumph over fear and superstition. If Hobbes describes the primary condition of man in nature as one of fear, it is only to celebrate the creation of all that we know as government as the solution to conditions of all-pervasive fear. Nowhere is fear the essence of the passions except where it is given as a drastic picture of what would have been the human state except for self-control (Stoicism), or except for the state (Hobbes and Rousseau), or except for faith and the mercy of God (Augustine and the Christian tradition down to Pascal).

Fear is what makes us relieved that each passion is only an episodic state and not a constant unchanging detail of our being. It is the essential passion to make us think primarily of relief from passion. This is why all philosophies that acknowledge the passions, but only with the goal of setting them aside decisively, do so by means of an analysis of fear. Unlike desire or anger, fear, which like all passions underlines from a certain direction the limits of the will, would seem to be the one passion that, had it been left out of human nature entirely, would have improved it, making it most godlike. Were human beings fearless, as trees are probably fearless, the entire apparatus of culture—the state, religion, science—would never have been required as a counterbalance against which to lean the human will.

When this much is said, it has to be added that the cultural attention to fear from romanticism through Kierkegaard and Heidegger is itself a pocket of self-doubt within a civilization of confidence, and even arrogance about the human will. The lyrical descriptions of the sublime, of dread, and of angst are themselves a local heresy within the technological optimism about the will and human power that has been the overwhelming fact of the past two hundred years. Emerson has written the passionate and lyrical mood music of this civilization, not Kierkegaard and Heidegger. It should be no surprise that it has been within a literary culture that has itself become marginalized within society that the disguised remnants of the religious thematics of profound fear—renamed the sublime, or Kierkegaardian "psychology," or existentialism—have found their strongest and perhaps their only audience.

The partner term to fear within this literary culture's account of the passions has been, since the time of romanticism, boredom, especially in its radical form, ennui. The spiritualization of this apparently trivial passion has been one of the striking accomplishments of that side of romanticism stemming from Byron and Stendhal. Both Baudelaire and Eliot spoke of ennui as the symptom of a stricken religious consciousness; that is, one in which religious impulses and needs were pervasive but could no longer be enacted. Just as Baudelaire called the dandy an "unemployed" hero, so too boredom can be described as the entire energies of the religious life, but now under the curse of "unemployment." Just as unemployment differs from leisure, so does boredom from religious faith. Boredom, which might be called the sexual impotence of religious life, marks out, as does the no longer episodic impotence of old age, an especially bitter terminal stage of a spiritual life no longer open to revival. Baudelaire and Eliot are the antithetical figures to those other religious outsiders, prophets. The prophet arrives too early but predicts just that entire range of enacted religious life that is bracketed on the other end by those who arrive too late. Their boredom is what occupies the passionate space of the prophet's fervid hope.

Like the strategic repackaging of fear as the aesthetics of the sublime, or later as existential psychology, the diplomatic reappearance of no longer employable faith as boredom—which led to the attempt to spiritualize the experience of meaninglessness—reflected a local heresy within the confidence of secular modernity. It amounted to one last attempt of the religious temperament to swallow its pride and offer its services to the new master in the same period that many a former duke or count clenched his teeth and tried his hand, reluctantly, at business.

Boredom and fear direct our attention to the passions along a decisive angle. Boredom and angst are best described as "moods." They are states rather than motions of the soul. The word "emotion," though itself a lessening of passion, drew attention to the agitation (the commotion, as Hume called it), the movement of the spirit typical of the passions. Running, the athletic contest, the endless movement in play of children and spirited animals like horses was from the start a feature of the passions. Achilles is the angry man but also the great runner.

Emotion and motion are linked. Agitation, perturbation (which is Cicero's Latin term for the passions—*perturbationes*), and physical expressiveness, all aspects of change, are features of the passions.

But fear and boredom, like the twentieth century's newly invented category within the passions, depression, are immobilized states in which the spirit feels inactive, incapable of motion. They are conditions in which the life energies seem injured. As immobility is a sign of damage to the body, so too the immobility of boredom, depression, or fear (which we speak of in the phrase "paralyzed with fear") directs us to a conversion of feelings or passions away from movement, toward the motionlessness of states. Whereas the passions were volatile, the states seem to have no internal ending: we speak of "interminable" boredom. Depression, fear, and boredom are all states from which the spirit needs to be rescued, precisely because within itself it knows no way out. Unlike the other passions, these seem never to be spent, nor do they lead to calm, as in Milton's line for the no longer enraged Samson, whose revenge is now complete once he has brought down the walls and killed his enemies: "Calm of Mind / All Passion Spent."

Among the most brilliant pages of Heidegger's eighty volumes of writing are the ninety pages that give an analysis of boredom in his lectures of 1929–30, lectures now translated in the book *The Fundamental Concepts of Metaphysics*. Clearly in the years of writing *Being and Time* and the lecture courses on which it was based, Heidegger had both fear and boredom in mind as states through which the world as a whole "disclosed" itself, to use his vocabulary. His very great analysis of fear in the lecture series just before *Being and Time* copied and spiritualized the precise terms of Aristotle's heroic analysis of courage. Deliberately moving from passions to moods, Heidegger restates fear without an object and without occasion—in the cleaned-out theological language of Kierkegaard, *Angst* or dread.

His one independent analytic contribution to phenomenology is the structure and phases of boredom.[17] It is easy to see a certain path within modernity, since the moment of Burke and Kant, that shifts the passions over into aesthetics and renews them through the mechanism of fear, while casting off the complex world of action that fear, when linked to flight or later to pity, had necessarily included. Mere states, like the experience of the sublime, were already halfway to being what we now call moods. The secondary interest in boredom as a spiritual condition confirmed the remoralization that was an undercurrent in the elevation of the sublime as a prominent category of experience over the last two centuries.

My argument in this pair of chapters on the template of fear began with the saturation of the political by fear within modernity, roughly since the time of Hobbes. Game theory, the prisoner's dilemma, strategic thinking in the style of Schelling, contemporary philosophy in the mode of Shklar's "liberalism of fear" or Nozick's general anticipatory fear—all these are, I hope, markers of that saturation.

I have tried to show that the legal and tragic uses of the shudder of fear as Aristotle proposed it, along with the links between fear and pity, on the one side, and shared fear, on the other, are permanent and profound ideas necessary to our legal system or to aesthetic thinking about works of art of the highest order.

I hope that I have not seemed to present the episode of the covert return of theology in the modern spiritualization of fear, along with the "invention" of boredom to hold in place the newly important category of moods in our century, as though it were the goal of this long winding river of fear; I see it, rather, as an episode within the persistence of fear as a template for the inner life.

The experience of terror, as we saw it in Homer's description of the failed spy Dolan, trapped by his enemies at night on a battlefield of corpses, might seem to emphasize the fiercely individualizing account of the passions as states in which reciprocity and an acknowledgment of the reality of others is suspended. In this moment of terror there is only one person left in the world.

What I hope I have shown here is that it was precisely through fear, a future-directed passion in which action of many kinds is possible, that a path to the imagination of the situation of others was opened. This path was opened through the relation between fear and pity, fear and sympathy, and above all because of what I have called the common experience of shared fear. In shared fear, the possibility opens of grasping the parallel state of another just because of the differing outcomes: some survive uninjured; others do not.

With Hobbes this idea is altered into mutual fear that founds all larger societies. The reciprocal fear of Schelling's armed burglar and armed homeowner depends on the projected imagination of the inner state of the other person, which I have claimed is the fruit of shared fear experiences. Reciprocal fear, as it guides the prisoner's dilemma or modern strategic thinking, makes evident to us a profound interdependence of wills in the forging of an outcome that both will suffer from, an outcome that will be reached by the process of reciprocal awareness, occurring in seconds of time, of the state and strategic options of the other.

Fear is, then, a surprising route through which reciprocity is broken off, the other valued at nothing, when we look only at the existential moment, but whereby an even more profound reciprocity then returns, through shared fear, mutual fear, reciprocal fear, anticipatory or volunteered fear. This process not only provides us with something far more important than fairness, at the political level—acknowledging the worth of the other's will. It reveals the interdependence of wills in outcomes shaped by fear and the search for either advantage or survival.

Finally, I also want to claim that the aesthetic importance of fear, from Aristotle's analysis of tragedy, and from tragedy itself, through the gothic, sentimental, and fright film genres, has the unmistakable prominence it does precisely because of the political imagination that locks our own state into play with the state of another—or of many others—and invents in fear an unexpected but crucial kind of civic energy.

NINE

The Radius of the Will

One of the most telling statements about the passions is the remark of La Rochefoucauld that there are many people who would never have found themselves in love if they had never heard other people talking about love first.[1] Like most wise and witty observations on the passions, this maxim draws a portrait, sponsored by the intelligence, of a subject that, as soon as the clear light of reason falls upon it, seems to disappear. La Rochefoucauld points only to "some people" who might never have thought up love for themselves, but if love is a kind of state they learned that they ought to feel, then might not the experience itself be as much a made-up part of ordinary life as the idea that time divides itself into "weeks" of seven days? We all find ourselves living week by week because other people have lived that way and have done so for centuries. If love is an artifact and not a fact, then haven't we found out, by means of one group of people, the only slightly more concealed case for the rest? And if for this one passion, love, which since the seventeenth century has more and more come to displace all others as the very meaning of passion itself, then wouldn't every other passion dissolve and reappear as a convention in the face of the same wit and doubt?

But what is telling about La Rochefoucauld's maxim is not the suspicion that it seems to open up about the passions. Instead, it is a difference between love and the passions that is made clear. We could not imagine changing his maxim to read: there are some people who would never have experienced fear if they had not heard others talking about it first. Neither anger nor surprise, grief nor wonder would fit into La Rochefoucauld's equation.

When Augustine asks himself in his *Confessions* what were the first sins that he committed as a baby, he points out that if we call a baby innocent, this is only because it lacks the strength and not because it lacks the will to do harm. He remembers seeing passionate jealousy in a baby who grew pale with envy whenever it saw its foster-brother at their mother's breast. How could this be innocence, he asks, when the child seems to resent a rival in desperate need and dependent on this one source of food, which, in any case, flows in such abundance?[2] The tantrums, tears, jealousy, and helpless anger of this child too young to speak testify to the presence of the will. The infant's jealousy unfolds in a spectacle of anger and in doing so reveals the core of anger or vehemence that is a constant oxygen within the combustion of the passions.

Since the will is ineffective because the baby lacks strength to bring about any of its own wishes, the important connection of the passions to the insulted or injured will, and above all to the limits of the will—to use the terms that I will spell out later—appears with unusual clarity. Augustine takes a baby as his instance of the passions because he wants to underline the fact that such passions are not, as La Rochefoucauld would have it, learned. Jealousy is already there before language, before observation, and prior to any imitation of others.

Charles Darwin used the facial expressions of the blind girl Laura Bridgman as evidence that we do not learn to express passions simply by looking at the faces of others.[3] Darwin also made ingenious experiments on small infants to show that the onset of emotional life was timed in a specific way. When he lightly touched the eye of an infant with a piece of cloth, he could see that tears were produced, but only in the one eye. These, he concluded, were tears but not the tears of the emotional life. When crying, infants do not produce tears until they are, as Darwin found, about 140 days old, and this, he claimed, was the first point at which emotional crying takes place.[4] Like Augustine, Darwin was particularly interested in establishing the exact onset of certain passions, as well as their appearance long before learning and imitation might account for their existence.

Augustine's use of a baby in his example also makes clear that our personal existence as a will can be seen long before we have any capacity to effect the purposes of the will. In this, Augustine demonstrates from one side what, in the literature of the passions, particularly in tragedy, is made clear by the choice, at the other extreme from an infant, of the example of a king. The king is the one man within society whose will is so completely enacted that any injury to his will comes to him with an amplified insult and surprise. He is also the person most likely to become confused about the limits of his will, even about whether there are any such limits. The traditional explanation of the choice within tragedy of royal or noble figures as central characters focuses our attention in the wrong direction. It is not the high estate nor the magnitude of losses, nor the depth of his fall, once the wheel of fortune turns, that distinguishes a king from an ordinary man and makes his fate, as we say, tragic. Rather it is the relation between tragedy and the will.

The passions occur at the contested periphery of the will, a periphery that for everyone is ultimately measured by the fact of mortality. We cannot will projects that require hundreds of years to accomplish, nor can we change in any way the fact that human life ends. But within everyday life, where our ultimate death is kept from sight, the radius of the king's will extends so far that it serves as a magnification of the ordinary human problem of the will. That problem can be stated as the ambiguity about just how far the will reaches. A king or tyrant whose decrees can move whole populations thousands of miles, declare war and raise an army to fight that war, plant rice where wheat once grew, order a new capital city built in what is now a swamp represents one clear example of how delusion could arise about the outer limit of the radius of a will that seems to be able to command anything at all.

Injury or insult to the will occurs because of a penumbra of ambiguity where we expect the will to operate but find it frequently baffled. Our two extremes, Augustine's jealous infant in its rage and the kings of ancient tragedy with their fatal mistakes about the will, make clear the topic of the will, and the specific problem of the insulted or injured will, within the passions. Epictetus spoke as a typical Hellenistic philosopher in stressing that "[o]f all existing things some are in our power and others are not in our power."[5] What Hellenistic philosophy and, above all, Stoicism isolated for attention and made fundamental to an analysis of the passions was just this problem of the will. What lies within our power? What does not lie in our power? Where does the border between the two realms lie? I have invented the term *the radius of the will* to describe this circumference. Inside the circumference of this radius of the will lies everything that is within our power.

But of course the exact boundary is ambiguous. It was one of the great insights of Stoicism that if we could be absolutely clear about the extent of our will, there would no longer be any passions, since the passions occur in a zone of ambiguity (on the one hand) or (on the other hand) in cases where we hold false beliefs and are simply wrong about the limits of the will or have forgotten what we know about those limits. The passions mark the point of injury to the will by the unexpected, the unwanted, and the threatening. By signaling that an insult or injury to the will has taken place, the passions mark out for us a point where we expected the will to be able to succeed. The passions are therefore a sign that passivity, powerlessness, and an attitude of hopeless acceptance of whatever will come are not endemic to our reading of the world. The passions occur around an active will, one that expects to fare well in the world and can, for that very reason, be startled, surprised, and even angered by insults or injuries to the will and its expectations about the future.

When we understand that passions like anger, fear, and grief are the response of an injured or insulted will, even of a baffled will, we take this to mean that such passions are themselves part of the will.

Duns Scotus, for one, claimed that this was the case.[6] Hope, for example, is a passion so clearly aligned with our will that it is, in effect, the will itself in the form of thought and consciousness. The same is true of the Stoic idea of desire, one of their four master categories within the passions.

That the passions react, as fear makes clear, to the unexpected forces us to recognize that the human will involves a second, ambiguous zone where much of what is predictable, foreseen, and expected has also been included in our plans, even if we know ourselves not to be the cause of the specific things that are predictable and expected. We become invested in the foreseeable so that when the unexpected happens, we feel an insult to the will that is hard to distinguish from a direct frustration of actions that we know ourselves to be the cause or source of. This is true particularly because any of our intended actions involves the presumed stability of a set of background conditions that enter into the success of our effectiveness as agents. We then end up including in a dangerous way many details that lie outside our will as though they fell within the will. The farmer's yearly plans include the assumption of "normal rainfall" and normal market conditions for his crop, among many other assumptions, just as he assumes that he will work as hard this year as last, using the full array of skills and energies that he knows he commands. He assumes tacitly that he will not break his leg halfway through the summer and, as a result, be unable to go to his fields. That he will work hard lies directly within his will, but normal rainfall, market conditions, and the accidents of life fall in three very different ways outside his control, even though his knowledge and expert adjustment to what he knows that norm of rainfall to be already place him in an ambiguous relation to surprise.

The will carries an enormous freight into action made up of what is expected, what is typical, what is lawlike, what almost always takes place. Bundled into the will, these domains, over which we in fact exercise no power, come to seem to us part of our will because every act of our will has to be allied with the expectation that background conditions will continue to be normal. Hellenistic philosophy insisted on, but had no program for clearly defining, the line between those things that are within our power and those that lie outside our power. The radius of the will has a penumbra of disastrous ambiguity of which this problem of background normality and predictability is only one part.

It is important to understand just why, historically, we needed to work out a sophisticated account of the will. I will claim that it is because of the needs of the legal system, where precise punishments and degrees of responsibility had to be distinguished and justified. It was in social life and specifically within the gradations of the law, and from the perspective of the judge, that we refined a theory of the wills of others in relation to their acts and our response to their acts. In this legal domain we forged a complex, nuanced picture of the will. Surprisingly, my own will, this most intimate fact about myself in our modern perspective, was not primarily a result of introspection. Instead, it arose as a social problem of observation directed at the acts—the crimes and offenses—and the presumed will of another person in the formal matter of punishment of deeds. Only then, and as a second, distinct step, was this account of willing applied to my own relation to my will as an introspective account, but now with features necessarily derived from interpersonal relations. These features carry forward the lack of immediate intuition that necessarily characterizes my description of another person's will.

We had no rival account of our own will, because we did not need one. The need occurred in the social realm as a problem posed by crime and transgression. We can see this in Plato's *Laws* and in the legal sections of Aristotle's *Rhetoric*,[7] where it is in the definition of the gravity of a crime and the degrees of responsibility for a crime that the most precise idea of a "deliberate act" is developed. The reason for its development and the shape of that development arose in the attempt to create a just and graduated set of punishments, including a clear idea of the unintended, the misadventure, and the distinction between remote consequences and proximate harm—above all for the set of cases for which no punishment at all should be assigned.

At some later point when we might need to evaluate our own experience, for other purposes, the only model of the will we find available is already saturated with the features made prominent by the topic of crime and punishment and degrees of responsibility. Christian theology spelled out freedom of the will and agent responsibility in its notions of sin, punishment, conscience, confession, the Last Judgment, Purgatory, and Hell—each notion importing into internal self-relation the judicial relationships that evolve between persons in a society, seen through the eyes of jurors and judges, and then only later becoming available as a package now modified for internal use in, for example, the idea of an examination of conscience.

The passions, above all anger, sponsor an alternative, presocial account of the will, but one that is also, in part, alert to transgression, especially to the invasion of a just perimeter of the self. But only in part. Anger and the passions embed that concern with justice within a wider topic of the insulted will, where losses and fears, the death of a child or a passenger's fear of a sinking ship, display the will humiliated by nature, by accident, or by the laws of life. The injuries suffered at the hands of another person who sets fire to my house are called arson by the legal system, but if lightning sets fire to the same house and burns it to the ground, the legal system is indifferent and calls the event an accident or misadventure. To the will maintaining the perimeter of a world, arsonist and lightning injure or insult the will equally. It is here that we can see that punishment, the only interest of the law, is a trivial matter to the will, and that the largest number of insults to the will—the death of one's oldest friend or of the best-loved person in one's life—fall outside the small domain of punishable harms. At heart it is this far larger domain of unexpected harms and injuries that trace the exact radius of the will of which we are notified by the passions. The judicial realm of punishable harms, or even harms that raise the possibility of punishment along with the task of identifying the agent of our harm, tends to overshadow the wider, more important domain. It does so because the accomplishments of legal precision have invaded and given their own color to a far larger territory, where they are often more deforming than illuminating.

Anger or mourning occurs where the will has been outraged, or we could say "irritated," by events that not only have not been willed but are contrary to what the will knows itself to want and to be in the process of accomplishing. The world does not follow the contours of the will. The man whom I expect to aid me opposes me instead. As a result my anger is incited. The child whose future much of my own effort is directed to forming dies at the age of seven. Profound mourning begins.

With losses that set off grief, the insult to the will is unmistakable. The death of someone loved, someone to whom the fabric of life itself seems linked, marks out one fundamental limit to the human will. That limit is mortality itself.

But a distinction should be made between our victimization by the external sources of an insult to the will because the insult comes from without and happens to us—whether it be some wild animal across our path that incites fear, or the sudden death of a friend that produces grief, or the opponent whose success at blocking our plans produces anger—and, on the other hand, the energetic and activist response that the vehement state of fear, grief, or anger in itself represents. A bland or passive fatalism could also have been the will's response to the wild animal, the dead friend, the opponent. The passions bring to light an element of experience in which we are, at first, passive in the sense that something has happened to us, and, in fact, most things do happen to us. The percentage of the will in daily life is small.

The passions themselves are evidence that the will has not so often been insulted that it has practiced defeat to the point of resignation. The passions locate precisely the level of expectation within us that the will ought to prevail. Functioning under the auspices of the will, the passions guard its periphery.

The Legal System and the Will

The point is often made that no clear concept of the will as a faculty of the soul can be discovered in Plato, Homer, or the Greek tragedians.[8] It was common to claim that we owe to Augustine and to Christianity the key features of our modern everyday account of the will and of our identification of ourselves with our will.

Jean-Pierre Vernant in an important essay has given a remarkable summary of the modern notion of the will that he, like many others before him, claims has no equivalent, as an ordered whole, within Greek thought. The next few pages will elaborate on Vernant's argument.[9]

To paraphrase Vernant, by the will we mean the person understood in his role as an agent. This implies that we understand each person as the source of his own actions, for which he is then responsible in the eyes of others. At the same time these actions are ones in which he feels himself intimately involved. Both the unity of the modern self and its feeling of continuity over time are closely linked to a concept of the will. By unity is meant the sense of having accomplished all that one has done. Even more, it is the constant choice to express oneself in words and deeds that manifest one's authentic being. The artist becomes an important model of authenticity because, working alone, he creates objects that more directly embody his uniqueness by means of acts of will than those who, in their working lives, cooperate with others (in a bureaucratic or factory world) and can find little or no trace of themselves in the objects that they produce. The artist is the hero of a society of the will.

For Vernant the continuity of the self is secured by the way in which we recognize ourselves in our memories as the same person who stands even today responsible for works and actions done long ago. When one remembers one's earlier self (as Augustine, Rousseau, Wordsworth, or Proust does), an even more powerful sentiment of self becomes possible because the memory creates an internal cohesion out of the sequence of acts and products. In its continuity this array of still acknowledged acts of the will makes up a history of the self that is, paradoxically, the strongest evidence for its integrity and continuity. This was a point made by Locke in a brilliant section on the self in his *Essay Concerning Human Understanding*.[10]

Within his richly articulated essay Vernant points out that the category of the will presupposes the following things: first, an orientation of the person toward action; second, a valorization of action and practical accomplishment in all their diversity; third, a recognition of the essential part played by the agent within action as opposed to chance, the gods, or the brute force of circumstance. The human subject is seen as the origin or productive cause of all acts that emanate from him. The agent therefore experiences himself in his relations to others and to nature as a center from which decisions flow out toward the world, and as possessed of a power to effect those decisions.

Insofar as we picture ourselves as a center of power, we locate the essential moment of that power in the act of making a choice or in the moment of resolving to act. In the moment of free choice both the autonomy and the responsibility of the self are concentrated. For modern man, as Vernant puts it, we see ourselves as beings who decide and act voluntarily just as we see ourselves as having arms and legs. The will is integral to what we mean by a person.

It is important to differentiate this modern and somewhat idealized account of the will from the operative Greek notion of *hekon*, which is better translated, not by the strong notion of voluntary, but by the weaker idea of willingly. *Hekon* occurs in opposition to *ákon*, which defines those acts done under external compulsion. The two important cases that show the distinction from the modern notion of free will are the passions and the actions of animals, both of which are *hekon*, that is, not caused by external compulsion, but also not within what in our vocabulary would be seen as acts of free will. The acts of an enraged man or of a hungry lion are, as Vernant puts it, in accord with his nature but not the outcomes of the reasoned choice that we expect in the case of the will.

Occurring too swiftly to permit reflection, the acts that are produced by the passions lie outside the deliberative acts for which Aristotle created the term *proairesis* (deliberation). The acts that in Plato's three-part soul result from the spirited self—*thumós*—and in which there is the closest possible link to the actions of animals, especially to such noble animals as the horse and the lion, are here designated as precisely those that bring into view a distinction between the modern notion of the free will and the far weaker Greek distinction between *ákon* (compelled) and *hekon* (uncompelled) acts. The latter would include many acts, like eating when one is very hungry, that might seem to be compelled, but where the compulsion arises inside the self and reflects its own nature. This internal compulsion is quite distinct from, for example, a moment in which a prisoner is forced by his captors to take a certain drug. For animals the modern term "instinct" exists to wipe out the uncomfortable similarity—for modern thought—between purposive and complex animal actions, on the one hand, and nearly identical human acts of will, on the other hand, to which they might seem related. If animals act by instinct, then there is no need to contemplate a realm like that of spirited (within the passions) or deliberate (within the will) where the overlap between human and animal realms touches on the central areas of what we now take to be, because of the influence of Christianity, uniquely human identity.

The legal system, in refusing to consider animals as guilty of crimes, draws a similar distinction between humans, who can be accused, and all other species, which cannot. Judeo-Christianity and the legal system, when taken together, undermine any interest we might have in the overlap between humans and animals that was always prominent in the topic of the passions.

The area within social life where the purification of a vocabulary of action takes place is within our systems of justice, particularly around the judgment of responsibility for homicide. Here the category of "premeditated" homicide, as it has been elaborated over time, has fenced in a cautious and explicit version of "free will" in which we can see clearly that it is the question of responsibility—which is itself driven by the problem of legitimizing acts of punishment—that drives the refinement of notions of agency and free will. As Vernant points out, the distinctions between *hekon* and *ákon* do not result from purely subjective or disinterested speculation. They are elaborated by the state with the purpose of regulating, and for the most part eliminating, private vengeance, and replacing it with a carefully developed set of gradations of responsibility for situations in which one person has brought about the death of another.

It is because the domain of action is transferred from the realm of the individual to the realm of society that the precise concept of free will and the attendant responsibility become solidly entrenched to the point that, at a later stage, they can have the most profound consequences for the individual's private relation to himself. This may take the form of "conscience" or the variety of pride that could be called "agent-pride"—the form of self-regard that results from considering oneself the primary source of one's own actions. These interior psychological features of the category of will, which might seem obviously prior to the social use within a legal system, should, on the contrary, be seen as an aftermath of the public fact, a repositioning of a social design within the individual.

Within the social system of justice the ever more refined distinctions follow from the need for a range of punishments that makes punishment itself seem legitimate. Within vengeance, or in general within acts driven by the passions, it is exactly the lack of any gradation of punishment that is most obvious. Within the immediate, rash response of anger, only the erasure of the source of offense by an act of killing seems adequate, as if by an act of magic it could undo the moment of offense itself, creating a world in which it had never taken place, since the very agent who might have done it does not in fact exist.

The elaboration as we can see it in Vernant of the notion of *proairesis* (deliberation) found in Aristotle, and of full legal responsibility within the laws surrounding homicide, point out just those features missing in the psychology that such a notion of the will replaces. The particular sector of the will with which Aristotle is concerned is the will subordinated to a planning reason. On the other side, the will as it comes to interest the state in laws governing homicide is a will already tethered to society and having its status defined by its acts that impinge on others who are considered to have equal standing as citizens.

The intellectualization of the will that occurs within Aristotle's notion of *proairesis* can be seen in the conditions that Vernant lists for the will:

> Beyond autonomy and free choice it (the will) presupposes a whole series of conditions: there must already have been delimited, within the mass of events, sets of ordered acts felt to be purely human that are linked to one another and circumscribed in time and space so as to constitute a unified conduct with its starting point, its unfolding, and its conclusion. It requires also the appearance of the individual and especially the individual understood in his function as agent, along with the correlative elaboration of the notions of personal merit and blame; the appearance of a sense of subjective responsibility replacing what one might call objective unfolding; and, finally, a beginning of an analysis of the various levels of intention, on the one hand, and of accomplishment on the other.[11]

A specifically adult, specifically human form of responsible action is at stake. Vernant concludes, "Obviously, *proairesis* bases itself on a wish or desire, but a reasonable desire, a wish (*boulesis*) saturated with intelligence and oriented, not towards pleasure, but towards a practical goal which the mind has already presented to the soul as a good."[12]

From the point of view of the passions it is important to note just how restricted such a reasonable will is. And at the same time how the autonomy of the self has been purchased at the expense of the autonomy of the will. The latter is now an instrument of the reason and not an independent faculty. Similarly, the constraints put on a notion of the will by the judicial interest in responsibility and punishment displace the interest of the individual in his own will. The social, external questions of accountability create a perspective from which the individual can come to regard himself, but which is quite different from the perspective of the will or the passions.

Anger and Diminution

To think about a version of the will designed by the passions and the spirited self, and not by the long history of our legal system with its spillover into everyday life and psychology, we need only replace the interest in responsibility, punishment, and reasonable effectiveness with a concern with the quite different situation that I have called the feeling of "injury" or "insult" to the will. A door through which we wish to pass sticks, blocking our route to the room we planned to enter; a fever takes the life of one's best friend; a storm at sea threatens to tear apart the deck of the boat on which we stand, putting at risk not just our voyage but life itself. These are moments that imply the will but mark out the radius of the will, the place where we would want the will to be operative but find experientially that it is not. The passions begin around a surprised and injured will, because passions flare out where our expectation that the will would prevail crumbles. When, in Homer's *Iliad*, Agamemnon reaches out to take Briseis away from Achilles, a line is drawn to mark where Achilles' will cannot prevail, a social line in this case, based on Agamemnon's power as the leader of the Greek coalition.[1] The irritation to the will arises over the indefiniteness of the will's boundaries. The passions arise from, marking for our notice and the notice of others, a militant state of the will, patrolling its own borders, or what it imagines those borders to be. The intensity of fear and anger, along with the tendency of formal descriptions of the passions to begin with either fear or anger, makes clear this negotiation of the radius of the will in which the self remains in a state of alert to any injury to the claims that the will makes on the surrounding world.

It is in the details of anger that these features of the will can be grasped most easily. Anger has been subjected historically to the most detailed scrutiny because of the acts of violence to which anger leads. Anger is the necessary bridge between a purely internal account of the passions and an interest in action, because it is with anger that the aroused state in the soul or spirit has the most immediate links to the physical acts of our fists or our body in the outer world. And it is with anger that we find, not just arguments against the passions, but explicit social intervention, through the legal system's response to violence. This response, we might say, ran away with the subject of the will, simply because, from a social point of view, the act of killing posed so dire a challenge to the well-being of others, that is, to their very survival.

It is to the analysis of anger as a template for the passions and for the aroused spirit that I will now turn. With the template of anger we need to put aside the kinds of instances that might leap first to mind from our own culture, where anger is thought of as a therapeutic problem. For our therapeutic, post-Freudian culture our keenest interest lies in controlling anger or understanding the roots of anger, or learning how displacement has concealed from us the actual target of our visible anger, which is often in modern culture imagined to be about something else, often some experience long ago in childhood. We need to step back from these twentieth-century topics of displacement, unconscious motive, and the preference for moderate as opposed to vehement states if we wish to explore an understanding of this passion that made it not only ethically desirable but a model for the impassioned state itself in its most positive versions. That is the understanding we find in Homer, Plato, and Aristotle, who, in combination, designed the larger account of the passions that survived until at least the time of Hume and Kant. Anger, as I will be describing it here, lies at the root of an intuitive and manageable sense of daily justice and is not to be confined to such primitive forms of justice designed for major crimes and offenses as the revenge or honor systems, which we pride ourselves on having replaced by our idea of a civilized life under an objective system of explicit laws and impersonal justice.

In Aristotle's classic description in his *Nicomachean Ethics* anger, properly understood, is itself not one of the extremes but a desirable mean. As Aristotle defined it, "The man who is angry at the right things and with the right people, and, further, as he ought, when he ought, and as long as he ought, is praised."[2] He continues, adding a term that surprises the modern reader, "This will be the good-tempered man." Our idea of the term "good-tempered" would entail the absence of anger, the very opposite of Aristotle's claim.

The capacity for correct anger is, like each of Aristotle's virtues, positioned between two equally negative extremes, one an excess, the other a defect. The excess of anger is obviously the bad-tempered or irascible man, the constantly or excessively angry man, the man enraged by trifles. But it is the defective extreme of anger, for which we have no word, but which Aristotle calls the "in-irascible" man, that excites Aristotle's close attention. The in-irascible man does not feel anger when he should. "[S]uch a man is thought not to feel things nor to be pained by them, and, since he does not get angry, he is thought unlikely to defend himself; and to endure being insulted and put up with insults to one's friends is slavish."[3] One detail of Aristotle's account of every one of the passions is the phrase "to oneself or one's friends," "oneself and those close to us." The passions are incited, as anger is in this definition, by what happens not simply to myself but to parents, to those I love, to children, brothers, sisters, friends, neighbors—that is, to those who make up our world. The importance of this extended world is a simple one. It is for various reasons easier to imagine just anger about insults or injuries to those we love, to a child, to a parent, or to a spouse than to ourselves, where we might accuse ourselves of egoism, of excessive sensitivity, or of a lack of perspective. We might expect of ourselves a standard of forgiveness and simple overlooking of injury that we never impose when what we would be forgiving or overlooking is an injury to one we love rather than to ourselves. Not to feel this just anger implies, as Aristotle says, that we have failed to "feel things."

Aristotle's inclusion of those close to us, our friends, family members, and certain others, in the structure of the passions themselves is one of the most important and accurate details of his work. It is also a detail neglected by all modern scientific work on the passions, which seemingly establishes the egocentric role of the passions in advance by studying fear, anger, or delight only in relation to things happening to the subject himself. From Aristotle to Hume the philosophical account of the passions always included the idea that the passions are incited by what occurs within a world of care and concern—parents, children, friends, those loved or close to us—as well as by what happens directly to us.

After Kant and Rousseau we find a different division of the world, along with a new attention to sympathy and pity as the first and only passions that reach outside the freestanding self to exhibit concern with the sufferings of others. But pity, we need to stress, extends the passions to strangers. It universalizes a generosity within passion that, in the modern view, is otherwise self-interested and stops at the boundary of the ego. This extension to all others, to persons unknown to me, is a significant part of a modern analysis of feeling. It lies at the heart of sentimentality, as well as of the democratization and universalization of what came to be known as a "feeling of humanity" after the eighteenth century. At the same time this extension to strangers in pity and sympathy had profound importance in explaining how in works of art we feel deeply the joys and sufferings of persons not known to us in our everyday life, in fact, fictitious persons.

But only in modernity do we contemplate a world made up of myself and what we call "others." The passions, as we find them described from Aristotle to Hume, are never universal in the Kantian sense. They do not concern my conserving for myself only what I will grant freely to all others. Still, the passions do concern a wider field of action than the isolated self. What happens to me and to mine, what happens within my world, is the subject of the passions, as Aristotle makes clear with his phrase "to me or to one of my friends." And it is this same line that Aristotle claimed determined whether, when we see something terrifying about to happen to someone else, we feel pity (if the other person is a stranger) or fear (if the other person is a friend or someone close to me).[4]

As I will argue later, it is by means of the passions that we come to know the periphery and characteristics of what we call "my world," as opposed to "the world," and come to know precisely who makes up the set of "those close to me." The passions concern two quite different peripheries that they both mark and reveal: first, the radius of my will; and second, the census of my world along with the exact contour of the phrase "me and mine."

To return to Aristotle's account of anger. Aristotle points out that the too-angry man is always condemned as a tyrant, but the inirascible man is called a slave and a fool.[5] The slave has no will of his own and exists only to execute the will of another. To be a free man or woman, capable of pride and self-regard, is to fall between the tyrant and the slave, and this middle ground between the two extremes is identified by, among other things, one's having the correct capacity for anger.

In both the *Rhetoric* and the *Nicomachean Ethics* the key feature of anger must be underlined: anger in its legitimate form has its source in the feeling and in the perception of injustice. Aristotle's initial definition of anger states that "[a]nger may be defined as an impulse, accompanied by pain (distress), to a conspicuous revenge for a conspicuous slight directed *without justification* towards what concerns oneself or towards what concerns one's friends" (my emphasis).[6]

In reminding us that anger seeks revenge and that it begins with a perception of unjustified damage or slight, Aristotle has returned anger to its roots in the prehistory of justice. Before there exists an objective legal system, justice is dependent on the personal execution of retaliation, which depends, in its turn, on anger. Even where a formal and impersonal legal system does exist for gross offenses, everyday acts of injustice and injury require small-scale retaliations, and these might amount to no more than a look, a moment of silence, a change of tone, or might include a warning or even an aggressive act. It is these small-scale and everyday occasions that make up the greater part of our lived experience of justice and injustice in daily life. Not speaking to someone who has insulted me or punishing a child who has been cruel to his brother or a child's shouting an insult back at the playground bully are local, everyday acts of justice still dependent on aroused anger. The largest part of our everyday sense of just and fair existence is not defined by the transactions of the courtroom and the prison system. Nor does it take its forms from that system. Instead, this everyday sense of just and fair existence has its source in the hundreds of sublegal moments of felt injustice and redress too small to interest society at large, in its institutionalized array of courts, judges, juries, and prisons.

The excitations of anger mark out the places where self-worth or honor has been transgressed. Any society based on honor requires each individual to be militant and alert to violations of his own self-worth, and it is anger that manifests both to himself and, outwardly, to others, the fact that an unacceptable injury to self-regard has taken place. Thus when Aristotle in the *Nicomachean Ethics* speaks of in-irascibility, he can do so only with contempt. Not to experience injury would be a sign of having no feeling of self-worth to be militant about.

By this route that has taken us from anger to injustice and to the necessarily alert and militant notion of self-worth, it is possible to see why Aristotle in his list of the passions in *The Rhetoric*, the key text for the entire later description of the passions, began with anger. Here again, it is important to add that each of these features applies to things done to myself and to those close to me.

A measure of self-esteem, or of endangered self-regard, is defended with the energies of anger that locate and announce that injustice has been felt and must be revenged. In other words, in anger the self itself and its world are at stake. Paradoxical as the claim may seem, when Aristotle begins with anger, his intention is identical to Hume's, although the latter begins his section on the passions in his *Treatise of Human Nature* with an analysis of pride.[7] Both Aristotle and Hume discuss first the passion by means of which the self has its own worth as its topic. That Hume can imagine this self-worth as a settled and expansive pleasure marks out a profound difference from Greek thought, where that same self-worth is conceived most powerfully in moments where it is challenged by an opposing force. To discover and defend a perimeter of self-worth that one will not allow to be violated by a slight or challenge to that self-worth is a sign of the Greek notion that only in struggle (*agon*) are the essential features and limits of anything revealed. Hume's relaxed pride, on the other hand, relies on a modern notion that even in the absence of a counterforce the characteristics and worth of something—including oneself—can occur to the mind. Hume's pride and Aristotle's anger both isolate a moment of asserted and felt self-worth as the primary ground of the passions.

In book 4 of Plato's *Republic*, in the discussion of the parts of the soul, it is by means of anger that the existence of a third part of the soul, the passions, is established, distinct from reason, but also from the appetites and desires. This third part of the soul discloses an intuitive and aroused sense of justice. Socrates asks whether it is not true that when a man knows himself to be in the wrong, he will endure sufferings like hunger and cold at the hands of someone whom he believes to be acting justly. The noble man will. But in the opposite case, where he feels that he has been wronged, the same hunger and cold will make his spirit "seethe and grow fierce." He will fight on for justice or accept death.[8] Here the spontaneous occurrence of anger or its absence demarcates a world of justice. Anger becomes, if we use a medical vocabulary, the symptom of an inner sense of justice that supports the judgment of reason or even precedes it. When he is wronged, a man's anger leads to endurance, willingness to struggle, a conversion of experience into strife where, in the language of athletics or war, one seeks victory or death. Here, just as in Aristotle's definition, the essence of anger lies in redressing a balance, but now without a vocabulary of revenge.

In Plato's final account of justice in *Laws* the angry or spirited self is fundamental to the indignation necessary for our insistence on justice; that is, not only must we favor or approve of justice, we must also seek justice and impose it wherever that is required. "For cruel and almost or wholly irreparable wrongs at the hands of others are only to be escaped in one way, by victorious encounter and repulse, and stern correction, and *such action is impossible for the soul without generous passion.*"[9] Reason alone cannot impose justice. It can write laws, but it cannot notice their violation in a specific instance. What is here called "generous passion" means that spirit or anger, and even what we might call militancy or fanaticism, is required.

Since for Plato in *The Republic* justice is the highest of the virtues of society as well as the most profound and encompassing virtue within the soul, it is now possible to see why anger is the passion that first makes evident the third part of the soul. Anger is, once Aristotle's account is considered, the most primitive and spontaneous evidence of an innate feeling for justice and injustice within human nature. Since the informal, everyday system of justice is utterly dependent upon anger and, then, limited by anger, the elevation of anger by both Plato and Aristotle can be seen as a way of looking back to the line between personal and impersonal systems of justice. For Plato as he writes his final work, *Laws*, vehemence is still, even within the most advanced and codified legal system, a necessary element of spirit that makes justice active and insistent within society. As Hume would write two thousand years later in one of his most provocative statements: reason is and can never be anything more than the slave of the passions.[10] In using the word "slave," Hume states a literal fact, and one that is clear from our previous argument. Hume means that reason is

■

178

not a part of the will and has no access to the will. The passions alone ignite the will. This repeats Plato's exact statement about justice. Only the aroused passions can set in motion our actions, and justice, among other things, is defined by actions that respond to the prior actions of others. Justice is not made up of opinions or thoughts about events.

In both Plato's *Laws* and Aristotle's *Rhetoric* it is in the description of murder and the degrees of modified responsibility for murder that the analysis of anger—or what we now call crimes of passion, by which we mean crimes of rage—takes its most acute form. It is because acts done in passion (*thumós*) can only partly be called acts "done by choice" or in our vocabulary, premeditated, that the law is forced to develop a psychology of intentions, agency, diminished responsibility, and fully punishable responsibility for acts. The law must also design a ladder of ever more serious acts that intersects with this ladder of chosen, not-quite-chosen, accidental, and compelled acts. A full theory of diminished responsibility for crimes of passion is clearly visible in Plato and Aristotle.[11]

That anger can, within the revenge ethic, only demand justice for oneself and for those extensions of oneself, family and friends, makes it, in the long run, a liability for society once the justice of every other citizen must be assured by means of a shared account of fairness and a system of punishment distinct from revenge. The transition from the militant awareness embodied in the formula "I (or someone close to me) must not be injured" to the impersonal "No citizen may be injured" is the transition from revenge to justice in the public world and for that small number of acts of justice taken into view by the public world.

In an impersonal notion of justice, injury is imagined to have occurred not to the victim but to the system of society as a whole, and its right to punish or to demand an accounting overrides the individual victim's private rights, which could be satisfied only by vengeance. The victim's anger becomes a hindrance to justice at this point because it claims to dispute with society as a whole the question of who has suffered more, the society or the victim. In addition to the objective system of justice, the ethical stress on forgiveness as it gains force through Christianity strikes an equally serious blow to the moral and psychological claims of anger.

In the specific features of an impersonal system of justice we can easily recognize, by negation, the crucial features of anger that are now being used but superseded. Let me quickly list these features here, because they outline the shadow of anger that falls across the idea of justice even by negation.

In a trial, the victim, even if living and present in the courtroom, is spoken for by a prosecutor. He or she does not present his or her own case. The injury is depersonalized by this measure. In anger we each present our own case. The jury and judge are yet more remote from the one injured, because they adjudicate between two presentations, that of the prosecutor and that of the defense. If guilt is determined, sentencing happens as yet another distinct act. The sentence, once imposed, is carried out by still other persons who played no part in any earlier stage, an executioner or prison guards and warden. The executioner, the judge, the jury, the prosecutor, and the victim divide up the set of roles bundled in a single person in acts of revenge. Finally, the very essence of the court system is to bureaucratize crime by hearing hundreds of similar cases. For each victim the crime that has happened to him or to her is unique and monstrous, but to the courts, forced every day to deal with drunken drivers, men who have killed their wives, bank robbers who shot a guard, the numbing repetition of long legal experience destroys the uniqueness, along with that part of the outrage linked to what every victim feels to be the unique monstrosity of what has happened to him or to her: the central matter for any person defending the perimeter of his or her own world in the immediate aftermath of an injury.

When we add all of these features together, they give a systematic portrait of the resistance of our legal system to the specific features of impassioned anger. It is precisely in the negation of the specific attributes of anger that our system of impersonal justice takes on the features that it now presents to us.

One final distinction between retaliation and our system of impersonal justice needs to be described at length. We commonly allow time to pass before holding a trial, often six months to a year. Anger acts instantaneously and cools with time. Our one-year delay outlasts anger, purifying the system of the initial disgust and rage we feel toward acts like the Oklahoma City bombing or the kidnapping, rape, and brutal murder of a small child.

Anger, Self-Worth, and the Radius of the Will

If we step outside the question of formal, institutionalized justice in its many forms—including the lynch mob, the modern trial by jury, personal vengeance, and the religious idea of the Last Judgment—we can see that what Aristotle makes clear through his definition is that anger is a territorial passion, and that justice is one, but only one, division of the world into territories—mine and not mine; deserved and undeserved; injury and honor. By generalizing, we can see that in anger we are alert to just how far our own will ought to extend. Earning and then maintaining our social worth in the eyes of others is only one of the projects of the will. Wrath is one of the primary attributes of both the Judeo-Christian God and the Greek or Roman head of the gods because the deity, in each case, is being described under the aspect of will. Because the will of God, in the Judeo-Christian religion, determines what exists and even that anything at all exists, along with the conditions under which it exists, any human recalcitrance—or, as it is called in Genesis, "disobedience"—implies an insult or impediment to the will of God. His is the one will that, in the nature of things, is without material limit. The wrath of kings, as we see it in *King Lear* or in the anger of Achilles or Oedipus, is, in a lesser sense, a sign of just how unlimited a will we assign to a king, a leader, a demigod, or a hero. What he wills or commands will commonly and widely take effect.

As we move down the scale of power, and therefore of effective will, from God to king to man, we expect to reduce the function of anger, since the further we drop toward a will that has a smaller and smaller radius of effectiveness, and a lesser and lesser frequency of finding itself in situations where it is likely to prevail, the less likely it is that the will's failure to prevail would taken as an insult to the will. If I will that it rain or that darkness cover the earth for sixty days, I do not become angry if these events do not take place. Most things lie outside my expectation or even my hope that my will might prevail. By contrast, when I hit a nail and it bends sideways instead of entering the wood, I often strike the already ruined nail a second, angry blow just because this simple act was, in my expectation, one where I counted on my will to be effective.

Whereas any act done by any creature or thing that is not in accord with God's will can be taken by him to be an insult to that will, an injury to his worth, and an implied diminution of his value, an ordinary human being would count only a very limited set of acts within his own circle of the will as implying any such diminution or insult. Anger is a relation of the will to that radius which it assumes to be within its control, or within which anything that happens either affirms or denies that territory. The radius of a king's will is larger than an ordinary man's, but even the king cannot order the winds and the tides to accommodate his fleet. Nonetheless a king, far more than an ordinary man, is likely to be confused about just how far his will does extend, since it does extend mysteriously far.

Within the radius of the will, the acts that we wish to do and then succeed in doing, maintain or reassert our presence in the full territory of the self. They protect its boundaries of freedom and effectiveness. Aristotle's initial definition of anger can now be seen in a somewhat wider light. He describes anger as "an impulse, accompanied by pain, to a conspicuous revenge for a conspicuous slight." The forms of slight that he lists are three: contempt, spite, and insult. As the translator notes in the Loeb edition of Aristotle's *Rhetoric*, "In Attic law *hybris* (insulting, degrading treatment) was a more serious offense than *aikia* (bodily ill-treatment). It was the subject of a State criminal prosecution. . . . The penalty was assessed in court, and might even be death."[12] Each of the three forms of slighting is defined by Aristotle as the actualization of the opinion that something is without value. The words or acts that slight and bring on anger amount to the notification of another that he is regarded as of little or no importance or worth.

In working out his examples of slight, Aristotle returns again and again to the fact that we feel anger in response to what we see as contempt, or as a sign of contempt. Achilles' wrath against Agamemnon begins with Agamemnon's act of taking away Briseis, the young woman who had been awarded to Achilles as his part of the spoils of a looted town. Because Briseis was given to him as an acknowledgment of his part in the raid, to take her away is to dishonor him, to show contempt for him. The very act of taking her away shows that Agamemnon asserts his higher place as commander and conspicuously (in front of all others) identifies Achilles as lower, as someone from whom something that had earlier been given to him as a token of honor can now be taken away.

The word that Aristotle uses for "slight" is *oligoria*, meaning to lessen, to diminish, or to make little of. It has a quantitative, almost physical meaning: to shrink the other. It stands therefore as the opposite of any act or word that honors or praises. Diminishing someone by slight or insult is directly opposite to some act like the giving of a gift that enlarges the sphere of the other. Slighting stands opposite, then, to the full range of acts that acknowledge, affirm, honor, praise, or increase the domain of the other, the radius of the other's will.

For Aristotle, anger is a response, an impulse to react and take revenge for such a slight. This implies that the choice to slight or to honor cannot be allowed to lie in the hands of the other. My anger implies an assertion that I have the right to be honored and not slighted. We can see here that an implied border of worth is understood by both people. It is not crossed accidentally. When it is deliberately crossed, this must be noticed or, from that time forward, a new, diminished perimeter of worth exists. This is the sense in which any slight diminishes the one slighted. Contempt is, then, the militant expression, not just of this momentary diminishing of the other, but of the intention to go on diminishing and slighting him. Anger, from the other side, is the militant expression of an intention to go on asserting a certain perimeter of self-worth. Both the slight and the anger are what we might call presentations of an idea of the worth of a person. And that person is myself or someone close to me and making up what I think of as my world.

Repeated Actions within a Shared World

It is by means of this clear notion of contested worth that we reach one of the most important features of anger: that it does not primarily concern isolated events and, in fact, has little relevance to our encounters with strangers. Instead, for anger, events and relations that are ongoing and actually or potentially part of a series of events make up the location in experience where the relation of anger to everyday justice can above all be seen.

When we think of fear, we think of unique, single events like a snarling dog on the path in front of me, an earthquake, a moment when my car begins to slide on an icy road, spinning out of control toward the oncoming traffic. In the case of anger the use of such onetime events involves a distortion. With anger we need to picture first of all a series of actions, and especially an anticipated future series of ever more serious acts in an ongoing situation. Fear is about the unexpected, the sudden. Anger in its ethical form requires us to think about expected, predictable actions in a series.

Here we are misled by the public institutions of anger: revenge systems, codes of honor, and our modern impersonal legal system. Retaliation or revenge we usually think of as a response to a single, complete, freestanding event. Should it be forgiven? Should it be ignored? Must retaliation happen? If retaliation happens, will it lead to a response and a spiral of violence that has no easy exit?

Similarly, our legal system, which depersonalizes vengeance and punishment, considers single events, not some ongoing stream of relations. A trial weighs the evidence for an actual crime. The legal system punishes only in situations where a completed act stands before us. Nothing can now be done to change it. The law can do nothing if I feel menaced by a neighbor, but once he has burnt down my house, it arrests him for arson and sends him to prison. Any onetime event, like a murder, a burglary, a rape on a street at night by a stranger, raises the legal system's attention and opens the question of guilt or innocence, punishment, retaliation, mercy, and forgiveness. It is exactly these questions that need to be put aside in the far more central everyday situation of acts in a series where what has just happened will shape the next and the next-on act after that.

It is in modern game theory and strategic thinking, especially in economics, that we find the best account of actions in a series. Game theory realized that the decisive question is not the single game but the iterated game, not a onetime prisoner's dilemma but repeated sessions of trust, mistrust, cooperation, and selfish defection over time and on into an indefinite future. What would the optimal strategy be for players who know that they will sit down again and again, on into an indefinite future and play further rounds of this game, seeking their own advantage, but only in ways that will work out as long-term advantages in successive games? Robert Axelrod in his book *The Evolution of Cooperation* has shown that the one strategy that is superior to all others is what is called tit-for-tat.[13] On the first move, act cooperatively, and if the opponent acts similarly, continue cooperating on your own next turn. Then make every later response mirror passively your opponent's previous move. If he defects from fairness, you must defect on the next turn. If he then returns to fairness or cooperation, cooperate on your next turn. Game theory, not the legal system or the revenge system, supplies us with the key premise of repeated actions that we need if we are to grasp the ethical intelligibility of anger as it has dominated discussions of the passions from Homer and Aristotle to the present.

The domain of intelligible anger is the domain of continual action or the anticipation of further acts just like the one or ones that have already occurred. Neighbors, men in an army barracks, school-boys who will be together day after day on the playground, children living in a family and in a house together, countries sharing a common border, a husband and wife: these are examples of situations in which the underlying facts are those of an indefinite future of acts always being shaped by the response to any one act that has just occurred. It is here that Aristotle's definition of anger as a desire to inflict pain because of a slight, an injury, or an insult has its most profound location.[14]

Between neighbors, the expanding on one side or the contracting on the other of a perimeter of rights and comforts takes place as a result of any one violation. The comfort and sense of well-being of next-door neighbors depends again and again on what the other does or does not do. If your neighbor makes a smoky fire every evening that fills the neighborhood and your house with smoke, or plays loud music, or has a dog that he lets run free, forcing neighbors frightened of that dog to keep their own children indoors, or forcing children at play to maintain a low-level fear and watchfulness because they do not know whether the dog is out, then, as we say, measures must be taken. As a first step he has to be warned or pressured (a mild kind of retaliation that at least puts the other on notice that some slighting or injury has taken place). Warning has as its only alternative what we call overlooking the transgression. There is no genuine alternative of ignoring it, because the neighbor must, at a minimum, be notified that you feel injured by the nightly smoky fire or the threatening dog.

Each neighbor, if we use Aristotle's underlying account of anger, is constantly expanding or contracting in minor or major everyday ways the domain of his will. In the examples that I have given, expanding any one neighbor's domain contracts or infringes on the freedom and enjoyments of others. Acts like these usually occur in an expanding series, like the schoolboys who tease one timid child, then slowly escalate to bullying, to hurting, to terrorizing, until the victim lives in a diminished world of the worst kind.

The legal philosopher Robert Ellickson in his book *Order without Law* has described how ranchers and others in a frontier existence handle, without calling in outside authority, these invasions of one another's sense of fair dealing that I am describing as actions in a series.[15] Calling attention to an infraction and making it clear that the act is seen as an infraction is one key step. This is certainly also the first effect of anger in Aristotle's definition. The insult or the act that diminishes me does not just pass unnoticed in the stream of events. The injury or insult announced or, we could say, proposed a diminished worth to the other neighbor. The stream of events is halted for a moment, broken off, and the event that just took place is isolated for attention. It is noticed and insisted on. The opposite would be "acting as though nothing just happened." Anger announces that "something just happened here." A warning is given. Anger within an ongoing series of actions does two things. It looks backward to put a frame around what has just occurred, and announces that a diminution of the perimeter of the self, of what I think I deserve, has just taken place. But then it also looks forward, putting the other on notice that any next action will be costly, and for that reason, just as in the strategy of tit-for-tat, anger imagines a future made up of escalating acts that might have taken place if this one had not been protested. Anger insists they not take place and attempts to make them unthinkable. In anger, the first injury is regarded as a test. If mishandled, it will lead to an ever more degraded situation among those who must go on living together.

In anger I insist and declare that I will maintain a certain perimeter of my own worth. Acts that injure or imply the diminishing of what one can expect from others will be noticed, pointed out. This is always the case among children in a large family who will have to go on living together for many years. And it is equally true for countries with a common border, or for husbands and wives.

Anger, when noticed by the other, announces to him and to onlookers that, in my eyes, an injury or slight has occurred. But even more important, my finding myself angry over something (or finding myself without anger, as the case may be) amounts in many cases to a discovery about myself and about just what kinds of slights or implicit opinions of my worth ignite my anger. Because it is not predictable in advance, in many cases, whether or to what degree I will be angry, I in fact learn about the extent of the radius of self-worth that I am committed to maintaining (or not) by what can at times be the surprise of finding myself enraged. Just as with wonder or grief, the passion of anger amounts to a discovery about a horizon line. I find myself notified of something by my anger in the same moment that my neighbor finds himself notified of a quite different thing by my protest or lack of protest.

Anger in any ongoing series of shared experiences marks a more important fact for the militant defense of some border of self-worth than it does in the simple case of an isolated act of insult or injury, the kind of single example that a law case is typically about—a murder, a burglary, a rape. Anger or outrage might be part of our feeling in these cases, but it plays a different role. Ethical examples discussed in philosophy prior to the study of iterated games typically invited us to make judgments of single events with no described past or future. The use of onetime events as ethical examples is a serious mistake, because it limits our ability to make sense of many of the most profound details of shared life—among them, and above all, the everyday value of anger in identifying for myself and for others the contours of a just, ongoing world.

Achilles and Agamemnon were part of a nine-year siege of Troy when Agamemnon insulted Achilles and brought on the anger of Achilles and the story of Homer's *Iliad*. Both men were subject to just this fact of iterated actions and the facts of cooperation over time, the facts of power and its distribution, of respect and honor or slighting, contempt and dishonor, under circumstances where on the next day and then on the day after that a joint project would continue and would need both persons. The border between them and the perimeter of self-worth that each man would need to defend against its progressive shrinking in the next and the next after that event was always present in the single here-and-now moment of this quarrel and this moment of anger. If this insult is accepted, a new, shrunken perimeter comes to exist that can in the third or tenth further-on action shrink one or the other into a contemptible "diminished thing." The mobile perimeters of interdependent self-worth of those living side by side over indefinite time are the real subject of the demand for justice in anger.

When we speak of King Lear's anger in Shakespeare's play, we usually mean his wrath at Cordelia when she refuses to compete with her sisters in making a declaration of love to her father in the ceremonial division of his kingdom. This is a onetime action, a unique moment, certainly the only moment in their lives when a husband will be chosen for Cordelia and Lear will step down and divide the country among his three children. Lear's wrath here is the kind we normally think of and use to define rage.

Several scenes later Lear's rage erupts even more violently against his other two daughters, and he curses them with almost unbearable words. But in this case a series of injuries based on escalating acts of diminution is taking place. Lear's man Kent has been insulted and put in the stocks, exposed to public ridicule. Each sister promises to shelter their father, but only if he reduces his retinue first to one hundred, then to twenty-five, then to ten. Soon the question will arise, why any retinue at all? Here we watch the successive iteration of insult, diminishing Lear's world and his worth in a few seconds of time, speeding up, as drama has to do, events that would more normally take place over months or years. If he does not stop somewhere in this ever shrinking world, will he be assigned a servant's room? Or put out to sleep with the pigs? Or fed on scraps from the table after the others have eaten because his manners are no longer presentable?

It is in this monstrous scene with Lear's daughters Regan and Goneril that we can see how anger has to notice and radically halt events that have a steady increasing pressure against self-worth. Here, rather than in the opening scene with Cordelia, the important mechanism of rage is brought into play, because here we see a sequence of actions taking place in front of our eyes.

Anger Begets Friendship and Love

With these ideas in mind about iterated acts over time we can see the logic of a very striking point made by Aristotle in his *Politics* where he is describing the character of those who would make up an ideal society. He speaks only of two traits, intelligence and spirit, or, in Greek, *thumós* (spirit, in the sense of passion understood as anger). Lacking spirit or vehemence, men are slaves. Just as he does in the *Nicomachean Ethics*, Aristotle defines the lack of anger at injury or slight or at the signs of another's contempt for us to be compatible only with slavery, the state in which we have no will. Here in the *Politics* the reasons for defending the perimeter of self-worth are not merely personal, even in that wider sense always used by Aristotle: myself and those important to me, including friends, parents, children, and the like. Here it is the larger shared endeavor of an ideal society that requires vehemence or spiritedness in addition to intelligence.

It is important to notice that there are many different perimeters of self-worth that can be maintained. Aristotle's slavelike man seems to imagine he deserves very little, and accepts this. But he also thinks so little of himself that he undertakes very little. At the other extreme, those Aristotle describes as great-souled, *megapsuchia*, demand and live for the highest honors and regard, and undertake great projects, as Sappho did in poetry, as Michelangelo did in sculpture, or as Napoleon or Caesar did in warfare. An ordinary person might be pictured as maintaining a perimeter of self-regard and a sphere of action so as to merit a degree of esteem somewhere between these two extremes.

The surprising claim that Aristotle makes in the *Politics* is that not only citizenship but love and friendship are linked to spiritedness, or *thumós*.

> Now, passion [*thumós*: vehemence, spiritedness] is the quality of the soul which begets friendship and enables us to love; notably the spirit [anger] within us is more stirred against our friends and acquaintances than against those who are unknown to us *when we think that we are despised by them.* . . . a lofty spirit is not fierce by nature, but only when excited against evil doers. And this, as I was saying before, is a feeling which men show most strongly towards their friends *if they think they have received a wrong at their hands.* . . . (My emphasis)[16]

The steps of Aristotle's thinking are surprising. First, passion (*thumós*) is the quality of the soul that begets friendship and love. Vehemence or spiritedness (*thumós*) lies at the heart of love and friendship. We more commonly think of spiritedness as grounding rage, wrath, enmity, hatred, war, and strife. But paradoxically, that is just the case here as well, because Aristotle's proof that *thumós* (spiritedness) underlies love and friendship is precisely that we more commonly feel anger at a friend or lover who gives a sign of slighting, injuring, or despising us than we do at a stranger who behaves in such ways. Aristotle uses here in the *Politics* the same terms he drew on in the definition of anger in the *Rhetoric*, where anger is the desire to retaliate for any undeserved sign of contempt or slight or injury. And this, in turn, is identical to the case given by Plato in *The Republic* to prove the existence of a third part of the soul, the *thumós*, or, as he said, the part with which we get angry. The contempt of a lover or friend wounds us, or their implied belittling of us wounds us, more than that of a stranger and calls on us to react or retaliate. We are most fierce toward our friends if we think we have received a wrong at their hands.

This might be true even if the stronger statement that *thumós begets* friendship and *enables* us to love were not true. We might think that even if it is true that we do react more vehemently to a slight from a friend or from one we love, this vehement reaction is an unfortunate, secondary feature of love. Aristotle claims just the opposite: the stronger feeling of anger when a friend injures us is not an undesirable dark side to love and friendship; instead this fact about passion and spiritedness enables love and begets friendship.

When slighted by a stranger in a town we are traveling through, and by someone whose opinion of us is a matter of indifference and, more important, without any future consequences or chances of any future series of encounters, we might find ourselves indifferent to the slight and ignore or overlook it. No slight or sign of contempt given by one we love and whose opinion of us we intend to go on caring about could ever leave us indifferent. Aristotle's seemingly odd claim can be restated as an argument that the sudden anger we feel driving us to retaliate also informs us of two things: first, that we have been held in contempt; second, that the person who has slighted us matters to us. The flaring up of anger informs us about how much we care for this person's regard, and how injured we are by any sign of contempt on his or her part. On the other side, our indifference to a slight lets us know that we care nothing about the person who slighted us. The flaring up of an urge to retaliate or the absence of such an urge draws a line, if we imagine repeated experiences, between those who matter to us and those who do not.

Of course, it is not only anger that draws such a line. We might also think of the line we draw between those we would spend a day helping at some task and those we would not, or those we commonly notice and praise when they do something fine and those we do not. These and many other ways exist to mark the line Aristotle is describing. But anger—and in public life especially anger, because of its militancy about how little or how much the other thinks of us in relation to what we think we deserve—draws that line in an especially intimate way.

We reserve our strongest feelings for the misdeeds toward ourselves of friends and those we love. We are angry at them if the injury concerns ourselves; we feel shame for them if the act that they have done is directed at another. In fact, by the stronger feeling of anger or shame toward people who slight us or injure another we in fact can come to know—to realize, in the strong sense of the word—that they are important to us. When their indifference or slighting incites vehemence, that sign itself proves that they are precisely the persons whose goodwill and esteem matter most to us.

We might see that just as with grief or wonder a horizon line is drawn in the mind by means of the sudden onset of the passion, in this case by *thumós*—vehement, spirited anger. By means of that horizon line we feel the difference between friends and those we love, on the one side, and strangers, on the other, between what we feel we deserve from another and what we regard as an injury or sign of contempt. It is this that accounts for Aristotle's need for vehemence in defining those who might make up an ideal society, whether in the large civic sense or in the smaller household of family, friendship, and love.

One of Wordsworth's best-known poems begins with the phrase "Surprised by joy." One thing that I have drawn attention to in this account of anger is the part played by surprise and notification within anger but also within each of the passions. Anger sets the other on notice. It announces and makes visible to others, including bystanders, that in my view an injury implying a diminished perimeter of worth has taken place. In most cases that same anger announces or discovers to me, insofar as I feel exactly this degree of anger, the contours or importance of my sense of self-worth, including the perimeter of my will. What is revealed in this moment could not have been discovered by calm reflection alone, nor by self-analysis of any kind. At the same instant anger divides the world into those close to us and those whose slights or injuries lead us to see that the contemptuous idea that they appear to hold of us does not matter to us, nor will it have any ongoing consequences.

Diminution: Humiliating the Will

The deep topic of anger can be summed up as the militant defense of a perimeter of personal worth and of an active terrain of the will. Both are insisted upon, and that insistence underlines the close connection between self-worth and the expectation that within the radius of the will choices and projects can be designed and, with effort, accomplished. By noticing and putting others on notice that injury or contempt has implied that they intend to think of us within a diminished territory of self-worth and activity, anger patrols the circumference of a certain radius of the will. By means of anger we can tell not only just how far we expected our own actions to work out, but also how far we would allow the balking of our purposes by others or their interference in those actions that invent our own future condition. A crime that victimizes me is only one publicly noticed level of serious injury or contempt to the just perimeter of my own will.

A formal legal system describes one part of the complex idea that we have of how and where a perimeter of self-worth is to be defended. The types of diminution prevented by anger involve another person, an agent, as we now say. As Aristotle's definition put it: we are always angry at a specific person about a specific recent act. Our legal system has this same structure: it accuses someone of a specific crime. Someone stands accused of the harm, injury, or loss that the accuser has suffered. In life most harms and most diminutions do not fall into this pattern. They have no agent. Accidents burn down far more homes than arsonists do in an average year. Crippling injuries from falls or car accidents diminish more active lives than do the few brutal assaults that the court system punishes. Few families lose someone to murder, but every person loses parents to age or friends and children to accidents or illness.

Hellenistic philosophers insisted on the many mistakes that our minds make over the limited domain of our will, and used these mistaken beliefs to discredit anger and the rash actions of the passions as a whole. The passions follow from false beliefs, they argued. To curse a rock after stumbling over it is to be mistaken about the radius of the will. Epictetus maintained that grief when a child dies is a similar mistaken anger at nature, a false idea of loss where we should say: I gave back that which was only lent to me for a time.[17]

Loss and diminution make up the structural center of anger when we understand anger as a combination of external protest and warning that follows on an aroused state which began by informing us internally that damage or injury had just taken place, much as pain notifies us of an injury to the body. The wrath of Achilles, for instance, is a way of picturing man, at the depths of his nature, as aggrieved, locked within an indissoluble mixture of anger and mourning. Achilles is "angry" as, within later definitions of culture—the Christian, for example—man might be defined as "free to choose good or evil," or "fallen as a result of original sin," or as in the definition of Nietzsche and Freud man might be "the sick animal." "Angry" is a term like "free" or "rational" meant to become the decisive adjective for man in the way that "immortal" is for the gods. Achilles' anger is not one state of feeling among others; it is his nature insofar as he is a man: that is, mortal and facing a mounting series of losses, which the state of war may speed up and multiply for consciousness, but which time itself, as only a gentler state of war, would otherwise exact. Anger is his material insofar as he can craft it into, or display it as, courage, vengeance, stubbornness, murderous pursuit, cruelty, grief, friendship, or pride. Courage, military strength, pride, grief, stubbornness, and rapacity are the revisions of anger as the leaf, oil, coal, and diamond are of carbon.

Loss, diminution, and the problem posed by the ambiguous territory of the will are not unique to anger, but by means of anger the larger structural core of a wide range of passions is made clear. That Plato or Aristotle, by means of the word that means both anger and passion in general (*thumós*), used anger as the template for the impassioned state itself depends, I think, on the clarity with which we are able to see in the experience of anger the combination of an actively defended perimeter of the self and a limited but personally asserted radius of the will that has an outer zone of ambiguity where it might or might not be correct to imagine that we are able to exert our will. Naturally, the extent of this radius of the will varies over the stages of a lifetime from childhood to maturity to old age to the final days of life that we call dying.

What anger makes clear about aroused passion carries over to fear, to grief, to jealousy, to pride, to shame, and to many other vehement states. Loss, injury, or diminution writes the script of grief or shame just as they do the script of anger. We can see this fact clearly in one surprising account of shame. In John Rawls's *Theory of Justice*, a book in which the passions play almost no part, and in which the objectifying veil of ignorance is expressly designed to let us imagine creating the social world dispassionately and impersonally, there does remain one extended discussion of a single passion: shame. Each person's happiness and ethical good depends on what Rawls terms a rational life plan that concerns, in the end, only our own self-relation over time, along with our own self-knowledge and set of desires. When we fall short of the design that we ourselves have made for our life, and do so through our own fault, we experience, Rawls claims, regret and shame. Shame, he points out, is evoked by "shocks to our self-respect" and implies "an especially intimate connection with our person and with those upon whom we depend to confirm the sense of our own worth." "Shame springs from a feeling of the diminishment of self" and results from "faults that wound one's self-respect."[18]

Defined in this way, the moment of shame discloses diminution and injury to a self-conception that we feel committed to maintain, but only in cases where that injury is at our own hands. The same injury at the hands of others, implying the same diminution, leads directly to the Aristotelian idea of anger as we see it illustrated in the anger of Achilles. Rawlsean shame restates, as a self-relation, the identical, active insistence on a perimeter of self-worth and a radius of the will, but now with, so to speak, self-insult or self-contempt revealed in the moment of aroused shame.

As Rawls stresses, moral shame cannot be reductively described as a merely social consciousness of the opinions others hold of our actions. We make this mistake when we contrast shame cultures and guilt cultures. But within shame, just as within anger, the constitution of an outer perimeter of self-regard is from the beginning known to us as something that includes others, both as potential and often even accidental sources of injury to that border, and as active partners in affirming or even in expanding what our will claims as its active terrain.

The diminution that a shameful act announces to us, in the very fact that we did, suddenly, find ourselves ashamed of what we just did, amounts either to a warning to ourselves about next-on actions or to an invitation to whittle down our self-regard so that if we wish to repeat similar acts, they will from now on be found outside the perimeter of self-esteem simply because we have, in a long-term way, shrunk the dimensions of what we expect of ourselves.

Shame, like anger, notifies us where a certain horizon line now stands, but that moment of notification does not control whether we defend that particular line against others or against ourselves when we are tempted to transgress against it. We often simply resign ourselves to the will's defeat and move the line in, making permanent the diminished sense of self-worth that the momentary flaring up of anger or shame had represented to us as a surprise, that is, as an unexpected and unwelcome event. In his description of anger Aristotle used a directly quantitative word to sum up insult, injury, and contempt. The word *oligoria* means to belittle, to lessen, and it is the same word that forms the stem of our word "oligarchy," rule by the few. It is a protest against diminution, or finding that we are from now on smaller in a precise and unmistakable way, that either anger or shame expresses.

ELEVEN

Grief

The civilizing of all terms connected to the passions is especially clear in the history of the word "mood." An Old and Middle English word that once meant ferocity and vehemence, *mood* came from the Germanic word for courage (*Mut* in modern German) and matched the broad range of the related German word *Gemüt*, once the main term for spirit or for the inner life of a person, the main alternative to the use of the word "soul" down to the time of Kant. Mood meant high-spirited, energetic, expansive being, best demonstrated in battle or in a race. It captured the same terrain as the Greek *thumós*, which Homer and Plato used for the energetic, spirited part of the self, the third part of the soul in Plato, distinct from the reason and the appetites. *Thumós* named the part with which we become aroused or angry and, by extension, the energy underlying all other impassioned states that could be understood along the model of anger. The words *mood*, *Gemüt*, and *thumós* designed the inner life itself—the psyche or the soul, as we might say—around the passions, and more specifically around the aroused spirit as we know it best in the experience of anger. English and German culture, along with the earlier Greek culture from Homer to Plato and Aristotle, reveals, in the use of these key words, a similar template for the inner life as a whole.

The word "mood" steadily shed the traces of vehemence from its early meaning of courage and anger, passion and bravery, finally reaching the modern word "mood," as we might use it in the phrase "mood music," where we imagine a low-level suggestion of state. Ever since the late nineteenth century, delicate, moody art like the paintings of Whistler or the music of Debussy would serve as fair examples of our own idea that mood itself is a gentle, low-energy condition, often sad or quietly pleased, but never given to dramatic, egoistic expression of the kind we associate with rage or grief.

In the earliest phase of the word's history, "mood," "moody," and "moodiness" were each terms for anger. They stand close to courage, to militancy, and to soldierly virtues. In Shakespeare's day, Golding, in translating Ovid, and, somewhat later, Dryden, in translating Virgil, used the English word "moody" to translate the Latin *ira* (anger) when speaking of the anger or wrath of a god.[1] As Plutarch put it in his life of Coriolanus: the Romans have only one word for virtue, and that word means manly courage.[2] A cutting edge of vehemence is then installed in any discussion of other virtues in Roman times because of this template. So too in England with the older meaning of mood.

An active, outgoing condition, mood is best visualized by means of courage, because courage is not a mere state but must, if true of a person, be proved by how he or she acts when challenged or in danger. Each of these features—activity, expressiveness, vehemence, high-spiritedness, the core of anger, tested by extreme circumstances and best expressed under those conditions—has been peeled away on the route to the twentieth-century term "mood," of which the inactivity of boredom, anguish, wistful dreaminess, regret, disappointment, annoyance, or quiet joy would be the natural examples. Only when we speak of "bad moods" as in the sentence "Watch out! He is in a bad mood today!" do we retain, by adding the word "bad," the vehemence, even the explosiveness, that was once intrinsic to the word "mood" itself.

The extreme conditions of the battlefield or of the more violent and power-driven parts of political life were not the only imaginable basis for the part that vehemence necessarily played in mood. If they had been, then a peaceful civic life, the marginalization of the warrior and of the ideal of a military life, along with the ethical thinking that characterized that life, might, in modern society, seem a completely welcome development. If the term "mood" shifted to take account of modern, more middle-class concerns, reflecting domesticity, the everyday ups and downs of a secure and predictable life circumstance, and did so because such stability had now been won for many people, then all that we find indicated in the passage from the older word "mood" to our own nuanced uses and meanings would be nothing but a gain.

But "mood" had a second domain, distinct from anger, courage, and ferocity, that preserved intensity and extremity. This second domain lay in the experience of grief, a meaning linking *mood* to the central Hellenistic term for distress (*lúpe*), the opposite condition to pleasure (*hedoné*). The vehement states might be less important as civilization progresses, but human mortality itself, along with the experience of loss and grief, would always remain the one fact never civilized into a gentle detail of everyday life.

If wrath and mourning are linked states of vehemence (as they are in Shakespeare's *King Lear*, Homer's *Iliad*, and Melville's *Moby Dick*), then the cultural progress from vehemence to gentle moods accommodates the needs of the ordinary and the everyday by toning down the violence, the wartime slaughter, and the acts of vengeful killing that take place in an angry world; but it suspends outside—ostracizes—the subject of mortality just as surely as it ostracizes the term "the passions." Along with mortality, we diminish or obscure by the same stroke the passions of grief and mourning that are the markers for human consciousness of and protest against mortality. In the same way that anger marks out and protests against injustice, and is the first and most important human experience of the boundaries of justice, so too mourning and grief, as states of vehemence, elaborate the experience of mortality both as a present loss and as an expectation and foretaste of each mourner's ultimate loss of his or her own life.

Each new moment in the history of culture refilters the passions. Certain passions, like envy or despair, occur in every possible description as dark spots within human nature. What we ask is how they can be limited or cured. On the other side, there are passions, like grief, that seem so fundamental to central human events and experiences that even the most radical cultural change can never alter their elemental place within the psychology of the passions. Unlike the case of fear or anger, we do not usually imagine reducing or applying therapeutic control to ordinary mourning or grief. In fact we regard as inhuman someone incapable of feeling and expressing loss, distress, and grief.

Against the claims of grief, two of the most sweeping but ultimately ineffective ideas of all philosophy were erected two thousand years ago as a barrier meant to disable grief. The first was the Christian promise of eternal life, with its claim that in fact death does not happen and that mortality is not a feature of human beings, because they will live forever. Complete and final death characterizes only the rest of the natural world. The second idea is the grand Stoic concept of nature marked by lawful, but constant, change. Since nature was for the Stoics the one true whole, the appearance of new parts and configurations, along with their return and reassembly into other parts, is not death but only change from one form to another in the ceaseless, but orderly, passage of time. The lawfulness of nature within which we participate only as short-lived parts, not wholes, attempts to describe a full, material universe in which it would be what the Stoics called a "revolt" for any part to complain against the laws that govern nature, including the universal law of the rise, short-lived existence, and return of an ever changing variety of parts within the stable larger whole called nature. The word "death" disappears within the Stoic's nature as surely as it does in the eternal life of Christianity.

Like the system of impersonal, formal justice, behind which we can recognize the victory over anger or at least the grounds on which all anger is forced to compromise its most vehement claims, the twin ideas of Christianity's eternal life and Stoicism's nature have for two thousand years, in a Western culture part Christian and part Stoic, pressed against the legitimacy of mourning and against the strong imagination of personal loss and mortality that grief sets in front of us, not as an idea, but as a profound physical and emotional experience.

We can see the details of the struggle over the legitimacy of grief in the face of the belief in eternal life in the early philosophical phase of Christianity. In his *Confessions*, Augustine describes how, when he found that he felt sorrow at the death of his mother, he struggled with his grief and struggled to understand how he could be feeling grief at all. What he reports to us is not precisely her death but her liberation from the earth and from her body, one of the basic reformulations of human existence in the light of eternal life. "And so on the ninth day of her illness, when she was fifty-six and I was thirty-three, her pious and devoted soul was set free from the body." He does not even need to say, "from the prison of the body." And yet, he continues, "I closed her eyes, and a great wave of sorrow surged into my heart. It would have overflowed in tears if I had not made a strong effort of will and stemmed the flow, so that the tears dried in my eyes. What a terrible struggle it was to hold them back! As she breathed her last, the boy Adeodatus began to wail aloud and only ceased his cries when we all checked him. I, too, felt that I wanted to cry like a child, but a more mature voice within me, the voice of my heart, bade me keep my sobs in check, and I remained silent. For we did not think it right to mark my mother's death with weeping and moaning, because such lamentations are the usual accompaniment of death when it is thought of as a state of misery or as total extinction. But she had not died in misery nor had she wholly died. Of this we were certain."[3]

She is now in Heaven, in the very condition of bliss that she and her son had earlier looked forward to together with such fervor. Even their separation will be only a brief one, and he will join her there forever in a few years. How could he now discover himself in a state of grief? These pages are among the most complex and moving in all of Augustine's writings. To find himself confessing to grief that seems to imply that he does not completely believe what his faith tells him is true would be the most serious failing of all those he has listed. It would be to confess that he lacked faith itself.

We could say that in the first moment of his grief something is disclosed to him, informing him of things about himself that he could not have learned by any other means than by passing through the moments immediately following the death of the single most important person in his life and finding himself in just this state. His grief educates him about himself, about faith, about the residual argument of mortality present even now in his convictions about eternal life.

To see the same fact of discovery and disclosure from the opposite side, I want to look briefly at Hume's arguments against the immortality of the soul, where he made a remarkable point about mortality but one that also turned on this idea of what our passions—above all, grief—disclose to us, what they inform us is the exact nature of our condition. In a footnote to his *Dialogues Concerning Natural Religion*, Hume wrote that when we examine our passions and our concerns, our ways of thinking, and examine also the scale on which we are able to imagine the future, we find that all the evidence points to the fact that we are finite beings, preoccupied only with units of time roughly aligned to the seventy years of our lifetimes, and to the time schemes of our projects and daily lives.[4] The passions that we find in ourselves and the objects of those passions pertain to this lifetime and no other. We find in our emotional lives no clue to the idea that this stretch of time in which we live is only a speck within an eternity in which we also live, and in which we will go on living once the short history of this kind of time is over for us. We are unequipped to be a person of that kind, even, Hume claims, in our imagination of time and duration.

We could say that Hume explains in this argument why Augustine found himself in grief. The signals of the spirited part of the soul, anger or hope or grief or shame, are features of this and only this kind of life in which we find ourselves here and now. Hume's argument amounts to what we would now think of as an almost Darwinian or biological account of human nature. Impassioned states refer to and reflect an adaptation of inner life to this kind of existence and no other, nor would the most common vehement states of our present lives prepare us to live in any other conditions of life.

Imagine, for example, that we could travel back in time at will to a chosen date in our own past to repeat it exactly as it was. Or imagine that we had the power to jump forward at will, skipping over any intervening days or years that we hoped to avoid. Just these two science-fiction possibilities would make obsolete and irrelevant many of our passions, along with our habits of concern and planning. We would also find ourselves with new passions unimaginable within our current way of living in time, in which we move only forward into the future without the advantage of skipping and without the option to return to relive, just as it was, an earlier moment, day, week, or year.

In other words, it is not only immortality that would require a world where many of the passions and conditions of life were other than those we now live within. The first and most important of those actual, present boundary conditions is mortality and a finite existence of just this particular length—seventy years. An existence limited to two years or one stretching typically to eight hundred years would also have entirely different passions and concerns from ours, even though they would be equally finite and mortal. Exactly this life under these conditions, Hume argued, has to be seen as presupposed by the extent of our thought, the kinds and intensities of our passions.

Grief is, once we put aside anger, the single best example of the role played by the passions (but not by everyday and moderate feelings, moods, or emotions) in articulating the boundary conditions of existence as finite, mortal, and limited by the wills of others. The importance of "mood" in its earliest uses was not the centrality of war or the conditions of war, in and of themselves, but the ability of war, because of the nearness of death, to give a compressed account of human existence where all action takes place within the ever-present, nearby boundary of mortality. Profoundly understood, the archaic word "mood" set up the path of vehemence and anger as the master key for grasping inner life itself and did so through the will in its condition of being contradicted by mortality. The will or, as Spinoza termed it, endeavor (*conatus*) presents the paradox that it strives to go on existing without limit of time.[5] Or, to put it another way, it is as though the will were unadapted to the fact of mortality and finitude. To think along the lines made clear by Hume, we could say that the will is the one detail of our makeup that does not show the prevailing boundary conditions of our existence. It is humiliated by reality into a knowledge that there is a radius to the will. So far and no further is it effective. But the second and more damaging humiliation of the will occurs at the hands of time and the small unit of time—seventy years—after which it will no longer be effective at all, even in those limited ways that it has learned to live with as the radius of the will: limits imposed, on the one side, by the wills of others, and, on the other, by the intractable material of the world that responds to some, but resists others, of our plans.

The close ties between anger and mourning as we find them in Homer and Shakespeare underline the fact that it is ultimately in grief and mourning that the template hidden behind anger is to be found. The final book of the *Iliad* begins with a description of Achilles' grief for his dead friend Patroclos, a grief that remains strong even though vengeance has already been taken and Patroclos's slayer, Hector, is now dead.

> All others turned their minds to supper, and the enjoyment of sweet sleep. But Achilleus began to weep, as he thought of his dear companion, and sleep that conquers all could not take him. He tossed this way and that, crying for the loss of Patroklos, his manhood and his brave strength, and all that he had worked through with him and the hardships they had suffered, threading the wars of men and dangerous seas. As he remembered all this he let the heavy tears fall, lying now on his side, now on his back, and now again on his face. Then he would leap to his feet

and pace distraught up and down the length of the sea-shore—
and he would see every dawn lightening over the sea and the
beaches. He would harness the fast horses to his chariot, tie
Hektor to it to drag behind the car, and pull him three times
round dead Patroklos' tomb: then he would rest again in his
hut, and leave Hektor flung face down in the dust.[6]

The physical details of grief are reviewed with an almost medical
interest: tears, sleeplessness, tossing and turning, discomfort, agitated
motion, inactivity alternating with pacing, and a climax of ritualized
repetitions of the insults and injuries done to the slayer, now by
Achilles' dragging Hector's body around the tomb and leaving it,
unburied and face down in the dust. Remembering and reviewing
his life together with his friend and all they had endured together
makes up the interior counterpart to the outer restlessness, tears, and
ritualized actions.

In the injuries done to the body of Hector, the residue of anger
within mourning reappears. Earlier, in the pursuit and killing of Hector, and the many deaths that accompanied Hector's, the full weight
of wrath within mourning had been measured out.

That mourning and anger are like two sides of a scale, where a
movement of the one requires a corresponding movement of the other,
can be seen as in some ways the central matter in the *Iliad* and *King
Lear*. What seems initially a work defined by wrath or anger is in the
end a design in which anger is transposed into mourning. The rage in
which Achilles or King Lear is first known to us becomes transfigured
after the death of Patroclos or Cordelia into a grief that, we might
say, reinvests the energies of anger in a new direction, while revealing
for the first time a content or topic within both anger and mourning
that makes them the two sides of a coin, where only one face of the
coin can appear at any one time. The coin is somehow defined by the
fact that one and only one of its two sides can appear. Yet when either
side is touched a certain way, the coin flips over, leaving us face-to-

face with the other side. The coin itself we cannot find by examining either anger or mourning. The coin itself cannot be seen; only one of its two faces can. The appearance of each surface has as its cost the invisibility of the other. What this image of a coin makes clear is the nature of a whole that can appear only consecutively in time, even though it itself is not temporal. It is only the limitations within our senses that force us to try to organize the wholeness of the coin out of the before-and-after glimpses that we have of front and back. This translation into consecutiveness could be called a Kantian limitation, one of the conditions within ourselves that makes experience possible, but a condition that corresponds, if at all, in only unknowable ways to the actual ground of experience. It is out of this Kantian limitation that the arts of time, as Lessing called them (poetry, music, narration, dance), take their necessity, because the arts of space cannot accommodate the complexity implied by unseen surfaces that must be displayed to the mind by means of consecutive events. That anger and mourning follow one another in time is our only access to them, and to the inner topic of which they are the two faces.

In anger we set aside the fact of death to focus on the cause of death, as though the merely static fact of loss were unendurable. The passive suffering of diminution is thrown aside in the active project of revenge. Because revenge might be taken, the suffering we experience does not have to be endured as something that simply happened to us. The revenge ethic is the single most powerful rejection of the damaging emotional detail of mourning: its helpless and inactive waiting. When Achilles rolls in the dust and weeps, he mourns Patroclos, but in setting out to kill Hector, he transposes mourning into vengeance. Most of all, he is able to set aside the paralytic passivity of grief that pays honor to death by simulating so many of its effects within the life of the mourner—his not eating, for example, or his refusing to continue with personal concerns, or being unable to feel strongly for others. In Hamlet's words, "How weary, stale, flat, and unprofitable / Seem to me all the uses of this world!"[7]

Grief and anger are alternative, active responses to death or to any loss. The most important split between the strategy of anger and that of grief occurs around the component of guilt and self-reproach within all mourning. A feeling of responsibility for the death, or at least a guilt at not having prevented it, hovers over every loss almost as a misunderstanding of death itself, or as a refusal of the passivity built into losses that happen to us, a refusal so urgent that it would prefer to imagine the self responsible if that would make it seem less passive. With anger and revenge the guilt is discovered to lie, not in the self, but concretely in the outer world where it can be attacked and punished.

Revenge and anger work out a simplification of grief in which the self denies responsibility and presents itself as the defender of the dead, replacing him in acts that, were he alive, he certainly would do for himself. Had he only been wounded by the one who succeeded in killing him, his first act would have been to retaliate. In revenge we execute for the victim the very acts that in the extremity of his suffering (death) he has been rendered unable to do for himself, like a victim who has subsequently been blinded by an attacker so that he cannot later identify him in court. In Shakespeare's play, the revenge that Hamlet is asked by his father to undertake is no more than the simple act that, if the movements of his hand could still occur on earth, he would do for himself. Or, to put it another way, had the poisoning in the garden been stopped just short of success, Old Hamlet with his own sword would have slain Claudius. Equally, he would have executed him on the spot had he discovered him in bed with Gertrude or overheard him plotting to usurp the crown. Hamlet, like all avengers, is the delegate engaged in carrying out those very acts that, had the victim's murder been incomplete, he would have done at once for himself.

Anger and acts of retaliation within mourning play out as though the death of the victim had never quite taken place, because the substitution puts the avenger in the place of the victim. In Homer's *Iliad* this is made especially clear because Patroclos had gone into battle dressed in the armor of Achilles. He died as a substitute for Achilles, and it is this that points to a second substitution in the later wrath and angry acts of Achilles.

The wrath within mourning that the climactic ritual act of dishonoring the body of Hector makes clear has its contrary experience at the very start of the *Iliad*, where, after his initial anger at Agamemnon, Achilles withdraws to weep, and in weeping over the loss he has suffered, he turns at once to think of his own fate.[8] His life is to be a short one; his death in battle is fated to occur soon. From anger, he passes to mourning over a loss (that of the girl Briseis), and like any loss, this local, relatively small external loss is seen as, above all, a small version of that larger loss he will soon suffer, the loss of his own life. At the core of his wrath over the injury done to him by Agamemnon's taking away part of his world is the anticipatory mourning over the projected loss of that complete world at the moment of his own death. At the same time, his injury at the hands of someone more powerful than himself brings out a second relation between anger and sorrow.

We do not feel anger against those so much more powerful than ourselves that their contempt for us or diminishment of us cannot be protested. This detail of the mechanism of anger was pointed out by Aristotle.[9] Where we do not feel anger at injury, we most commonly feel sorrow instead. Where sorrow appears in the place where we might expect to see anger, a resignation of the will to its own inability to police or to insist on a certain radius of self-regard is made clear. Grief is, in this way, even more than shame, an articulation of a line where loss has occurred, and where the world is, for that reason, smaller. Like the relations among pity, fear, and terror that were discussed in chapter 8, this situation in which either sorrow or anger might appear, but in the end just this one and not that one does appear, articulates the web of relations among persons and events—

in this case, relations of power—that are disclosed only in the middle of circumstances and could not have been predicted in advance. When Augustine finds himself giving way to grief, a disclosure that can never be forgotten or denied has occurred, but only by means of a situation in which an impassioned state occurs or fails to occur, or occurs in one form (anger) or in another (sorrow).

One reason to consider carefully the features of grief and mourning within the passions lies in the philosophical challenge that we can locate in this particular passion to most or even to all of the angles of attack on the passions in Western philosophy. For example, Aristotle's description of correct passions as a mean between two extremes would, in the case of genuine grief, nonetheless embrace a strongly felt, active, dominating experience of mourning as the very nature of that mean. The avoidance of extremes would not leave us, as we often imagine, with only a mild, controlled, or inexpressive level of feeling that we moderns might assume to be the mean between two extremes. Moderation would, in fact, define a significant state, a vehement condition. It is by means of the case of grief that it becomes possible to see that in all cases, including anger, what Aristotle meant by correct anger, or by his more general idea of the mean, is not a disguised way of saying "just a little."

Grief also lets us see just why it is not the excess of a passion that is, in the most important situations, the troubling extreme. The passions are commonly discussed within practices or therapies that urge restraint or the elimination of the passions because it is the problem of excessive anger, jealousy, fear, or envy that is being considered. Instead, it is the defect, the lack of grief or anger—the cases where someone who clearly ought to be strongly overtaken by grief or by anger seems unaffected, seems, we could say, even not to have noticed—that testify to the far more important problem: the lack of fully developed human character, what Aristotle calls slavelike response, the response of one whose larger life is defined by his having been deprived of his will.

When thinking of grief, we naturally have in mind actual and essential experiences of loss, like the death of the best-loved person in one's life: the death of a lover, a child, a close friend, a parent. Because these are our natural instances, we can see that with this passion we think first of extreme or vehement cases. We avoid trivial or slight instances of the kind we might use for envy or fear or anger. We also avoid the problem of false belief that played so large a part in the thinking of Hellenistic philosophers and made up the heart of their opposition to the passions. Othello, in his jealousy and murderous rage, is mistaken in believing Desdemona unfaithful. Romeo kills himself because of his incorrect belief that Juliet is dead. Even an hour of prudent delay would have saved his life once she awoke and told him about the potion that let her fake her death to come to his side. The vehement state that followed upon false belief, as we see it in these two plays of Shakespeare, implicitly makes the claim that all impassioned states are, if examined closely, based on false beliefs. Once knowledge is given time to correct the false belief or false opinion, we are able to awaken from the dream and live without passions.

With grief, we seldom think of the rare cases where we might be mistakenly informed of someone's death, just because such cases are both rare and irrelevant to the universal experience of having undergone the death of someone close to us. Because vehement jealousy, anger, envy, ambition, or fear is typically felt by some people and not by most others, we can take the majority of others as the correct norm and imagine that the right stance toward such extreme states would be to control the few in the interest of a human norm represented by the many. But whenever we see someone else suffer a great loss, we are brought to think of our own greatest losses, because no one is free of some personal experience of loss and death, along with the sharp experience of grief and mourning that followed. Even more important: the grief we feel for the death of another previews for the will the damage it has not yet had to imagine in its own case. Grief felt for the most important losses that we experience in the course of our life is the single most important way that we acutely imagine our own future death. One component of all mourning is an advance payment of grief for ourselves that will be unpayable once that death has actually occurred, because we will not be in existence to feel the sorrow of the greatest loss of all, that of ourselves.

We might say that there are no trivial, slight, or mistaken cases, because in each of these instances we in fact do not find ourselves in grief at all. To think of grief, we have to define it, as Augustine did in his *Confessions*, by speaking of the death of the central person in his life. Diminution is clearly the heart of the matter of grief. One person is now dead, but as the example of Cordelia in *King Lear* or Patroclos in the *Iliad* makes clear, the world itself is so deeply altered and changed forever by certain deaths that it is not a question of one person's subtraction but of this event's changing everything, striking at the heart of life. Such a loss is as close as can be imagined to experiencing one's own death. There is no world anymore with my own death, but with the death of a person who is the center of every thought and plan, every pleasure and structure, there is a near-death of the world itself, that is, of "my world." In the aftermath of such a death a new life has to be built; some other life has to be started.

Grief is the easiest way to see the central fact of diminution in the passions. Fear is clearly fear of death or of extreme harm, of loss. Jealousy is fear of diminution through the loss of the beloved. Aristotle's account of anger makes it a militant attempt to notice and prevent and require compensation (plus acknowledgment) for any insult or injury (any belittling or diminution) to oneself or those close to one—that is, one's world. John Rawls's analysis of shame defines shame as an experience of diminution. One reason to take grief or Stoic distress as a template for the passions as a whole relies on the fact that it is through grief that the structure of loss and mortality within the passions becomes clear as an experience of the diminution of the world. It is also through mourning or grief that the larger intellectual work of the passions is made unusually clear. The passions make the contours of a personal world intelligible by means of a series of horizon lines, lines of demarcation.[10]

In mourning or grief, we are made to see for the first time, in the act of grieving for someone, that this person falls within the inner circle of those whose deaths stop our world for us, diminishing us and casting a shadow over all experience for a time. Outside that circle are those whose deaths we take in simply as information, as ungrieved death. Every day in the newspaper we learn of many deaths that have no effect on us at all. We find ourselves notified about what must be other people's losses. In our own everyday world a neighbor might tell us of the death of another neighbor whom we knew, yet we find ourselves without strong feelings of grief now, in the moment when we learn of his death.

When we find ourselves beginning to grieve, we realize, in that moment, and in a vivid, unmistakable way, the value we placed on the person who has just died. In some cases, we find ourselves grieving not only for those obviously important to us—a lover, parent, close friend, or child—but for a person who, until the moment when his or her death sets loose in us grief and the immobilizing sorrow of mourning, we have never before been aware of as belonging to that inner circle of persons out of whom the fabric of our world had been secured.

On the other side, we sometimes learn when we hear of the death of a relative, or someone that we think of as making up our world, that we feel surprisingly little. The world does not seem very altered, and we do not enter a period of mourning. Both kinds of cases surprise us with new facts about our world at the moment of a death. The grief that does or does not surround us suddenly, or the intensity or thinness of that grief, along with its duration and stubbornness, discloses new knowledge about just how our world was constituted. Only the moment of learning of this particular death and our unpremeditated response to that moment could ever give us this knowledge. Grief or mourning draws a horizon line between those who do and those who do not make up our world. Grief discovers or reveals a bright line between those who are and those who are not really part of the inner fabric of my world. Anger, as Aristotle noted, draws this same line, a line that makes visible, he claims, love and friendship. This complex by-product of anger I examined in the previous chapter.

The details of this process of demarcation in the example of grief need to be listed in full, because through this case the corresponding effects of wonder or envy or anger can be implied. What is at stake here is the fact that the passions inform us of the unmistakable geography of our world, revealing information to us about that world that could not have been reached by any other means. No speculation in advance of battlefield experience could let us know anything about the fear or courage we will, in the aftermath of the events, learn we displayed. And so with wonder or jealousy.

In the example of grief and mourning a line is drawn that narrows the domain of our world to just the small number of things or persons that have over time elicited this state. The particular death that sets off grief and mourning notifies us that this person is one of the small number of persons making up the heart of our world, just because, in the moment of his or her departure from it, that world pauses to accommodate the suspended activity of mourning. How many people might make us grieve? We cannot tell in advance, although for some small number we could be almost certain that their death would set off grief and mourning. Other deaths, we are convinced in advance, will fall outside this line and count for us as mere deaths. But where many others would fall we cannot tell in advance of the surprise of their death. The bright line cannot be set out by speculation or by thought alone. Passing through the event at a certain moment and learning how strong a shadow it casts over the succeeding days, weeks, or months is the only way to reveal just where the line falls. Many people learn through the intense and prolonged grief that they experience at the death of a pet or of a political leader or celebrity that this person or pet was more important to them than many friends and acquaintances.

The intensity or the lasting on and on of mourning reveals a second set of facts about the stubborn importance of this particular person in our world. Once again, in advance we could not predict just how long our world would stop with grief, or how stubborn that state of mourning would be. By being just so long and just so deep, it informs us of the importance of the death to us just now at this intersection of our life, and this is something that we could only have speculated about in advance.

After many experiences of the deaths of a lover, a friend, a parent, a brother or a sister, a child, a companion, a colleague, or of one of those many people who are fixtures of our daily life, we come to learn on a very nuanced scale the extent to which each of these, at the moment of his or her death, truly made up the fabric of our life and tore that fabric by dying. A nuanced scale emerges over many experiences of differing intensities and durations of grief that informs us about our world and the weight that those important to us have had in it. All of this is made clear through the gradations of grief. What is true of these three epistemological features of grief is equally true of each person's individual experiential history of wonder, anger, fear, pity, or sympathy.

The gradations of mourning or sorrow as we come to know them through a sequence of losses amount to one side of a scale that gives us, in the end, an intelligible world. On the other side the array of possible claims on the energies of inner life from a competing set of impassioned states also provides, in the end, an articulated world. To show how this works I want to consider for a moment the claims of grief that Shakespeare used to measure out, by means of a long and complex plot, the sequence of challenges or alternatives to grief in the case of Hamlet.

Hamlet's mourning or grief for his father is precisely measured out in the action of *Hamlet*. His love for Ophelia seems unable, as Gertrude's passion for Claudius had been, to push quickly aside the fact of the death of the old king, his father, Gertrude's husband. Hamlet has refused to "cast [his] nighted color off." What the new king sees as "mourning duties" should last only a certain time, beyond which grief becomes "obstinate condolence" or "stubbornness." After a time "unprevailing woe" must be "throw[n] to earth" and life resumed with a "new father," just as the state has taken a new king and Hamlet's mother a new husband.[11]

The features of stubbornness, invariability, and withdrawal from an ever-changing social life to pursue in solitude the course of his passion make Hamlet in his grief a classic picture of an impassioned man, but one whose vehemence is the vehemence of mourning. What seemed at first his callous response to the deaths of Ophelia, Rosencrantz and Guildenstern, and Polonius might be described as the grip of his deep and primal mourning for his father, whose death makes all else trivial. Just as Achilles kills twelve prisoners at the pyre of Patroclos, kills and mutilates the body of Hector, and slaughters his way across the Trojan army, all of these killings counting as nothing because of his pervading grief at his friend's death, so too Hamlet's carelessness with death in bringing about the deaths of Ophelia, her brother, and her father might count as little in the face of his all-consuming mourning for his father, a mourning that ends only with his own death.

Could we go further and say that not only less important grief—as for Ophelia—but all other possible impassioned states are frozen out by such a stubbornness of mourning as Claudius describes for us in the play's first portrait of Hamlet? His inability to enact vengeance might then be seen, not as a consequence of a paralysis of thought, or doubt, or self-consciousness, but as the stubbornness of a more compelling passion (grief), which holds its own against not only pleasure and the distractions of social life, but against love in the presence of Ophelia, and wonder in the presence of the natural world, but, above all, against the anger that the murdered father hopes will activate vengeance.

It is in these varied temptations against mourning that the scale of Hamlet's personal world is measured by the array of impassioned states that he neglects or seems even to fail to feel. The bright lines drawn in the world by his state disclose to him, and to us, refined information about his world similar to what Augustine found disclosed to him by the paradoxical mourning he discovered in himself in spite of his faith in eternal life and in the blissful happiness to which his mother had attained in casting off her earthly existence and passing to the sight of God in heaven.

By means of this articulated world we learn that the vehement states are not universal or democratic. We do not feel them equally for everyone or for everything. They are unfair, because the benefits of the care that they extend are unfairly distributed. In philosophical terms grief and anger, pity and fear are not Kantian or universal features of our moral world. They are also not reciprocal. We do not necessarily grieve strongly for those who might grieve most strongly for us. Nor are we angered by the slight or injury of just those persons who would be most angered by our injuring them or showing signs of our indifference to them. The lack of fairness, of universality, and of reciprocity is a fundamental fact about the passions and distinguishes them from reason.

The passions favor a narrow band of concern that is precisely what we mean by a personal world. This is what we intend, in the strong sense, by the phrase "my world" as opposed to "the world." The impassioned states prove to us that what we need to think of as nonreciprocal intimacy is far more important than civic reciprocity or even reciprocal intimacy.

Each of us can explore the personal geography of fear or wonder, grief or anger, only in the aftermath of having found himself or herself feeling wonder at this but not at that, anger at this but not at that, intense or mild fear in this situation, unexpected grief over this death or none at all over that. The terrain of this articulated world comes to be known by our passing through events in which surprise plays an unusually important part. The opening words of Wordsworth's poem—"Surprised by joy, I turned . . ."—need to be extended in every possible direction: surprised by grief, surprised by anger, surprised by fear, because only through these moments is a personal world, unknown until that moment of surprise, articulated.

Stoic Rehearsal for
Grief and Distress

The most significant revision of the account of the passions within philosophy was not the Aristotelian development of the virtue of moderation but rather the Stoic description of the self as character. The primary threads of anger, grief, the position of the will, and the account of mortality recur within Stoic philosophy, but altered so as to devalue the passions, and even, insofar as it is possible, to bring about their defeat by proposing that, as a result of Stoic practice, they might come to be seen as unreal. At the heart of the Stoic assault on the passions was the disarming of grief or distress. As Epictetus said of the philosopher, "His true work is to study to remove from his life mourning and lamentation."[12]

The Stoics listed four primary categories within the passions. Desire and fear they listed as the two anticipatory relations to what lay in the future. Pleasure (meaning delight or joy—*hedoné*) and distress (*lúpe*) were the two present-time, reactive impulses in the face of what had already taken place. Distress, grief, and suffering constituted a broad negative category of response that included such subdivisions as malice, envy, jealousy, pity, grief, worry, sorrow, annoyance, mental pain, and vexation. The central case was that of mourning or grief, which played the key part that it did in Stoic thinking precisely because of the resistance of grief to the therapies that might seem both legitimate and effective in thinning out the vehemence of anger.

Stoic control over the passions was achieved by means of a retraining of the habits of response, above all by eliminating the part played by surprise and suddenness. What Stoicism recommended was a constant practicing of response long before a sudden loss or occasion of anger occurred. Steadfastness was won through repetition and a form of practice that had at its center the act of repicturing or renaming experience so as to cut it off from self-reference. Epictetus's advice in his *Manual* is a typical example of the self-preparation and repicturing that would, once the blows of experience occurred, make the self immune to passionate response.

II.

Never say of anything "I lost it," but say, "I gave it back." Has your child died? It was given back. Has your wife died? She was given back. Has your estate been taken from you? Was not this also given back?[13]

This radical repicturing aims at the reversal of the component of the will in experience. Its key step lies in the restructuring of experience away from possession. Even "my" life or "my" self can be cut free by this mental practice. The will has its sphere reduced as a step toward silencing the passions. The Stoic account is the first to notice the extent to which language is an act of the will by means of which we build ourselves into the world so as to intercept experience at a fixed angle. To learn and then to use new words is to relocate the self's angle of intersection with ongoing life. One of the primary words of distress within experience is the word "loss." Marcus Aurelius replaces it in this way. "Loss is no other than change; this is a source of joy to the nature of the whole and all that happens in accordance with it is good."[14]

To rename loss "change" is to trade in the perspective of the self for the point of view of the whole, or nature, in which whatever is lost here is relocated there. Matter, now in one form, now in another, is never lost. The concept of nature and its point of view disconnects the passions just as radically as does the notion of objective justice once it has replaced anger and the ethic of revenge. The imperturbability that Stoicism seeks, imagining itself surrounded by indifferent things, is a form of calm won at great cost against the passions. The need to practice and inoculate the self in advance is a sign of the energies that are forced into this often hopeless battle.

In remaking language away from the centered self and simultaneously away from the passions, Stoicism implicitly concedes that it is precisely by means of the passions that the world becomes "my" world. The self becomes centered in itself by structuring the distances around itself in terms of anger at this, fear of that, hope for this, and regret or grief over that. The language of this possessed world—the world as "mine"—would seem at first to be the natural and inevitable language of experience. The perception and point of view that shape it would seem to be instinctive. If so, the Stoic practice would be an unnatural and violent decentering of the world. But, of course, it is just here that Stoicism, against the passions, can seize back the word "natural" for itself and see the everyday, personal world as "unnatural" in the sense that it is not in accord with the obvious laws of nature taken as a whole. Change, not loss, is the natural fact.

The language of the passions stands revealed in Stoic thinking as an artifice to set in place a personal world. Looked at from the outside, the Stoic assault on the passions has a second side in which it implicitly affirmed the interdependence of humanism and the spirited self, each of which insists on a centered world. Within Stoic practice a division of the self occurs that actively pits aspects of the self against one another. The self has to be, in Stoicism, reminded to be itself. It must be recalled to itself. The steady state to which it is called back is known as character, but what is meant by character is a crafted object, set in place by means of training and philosophical self-education, and then carefully maintained.[15]

Like Hamlet, the Stoic has given up self-identical being, which I have earlier called thoroughness. One aspect of the passions, with their unquestionable reality, is the thoroughness of self that they embody. The anger of Achilles, the rage of Lear, the jealousy of Othello are states in which the self floods out to the limit of its reach without reservations or counterthrusts. In the act of engulfing the self, pushing aside all other considerations or goals, the thoroughness of grief, extreme fear, or sudden wonder reinstates the full individuality of the self at the center of its world.

The Stoic attack on the passions became later in its history one part of a wider attempt to make distinct the outer and inner worlds, enlarging the sphere of the inner world of feelings as a world of privacy. Feelings that are not visible become aspects of a sensibility, a rich consciousness that is available only to the person in the state of feeling. Where expression becomes a matter of choice, each feeling can be either social, as when grief is expressed outwardly through sobs; or private, as when behind an unchanging manner the deepest and most rapidly changing states of mind and feeling are taking place. Part of the Stoic goal is control over the self, but an equally important goal is the shrinking of the public world so that many of the deepest matters take place in the solitude of the mind. No clues are given in either words or gestures of the anger, delight, or grief within. Instead, consciousness and a self possessed of its own experiences come into being. The domain of the private self is expanded as whole territories are withdrawn from the communicative, shared realm of signs of feeling: sighs, tears, blushes, shouts of anger, rapid movements, and words.

Stoicism and Hellenistic philosophy thought in terms of the normative domain of everyday life and, with it, the ordinary emotions and a level of appropriate, reasonable response to the regular conditions and experiences of life. It was here, in the domain of ordinary life, that a rational person could be said to need, above all else, to control or even to extirpate anger, fear, hope, shame, grief, attachment; that is, the passions per se. It was in what we could broadly call the economy—whether of family life and the level of the household or the larger life of the state, now understood as an economy rather than a place of war, conquest, and honor—that the passions were best imagined as perturbations, short violent dislocations parallel to fever or illness or disease in the economy of the body, where the norm is the everyday physical equilibrium that we call health. The analogy of health should make us see that health is not a true positive term; it is the negation of a negation—freedom from illness, disability, limitation, disease. If there were no diseases or illnesses, we would never have had an idea of what we call "health," because in itself it is not a state we would notice except by contrast and gratitude for not being sick. If we think of the terms "happiness" and "unhappiness," the opposite is the case. Happiness is a genuine and noticeable positive state, and unhappiness is the absence of that state. With health the noticeable, prior state is illness, and it is because of illness that we develop an idea of being "healthy." In fact it amounts to no more than saying that our ordinary functioning and mood are not being interfered with at this time.

This distinction is important because of the analogy of bodily health, and the temporary interruption of that health by states of illness, that was the primary analogy for the passions in Stoic thinking. If the passions are in fact a decisive part of that normal functioning itself, and if no genuine image of ordinary functioning could be given without an assumption of the activity of the passions, then the strange consequences of the invocation of the model of health and illness become clear. That model has as one of its most troubling problems just this fact that health, unlike happiness, is not itself a state but a back-formation from illness.

In a striking parallel with Stoic thinking Albert Hirschman's analysis of the seventeenth-century's replacement of the passions by the interests identifies the economy, understood as well-being within ordinary life, as the location where the issue of the passions needed to be debated.[16] Not the moment of war, as the *Iliad* had staged the question of the passions, but peace. Not the singular man, Achilles, claiming and defending his singularity, not the wrathful God of the Judeo-Christian Bible, but an ordinary man under daily conditions and subject to those two essential Kantian rules of all ethical, ordinary life: reciprocity (what I expect of you, you may expect from me) and universality (what I claim for myself, I affirm for any other person).

The Stoic and Hellenistic relocation of discussion of the passions within the conditions of ongoing, normal life with its annoyances, rather than its tragedies, its attachments, and its larger commitment to life itself—this deep commitment to the ordinary, as well as to an ordinary level of offense, of perturbation, of fearfulness, seems correct.

Why should the singularity of Achilles' wrath, of Captain Ahab's vengeance, of God's or Jove's anger define the location for debate about the passions? Why not instead a man whose car doesn't start on a winter morning? Or a person giving a dinner party who watches a servant carelessly break the most precious vase in the house (the type of example used by Seneca in his book *On Anger*).

The reasonableness of using jealousy or social envy or avarice or Hume's example of pride in a new suit of clothes as our entry point for an examination of the passions seems at first persuasive. Yet the topic of the passions enters philosophy, ethics, rhetoric, and psychology by means of the opposite kind of instance: the wrath of Achilles, the fear of a soldier advancing toward the enemy and toward likely death on the battlefield.

It might seem at first that it is because of the singularity of Achilles, Oedipus, Job, Medea, and the other tragic or religious examples of nearly transhuman circumstances and dimensions that the passions were argued out by means of what I have been calling vehement or extreme states of wrath or fear or grief. We might also say that it is the magnification of war and the battlefield, as Aristotle uses it to define courage and fear, that gives the vehement dimension to Homer's description of the passions and then, as a result, to Plato's and Aristotle's grounding discussions. War and the moment of battle within war is to peace and to ordinary life just what the extreme and singular person—hero, captain, king, or god—is to the everyday man or woman in ordinary life.

The persuasiveness of either the state of war or the singular king-like being as a norm would vanish in our later world of citizenship, of reciprocity and universality, in our democratic world of ordinary women and men with their everyday experiences—it would vanish except for one thing. If we imagine that it is not the singularity of character—king, captain, god, or hero—nor the singular intensity and finality of war that is at the heart of the original choice to use extreme states as the norm for discussion of any states whatsoever, then we have to consider a third possibility. Namely, that these two forms of singularity and vehemence stand in for and shadow, or are made exigent by, the presence inside each individual life of certain moments or, perhaps, of just one experience that, in its power to define all other moments and experiences, plays the part within each life, by necessity, that a king plays in a monarchical state, and that war plays within the conditions of life.

That singular condition, with its necessarily vehement state, is that of being about to die. The absoluteness or radical importance of this one passage of experience puts it in the same relation to ongoing, daily life as kings or gods are to the worlds that they rule and define by their existence. Being about to die is not subject to equivalence, and, above all, it is not subject to Kantian conditions of reciprocity and universality any more than kings or gods are.

Whatever grandeur Achilles has because of his military feats, he is known to us from the start as one who, as soon as he enters battle, will bring on the chain of events that will lead to his death at Troy. He is or will be "about to die" in the near-term way that someone who learns he has a fatal, untreatable cancer has learned that from this day on he is "on his way to death." This is the condition described in Tolstoy's story *The Death of Ivan Ilyich*, where we take the words "the death of" to mean the interval between that first instant when ordinary life is over because we know that it will never be resumed, and the actual instant of death some weeks or months later.

The primary vehement states of anger, fear, and grief array themselves, in their extreme forms, around the singularity of the experience of dying rather than around the singularity of heroes, gods, or the conditions of war. In fact, all of these singular conditions are needed, just as kingship is in Shakespeare, to transfer to these external conditions the nature of the central experience of mortality.

If we step back and use grief or mourning for the loss of one of the small number of persons who make up the heart of our world, then we can see that even if in ordinary life there is not necessarily any wrath equal to Achilles' or Lear's, nor any terror like that of a soldier on a battlefield, still there is one common experience, grief, where full vehemence exists and deploys itself around the central fact of mortality, illuminating the topic of mortality shaded or hidden within the other impassioned states.

TWELVE

Spiritedness

If the experience of mortality is anticipated in everyday situations by the undercurrents of diminution, loss, and the threat of loss present in fear, jealousy, and many other states, then this secondary detail of each of the impassioned states—the anticipation of mortality—signals one of the most important structural facts about vehement states, no matter what their local content might be. All such states are states of loss.

The vehement states are, at the same time, no matter what the local content might be, states of arousal. We preserve in our clear ideas of sexual arousal or the arousal experienced in competitive races a model for the larger fact that fear, shame, wonder, grief, and anger are states of arousal. For competitive, high-energy states we prefer to speak chemically and say "the adrenaline was flowing." Behind our use of "adrenaline" or the quasi-physical but always psychic idea of sexual arousal, our modern vocabulary does not supply a common term for spiritedness, or for the underlying notion of a spirited self that is evoked and defined by vehemence and the impassioned states. Along with the advance preview of mortality present in many experiences of what I have called the injured will, a second larger topic, that of spiritedness, enters experience through the passions and the strong emotions, and it does so through the fact of arousal. Spiritedness sets up a boundary condition for human experience equal in importance to rationality and to desire or appetite. We will be able to give an account of this state of arousal and spiritedness by looking first of all at its well-defined opposite, the lack of spirit.

Our medical term "dysthymia," which marks a mood disorder in current psychological classifications, is defined as a condition involving low spirits, lack of interest, depression, sadness, lack of energy. The identical term and range of meaning appeared in Hippocrates and in the Aristotelian corpus, along with athymia, which we now use for milder episodes of listless, prolonged sadness or lack of affect.[1]

What we no longer have are the words that these negative states invert, "euthymia" or *thumós* itself: high-spiritedness. It is as though we had the term "disorder" without any concept of order, or "displeasure" without the grounding concept of pleasure, or, more to the point, the idea of dispassion without the idea that it disowns, passion.

Because low-level background consequences of Stoicism persist in our culture, the passions are best known to us through surviving negative ideas. The word "apathy," the single most important concept of Stoic ethics, still bundles together, two thousand years later, the same four matters: lack of passion, or even freedom from the passions; lack of energy and excitement; lack of interest in things; lack of activity or action. By deprivation, the Greek letter *a* in "a-pathy" implies the missing alternative: an opposite realm of impassioned, energetic, interested, active liveliness—the realm of spiritedness and the passions. What the idea of apathy makes clear is that its opposite would involve not only strong feelings but activity, energy, interest, and excitation. The alternative would not be passive, as we often claim, still speaking out of the residues of Stoicism, when we equate the passions with passivity or think of actions and passions as contraries. The passions constitute a highly active, aroused, focused, and energetic domain within inner life.

Darwin's grouping of the emotions described one set generated by what he called low spirits: grief, dejection, anxiety, despair.[2] One physical detail of these states should be noted: motionlessness. The opposite world of high spirits and of both motion and emotion—laughter, joy, love, devotion—is the subject of Darwin's following chapter.[3] Modern medical psychology reminds us that "athymia" and "dysthymia" were also words for melancholia. In Greek medicine the details of the state of melancholia were closely modeled on the symptoms of malaria—low energy, indifference, dispiritedness. Malaria was the greatest medical plague of the ancient world, and, by analogy, melancholia came to be used for "any condition resembling the prostration, physical and mental" produced by malaria, one form of which was supposed to be caused by "black bile" (melan-cholia).[4] These details of melancholia have been transferred intact to our modern preoccupation with the condition that we call depression, one of the most widely diagnosed syndromes within modern psychology. Our thinking has neglected the contrary term of exhilaration opposite the negative territory of melancholy, depression, apathy, dysthymia, and athymia.

If the strands of perception held together in the uses that Homer, Plato, and Aristotle made of the word *thumós* had lasted as successfully as the much less important negation, "dysthymia" or "athymia," we would have a cultural or temperamental notion of spirit, energy, courage, anger, and passion. This single notion would be the complement or opposite to the idea of melancholy.

In the work called *Problems*, not written by Aristotle himself but printed within the Aristotelian corpus, can be found one of the best early descriptions of melancholy, a discussion of dysthymia and athymia, but above all of *thumós* and *euthumós*, spiritedness and high-spiritedness.[5] It is in these pages that the well-known remark—every animal after sexual intercourse is sad—occurs, and the word here is *a-thumia*: dispirited. The opposite moment of arousal and pleasure before and during sexual intercourse is implied by this aftermath and would naturally be termed "spiritedness."

Our culture's theory of melancholy is a minor branch of a profound river that is no longer shown on our maps, and the missing notion of spiritedness, high-spiritedness, or *thumós* is one of the most revealing absences within our thinking. The Greek word *thumós* means, according to Liddell and Scott's Greek lexicon,[6] the soul or the spirit, the principle of life, feeling, thought. The word covers especially strong feeling or passion and stands closest to our use of the word "heart"; but where we, in our modernity, think of the heart primarily as the seat of love and affection, the Greek meaning begins by picturing it as the seat of anger. The passions are, by means of the word *thumós*, set in inseparable relation to wrath, as in the modern period they would be to love or desire. The related word *thumoun* means to make angry or to provoke, and, in the case of animals, to be wild, restless, or fierce.

The Stoic shadow fallen across our vocabulary has one important piece of evidence in the survival of the term "apathy" and in the link we make between passions and passivity, as opposed to active, energized spiritedness. Within the term "spirited" we have to imagine the combination of high energy, youthful freshness, capacity for delight, cheerfulness, confidence, proneness to anger and to competitiveness, pleasure in motion or dance, in athletic contests, in running as opposed to walking or standing motionless. This combination in its spiritual coherence has not endured. Lost to sight, it has been proposed or invented again and again from Homer and Plato to Shakespeare, whose "skipping spirit" and passionate figures with their verbal wit and quickness define the best modern synthesis. Spinoza, Stendhal, and Nietzsche celebrate, under different vocabularies, modern versions of high-spiritedness, as Hazlitt did in his use of the term "gusto," but no later formula has ever had the stability of the victorious opposite: melancholy. Spinoza was unique among modern philosophers in placing an overall feeling of increasing power—"delight," as he called it, or in Latin *laetitia*—as the highest state within his *Ethics*, but this is because Spinoza, like Plato or Homer, was a philosopher of power and capacity.[7]

The term "spiritedness," or *thumós*, then, sums up what is defended about a notion of inner life when one thinks of the passions as one of the three determining features of experience, equal in importance to the activity of reason and the activity of the appetites and the desires. As one final step, we can reverse direction and look closely at just what is filtered out by the most important attempts to reduce or marginalize the vehement states.

We can pass in review most easily the features of the vehement passions by watching carefully the angle of attack directed against the passions that singles out just this specific feature as the core of the passions themselves, now seen as the decisive point that, if defeated, will suspend the action of the passions as a whole. Aristotle's emphatic and sometimes mechanical concern with the correct state of the passions as lying in the mean between two extremes makes clear the feature of excess and extremity, vehemence, as I have called it, that seems a fundamental feature of fear or anger, grief or envy. To call for a close attention to the mean, sometimes read as moderation, reveals the true nature of the case: the impassioned state itself is absolute and violent in the absence of our conscious attention to and training toward the mean. But for Aristotle a second opponent is also in view that slips from attention in most later reports or uses of his idea. The most revealing and degrading condition is to feel too little anger or none at all—in fact, not to be aroused to anger by injustices to oneself or those close to us that need to be noticed and made clear to others as felt injustice. The defective state is more puzzling and more dangerous than the state of excess in many cases. The idea of the mean as an angle of argument against the passions throws into sharp light these two aspects and singles them out for our notice.

When the Stoics developed their elaborate training in advance of experience, they taught that we must practice response long before the sudden and unexpected events that most commonly set off impassioned states. Practice saying to yourself when looking at a child: this child will die. Use the sentence "I gave it back" whenever you would ordinarily say "I lost my home in a fire last week, " or "I lost my brother in the war," and by means of practice you will become so used to the idea of "returning" rather than "losing" that the death of someone near to you will not, the Stoics claimed, set off grief and mourning. The accidental breaking of a prize vase will not set off anger if we say, "I gave it back."

Stoic practice, consisting, first of all, in the act of renaming, attempts to install in experience a protective way of seeing events, a way that addresses two fundamental features of the passions which become clear to us precisely because of this therapy and rehearsal. First, the passions are particularly strong in the face of sudden and unexpected events. Practicing in advance how to think about the very things that, when they happen, will happen as suddenly as a blow illuminates this feature of the passions by attempting to go to war against it. Second, Stoicism saw that the language through which we think of things already has memorized a philosophy of experience, and that the hidden philosophy in everyday language is committed to the perspective of the passions. If we could stop saying "my vase" and said only "the vase lent to me for a time and which someday will be called back," or instead of "my child," "the child lent to me for a time," and expanded throughout our language the everyday phrases of a new philosophy, we would already, in advance of individual moments of experience, have sapped their power to impassion us. Language reminds us of our understanding of the world. A new language for experience, once naturalized, would remind us of and hold in place a new version of experience.

Stoicism neglected to consider what would occur if its new language never came to seem natural. Many hypocritical and pious phrases stock our minds with a pretended or half-believed account of experience. In the end Stoicism contributed to the demimonde of this empty language and fell under the ridicule reserved for all failed spiritual revolutions, with their terminal condition of mismatch between words and stubborn realities.

In modern philosophy, two proposals, one by Spinoza, the other by Kant, isolate for attention essential features of the passions just as Stoic practice and the Aristotelian idea of a mean between two extremes had in ancient thought. In Spinoza's *Ethics* it is the element of time within the passions that his most cunning thought experiment filters out for our notice.[8] As my earlier analysis in chapter 5 showed, we ordinarily react in radically different ways to an event or situation—a threatening wild animal, a valuable gift, a family death—if we know that the event is now taking place, or took place ten minutes ago, took place forty years ago, will take place ten minutes from now, will take place fifteen years from now. The temporal location that we add onto the event in describing it as an event of the past, the present, or the future determines most of our emotional state about the fact or the event. Spinoza proposed that all things be regarded as if we did not know about them whether they were past or present or future. They are to be regarded "under the aspect of eternity" or *sub specie aeternitatis*. By "eternity" Spinoza meant just this fact that we do not know or take into account the temporal proximity or remoteness and the temporal direction away from the present of the event. Is it about to happen? Did it just happen? Did it happen long ago? Or will it happen, as we say about the unclear future, "sometime"? The erasure of detailed temporal knowledge makes up, in this case, Spinoza's meaning of the word "eternity." His perspective, or aspect, of eternity erases the passions from mental life.

If we consider for a moment having an unpayable and crushing debt in the past, the present, or the distant future; being crudely insulted thirty years ago, just now, or thirty years from now; being in grief and mourning ten years ago, or now, or ten months from now, we can see that the passions are locked into a temporal structure that is fine-grained. The sudden wonder that fades, the anger that burns through us and then declines, the shame over a terrible mistake that eases after a time—such experiences are time-bound to so great an extent that it is by means of the sudden eruption of such passions and their fading that, as human beings, we know time and the passage of time most convincingly.

To regard events as though we did not know about them whether they were past or present or future is to set up a "veil of ignorance" (to use John Rawls's phrase) but one that amounts to an act of self-divorce, because by stripping away time, we have taken away a large part of what arouses us within experience. We might as well say: consider an unpayable and crushing debt as though you did not know whether it was your debt or the problem of a person unknown to you. Consider all experience as though you could not be certain whether it was your own experience that you were thinking about and reacting to. Not knowing the temporal location of an event is just as radical as not knowing which person it happened to: myself or an unknown stranger.

By isolating time in his thought experiment, Spinoza makes only more compelling the central fact of precisely articulated time within the passions. With this weapon against the passions, he illuminates their structure just as Stoicism had or Aristotle had in their very different earlier refined targeting of crucial aspects of impassioned states.

Spinoza's proposal depended on taking a position about our experience that within religious cultures already existed but was not our own human position. It is God who sees all things under the aspect of eternity, a condition that is made humanly comprehensible when we think out the implications for justice of the idea of a Last Judgment, as I did at the end of chapter 6. Spinoza's thought experiment requires us to imagine ourselves to be God-like in relation to our own daily experience in time. We could say, for that reason, that Spinoza's proposal was not a new invention; it simply extended in unexpected and telling directions one detail of a religious universe.

Within our secular culture it is in the work of Kant that we find the strongest, most enduring, and most telling modern assault on the passions. As one individual, Kant achieved as much as the entire history of Stoicism, and he was able to do this because he never made the inhuman or improbable demands that Stoicism at its most radical imposed.

One of Kant's best-known formulations is that the only thing which is good without restriction or qualification is a good will.[9] Since the passions make up part of any theory of the will, we might imagine that a good will would, in fact, be something quite different from the will as we commonly understand it. To explain what he means by a good will, Kant creates in its shadow the very idea of the passions and, even more important, the idea of the spirited self—the Homeric and Platonic *thumós*—that he plans to brush aside. When Kant speaks of the gifts of fortune he says, "Power, wealth, honour, even health and that complete well-being and contentment with one's state which goes by the name of '*happiness*,' produce boldness [*Mut*] and as a consequence often over-boldness [*Übermut*] as well, unless a good will is present by which their influence on the mind [*Gemüt*]—and so too the whole principle of action—may be corrected and adjusted to universal ends. . . ."[10]

The three words of danger that Kant uses—*Mut, Übermut, Gemüt*—are the words for courage, for spiritedness and high-spiritedness, for heart and spirit, exactly the inner states that lead to rash actions, self-confident, aggressive, driving energies, self-expansion, and all of those actions "not adjusted to universal ends" because they have the energies of the self and its expansion in play. Kant begins by pointing out the grave spiritual danger of all of those many gifts of fortune that we usually think of as good in themselves, like health or uninterrupted good fortune, because, as Kant sees, they breed self-confidence and energetic optimism about the future projects of our will. This very optimism, funded by past success, is what normally makes the human will eager and active in reaching out to act in the world. What Kant is really describing here is the undefeated or not yet humbled will.

Happiness, the highest of these, and the goal of human action in Aristotle, Kant is eager to expose early on as dangerous, and not good in itself, because happiness will be throughout Kant's ethical writings the icon that he will shatter and replace with duty. One of Kant's goals is the replacement of the term *Gemüt* (heart or inner spirit) with the new moral term *Persönlichkeit* (personality or personhood) as the name for the self.[11] Our *Gemüt*, as he invokes it on the always quoted final page of the Second Critique—where it denotes our being, insofar as courage, pride, the heart, and energy make up our being—stands opposed to humiliation and the process of humbling (*Demütigung*) and to *Kleinmut* (to lose heart or confidence).[12] *Gemüt*, a common term for the inner self since at least the time of Meister Eckhart, points to spiritedness, as in a spirited horse, and it naturally leads to concepts that link pride, courage, and, in the end, arrogance, which we see spelled out in the idea of high-spiritedness: *Hochmut* These words, taken together, bundle a strongly positive account of energetic inner life that is expansive, self-confident, willful, and, at some level, incandescent in feelings, passionate.

"Personality," as Kant uses this new term, is clearly and specifically the moral self and the self in self-division. The personality, through its alliance with the moral law and in its stance of duty and respect, finds itself in tension with our inclinations and desires. Personality is not just based on a tension with self-oriented will but begins by accepting the humiliation of that notion of self devoted to its own interests and self-love. Where the passions are a sign of thoroughness, the term "personality" calls our attention to the finite, incomplete self and to its distance from itself, insofar as that lower self is guided by its desires, happiness, inclinations, and self-love. It is equally divided from any spontaneous or natural relation to the moral law. It is bound by duty, since it must be commanded. The reason that it must be commanded lies in the fact that it is never naturally aligned with the moral law. As Kant wrote, "This idea of personality awakens respect [*Achtung*]; it places before our eyes the sublimity of our own nature (in its higher vocation), while it shows us at the same time the unsuitability of our conduct to it, thus striking down our self-conceit."[13]

The main attack of the Second Critique is an attack on the moral value of happiness, and on all ethics based on happiness from Aristotle to what would later be called utilitarianism. Happiness, for Kant, is the goal of our existence only at the level of our system of desires, our inclinations (habitual desires), and our fears (aversions). "To be happy is necessarily the desire of every rational but finite being, and thus it is an unavoidable determinant of its faculty of desire. Contentment with our existence is not, as it were, an inborn possession or a bliss, which would presuppose a consciousness of our self-sufficiency; it is rather a problem imposed upon us by our finite nature as a being of needs."[14] Kant rephrases the entire history of the idea of happiness by stating that our moral goal is not to be happy but to be worthy to be happy. He writes, "[A] rational and impartial speculation can never feel approval in contemplating the uninterrupted prosperity of a being graced by no touch of a pure and good will, ... consequently a good will seems to constitute the indispensable condition of our very worthiness to be happy."[15]

The Feelings of
Respect and Humiliation

Kant discusses the experience of respect or reverence (*Achtung*) for the moral law as the only possible moral feeling; that is, the one feeling that defines human nature as "personality" rather than a mere assembly of inclinations directed toward happiness. Respect, the one moral passion acknowledged by Kant, is seen by him to be related to wonder and admiration. Respect (*Achtung*) occupies the unique place in his moral system that anger (*thumós*) does in Plato or that Wonder (*L'Admiration*) does in Descartes. Respect and its counterpart, the destructive blow to self-conceit, self-love, and pride that he calls *Demütigung* (humbling or humiliation) is constitutive for moral identity, for location in the world, for Kant's new term for the self, "personhood." Just as man learns in Descartes, or just as man, angered, pursues justice in Plato, so here the respect addressed to the moral law and the humbling of the self that follows is the single constitutive experience involving the passions. "Reverence [*Achtung*] is properly awareness of a value which demolishes my self-love."[16]

Demütigung is a far stronger word than "dispiriting," even though the central part—*mut*—is clearly our English word "courage," and *Gemüt* is the spirit or heart. Equally, our word "disheartened" would be too mild for the German *Demütigung*. The German word carries the sense of being dejected, cast down, humble, meek, submissive, lowly— all the words that are the antithesis of pride or self-worth. The phrase *sich demütigen* means to humble, prostrate, abase, or degrade oneself; to grovel before, submit. Kant's choice of this one approved feeling is a powerful, even a distasteful, medicine. Like Hirschman's evocation of avarice as the one passion in an economy-driven culture that turns back against all others, taming them in the interest of the Interests, Kant has defined a therapy against the passions, desires, and inclinations that arises, not from reason, but from an impassioned state, humiliation, that is affirmed just because it undermines all other vehement states based on self-love, pride, self-affirmation, or any merely personal search for happiness. The moral law humbles and humiliates our self-conceit. It reverses the self-expansion of the spirited self and denies the value of those acts that define the self as energetic and confident.

The moral term "respect" or "reverence" (*Achtung*) evolves out of and deforms the classic passion of wonder (*Bewunderung*). Both passions look up; both register a highly intellectual idea of norm and exception, a pleasure in and fascination with something outside the self, as love does. Reverence, wonder, and love are three passions in which the value of a person or thing outside the self is experienced as equal in importance to the very self that finds itself under the sway of this external power. In Kant, respect or reverence is defined by reference to wonder in this passage from the crucial third chapter of his Second Critique: "Respect always applies to persons only, never to things. The latter can awaken inclinations, and even love if they are animals (horses, dogs, etc.), or fear, as does the sea, a volcano, or a beast of prey; but they never arouse respect. Something which approaches this feeling is admiration [wonder] and this, as an emotion (astonishment) can refer also to things, e.g. lofty mountains, the magnitude, number, and distance of the heavenly bodies, the strength and swiftness of many animals, etc. All of this, however, is not respect."[17] Only moral righteousness found in a supreme moral example elicits, and even requires, reverence and respect. Martin Luther or, in our century, Gandhi would be instances. But to reach this definition, Kant has passed through exactly those examples of the sublime and the powerful that classically were said to elicit wonder. His moral concept *Achtung* is a kind of moralization of wonder, a back-formation from its aesthetic and intellectual elements, and from its connection to surprise, suddenness, the way of taking the will by storm in the spontaneity of wonder.

One of the best-known and most eloquent sections in all of Kant's works, the conclusion of the Second Critique, sets wonder and his new term *Achtung* in exact relation. In this section Kant sets out respect and humiliation before the moral law as the fundamental successor experience to the now outdated scientific experience of wonder that we find in Descartes. In the passage that follows, Kant situates himself side by side with Newton. An ordered image of the universe had been set before the mind by Newton. Now Kant imagines himself to have added the equally compelling order of the moral universe within us and its simple fundamental laws.

> Two things fill the mind with ever new and increasing admiration and awe, the oftener and more steadily we reflect on them: the starry heavens above me and the moral law within me. I do not merely conjecture them and seek them as though obscured in darkness or in the transcendent region beyond my horizon: I see them before me, and I associate them directly with my consciousness of my own existence. The former begins at the place I occupy in the external world of sense, and it broadens the con-

nection in which I stand into an unbounded magnitude of worlds beyond worlds and systems of systems and into the limitless times of their periodic motion, their beginning and their continuance. The latter begins at my invisible self, my personality, and exhibits me in a world which has true infinity but which is comprehensible only to the understanding—a world with which I recognize myself as existing in a universal and necessary (and not only, as in the first case, contingent) connection, and thereby also in connection with all those visible worlds. The former view of a countless multitude of worlds annihilates, as it were, my importance as an animal creature, which must give back to the planet (a mere speck in the universe) the matter from which it came, the matter which is for a little time provided with vital force, we know not how. The latter, on the contrary, infinitely raises my worth as that of an intelligence by my personality, in which the moral law reveals a life independent of all animality and even of the whole world of sense—at least so far as it may be inferred from the purposive destination assigned to my existence by this law, a destination which is not restricted to the conditions and limits of this life but reaches into the infinite.[18]

Kant has modified the topic of Pascal, whose play with the worlds upon worlds of infinite space had reminded him of the speck of matter that made up his body. The visible world of traditional intellectual wonder—the starry heavens—is placed second to the invisible but necessary moral universe of the moral law. The contingency of this universe with this tiny planet and with my even tinier body is, for Kant, inferior to the necessity of the formal law of all laws: that we must act always as though in acting we willed the same principles of action for all rational creatures.

In German, Kant's passage begins by saying that two things fill the spirit (*Gemüt*), not simply the mind, with awe and admiration. The reverence and respect (*Achtung*) that Kant defined as the spontaneous response of personality to the moral law produces, as its secondary effect when we turn back to remember the extent to which we fall short of it, humiliation (*Demütigung*) that disheartens or dispirits us. Wonder inspires, increases spirit, as anger or courage does. Wonder intoxicates. Respect and reverence dispirit and humble self-regard.

The Kantian progression from the starry heavens to the moral law moralizes and sobers the experience of wonder, breaking its mood of elation, by means of the calm, thoughtful submission accepted within the solemnity of modern moral life, with its new term for the self, personality. It is this that Kant celebrates in his justly famous concluding passage.

In his moral writings Kant is so strongly committed to practical reason that the place left over for the feelings is narrow and peculiar. His language is aimed at the system of desires, the impulses and the settled desires that he calls the inclinations. Since the subject of his moral philosophy is the good will, he uses "impulses" and "inclinations" as terms for the self insofar as it seeks happiness. The system of personal inclinations, if we imagined them satisfied, would be happiness. Over against this, Kant erects the austere world of moral law, submission to that law, the categorical imperative, a strong clear notion of duty (*Pflicht*), and the single moral feeling of respect or reverence (*Achtung*) for the law and for those who are morally exemplary.

All other feelings Kant categorizes as pathological. For example, in speaking of incentives or motives, he calls both sympathy and self-love pathological incentives. Benevolence in the eighteenth-century sense of the term would be a pathological incentive. When he speaks of the commandment to love God, he notes that this is not an inclination (pathological love) because "God is not an object of the senses." The realm of self-love that Hume would have called pride is dismissed with words that show this new idea of the pathological.[19]

"Now everything in self-love belongs to inclination, and all inclination rests on feelings: therefore whatever checks [as respect does] all inclinations in self-love necessarily has, by that fact, an influence on feeling.... The negative influence on feeling (unpleasantness) is, like all influences on feeling and every feeling itself, pathological."[20] In a startling passage Kant gives a reading of the scriptural command to love thy neighbor as thyself.

> It is doubtless in this sense that we should understand the passages from Scripture in which we are commanded to love our neighbor and even our enemy. For love out of inclination cannot be commanded; but kindness done from duty—although no inclination impels us, and even though natural and unconquerable disinclination stands in our way—is practical, and not pathological love, residing in the will and not in the propensities of feeling, in the principles of action and not melting compassion; and it is this practical love alone which can be commanded.[21]

This has what might seem to us to be the odd feature of making commanded and reluctant love seem higher—that is, of greater moral worth—than any mere pathological love. Love freely felt and offered, arising out of the feelings, even those of sympathy and compassion, has no moral worth, and Kant always speaks as though sympathy and compassion were disguising themselves to appear to have a right to claim this worth that belongs to duty alone, never to inclination or feeling.

Only respect for others and the moral law (*Achtung*) and its correlative humiliation (*Demütigung*) are exempt from this pathological characterization. Kant calls respect or reverence "this singular feeling, which cannot be compared with any pathological feeling...."[22] The term "pathological" is the final resting place in this world of reason for the passions, along with the system of passions as we find them in Plato, Aristotle, the Stoics, Descartes, Spinoza, Hobbes, and Hume. To preserve a strict moral account of the good will, Kant has pushed roughly to the side these elements of the proto-will, the passions, so as to isolate the sublime freedom and servitude of a will submitting to laws that it itself has made and made universal for all men.

Once we have considered Kant, it becomes clear that the picture I have given of the passions in relation to singularity, to extreme individualism, to unique claims, to the implied uniqueness of only one person in a monarchical state, and to suspended reciprocity, to the ignoring of all social claims, is too narrow. Such terms imagine a contrast between, on the one hand, the world of only one person—the angry man or woman, the man or woman in a state of fear or grief—and a social world where the claims of others count equally with my own self and its claims. This social world objectifies claims by putting them in the hands of neutral, objective parties as a court of law does. The highest mark of the social world is reciprocity. Such reciprocity often includes bargaining: if you let me do this, I will let you do that. In bargaining the two acts are not necessarily the same, but each side will gain and regards the contract as fair. This is one meaning of an ethical world characterized by fairness. Distinct individuals remain, but they each count. In the monarchical world of the passions many individuals exist, but only one counts.

Kant requires something far beyond fairness and reciprocity when he speaks of acting only insofar as I will make my action a maxim applying to everyone at all times. His demand is that we universalize. In universalizing, I erase my individual will. Under the moral law every good will must be identical to every other good will. Distinct individuals no longer count except as they fall short of the moral law.

In everyday thinking it is the will that we take to be the essence of our individuality. In willing to do this (or in refusing to do that), I define myself and only myself. My uniqueness is tied into the set of acts that I have, over the course of my life, willed to do and refused to do. Presumably, this is a very different set of acts from those of any other person. In this location where our individuality exists and, in essence, our unique identity arises and can become known to us as we recall the history of our own willed deeds, Kant forces us into a universal posture. To act, we have to choose this for all humanity, forever. We now view each act, in the very moment of willing it, as abolished in its aspect of uniqueness and self-definition, because we usually take self-definition also to mean difference from others.

The array of willed acts is a higher definition of selfhood than the sum of desires or the set of determinants; that is, the external facts about myself. Kant cancels just this higher version of uniqueness and does so in the name of universalization of every act of my will.

In an earlier section I described the passions as singular in their revocation of reciprocity. The passions are monarchical in asserting the reality of one and only one spirit, one and only one account of the world—that of the jealous man in his state of jealousy, that of Miranda in her state of wonder. The passions interrupt the ongoing, everyday social world of relations, as Achilles' anger does the every-day workings of the Greek allied forces outside the walls of Troy. Later, his mourning for Patroclos suspends all ordinary relations in just the way his earlier anger had. Mourning, jealousy, fear, and anger are the classic examples of a vehemence that retracts all bonds and cancels exchanges with others by claiming absolute rights for one individual.

When we think of the Hellenistic and Christian notion of the will as a key step toward modern notions of individuality, responsibil-ity, self-definition, and moral life, then the outcome in Kant's categori-cal imperative is a surprising one, both in terms of the individualism of the will that we identify in the notion of freedom of the will, and in terms of the individualism of the passions, the complete, thorough identity with the moment of anger, jealousy, grief, or fear that in the philosophy of the passions also defined a distinct selfhood outside and prior to social life. Kant makes into the fundamental moral law the principle or the commandment that I must act on every occasion in which I must choose and then engage my will as though my act were making a maxim or law for every other rational creature on every occasion. I cannot claim to be an exception, nor can I claim that this circumstance is exceptional.

Individual will no longer exists under this rule. We always will for humanity as a whole and for all times. The will is universalized, socialized, and every act occurs only with a consciousness of all others. We cannot imagine acting alone. All others are pictured not simply as the spectators of our will and its acts, as they might be in a culture of shame. We ourselves, as individuals, might be pictured as later spectators of our own acts in a culture of conscience. Instead all others are instructed by our acts, and every act becomes pedagogic. In every act we consider the acts of all others and, as Kant put it, "Reason thus relates every maxim of the will, considered as making universal law, to every other will and also to every action towards oneself."[23]

The Kantian moral law cannot stop short of making all individuality defective, since if we conformed to this law, we would lead a model life, as would all others. In willing for all others at every moment, we would become identical with one another, except in our distinct failures to live up to this moral standard. The will itself has been used by Kant to carve out a shared humanity. Every personal will has been imprisoned in the collective web of wills, those of all men and women, now and in all future experience. "I ought never to act except in such a way that I can also will that my maxim should become a universal law."[24]

The well-deserved success of objectivity and impersonal, systematic justice in our legal system can blind us to the costs and losses in the victory over anger and impassioned spirit on which this civilizing accomplishment was based. Objectification and the disowning of the merely personal world have many more victories to show than this one triumph of impersonal justice over retaliation. The guiding Kantian ethical ideals of reciprocity and universality; the concept of a rational life plan as we find it in Stoicism and in Rawls's *A Theory of Justice*; the requirement to act from an integration of one's inclinations, as Kant insisted, and not from any one strongly felt momentary passion; the plural notion of the interests that Albert Hirschman has described as the successor topic to the passions; the premise of rational choice theory that all units of future time have equal value: these are only a few of the posts and beams supporting the structure of a dispassionate world—*the* world, as we could call it, by contrast to *my* world, or *your* world. The dis-impassioned world of modern philosophy and culture has as strong and prominent a set of consequences as the more widely recognized "disenchantment of the world" described by Max Weber.

The failure of a few extreme proposals demanding almost inhuman objectivity should not hide from us the wide success and ongoing pressure toward this goal of depersonalized, fungible description. Stoicism did not prevail with its profound concept of nature, lawful long-term processes, and a repicturing of loss as transformation. Spinoza did not succeed when he suggested that we think of every event as if we did not know whether it had already taken place long ago, had just happened, were happening right now, were just about to happen, or would happen in the distant future. He knew that if we could picture events in this way, the passions would disappear from experience. In a small, purely negative way we would all become like God and view our own experience under the aspect of eternity, at least so far as that could be done through our not knowing whether it were past or present or future.

Spinoza's thought experiment and the framing proposal of Stoic thought about nature—to regard myself only as a part and never as a whole—implied such thoroughgoing erasure of the very terms of human experience that they exist now only as markers of how far we might imagine going down this path. For no one do they exist as ways of living in time.

But in recent years John Rawls's veil of ignorance, behind which we imagine making choices about lives without knowing which of those lives is our own, and rational choice theory, which attempts to implement one part of Spinoza's veil of ignorance about time by applying it to the future only, have pushed the horizon line of the world several post-Kantian miles further. Albert Hirschman's plural term "the interests," when we apply it back to the individual and not just to the varied interests of political groups or actors, could be said to impose on us the integration of our own varied interests in each local action just as strongly as does Kant's insistence that only an integration of all of our inclinations, in their just proportions and weightings, should be a correct motive for action, never one inclination, never one emotion. For Kant emotion is local in time and extreme in intensity, disruptive of the planning self, which in its idea of the future has integrated its desires and inclinations for the optimal combination of satisfactions. In a certain way the interests are inherently plural, but passion is, at heart, best spoken of as it occurs in time, singular, one at a time, never subject to integration or combinatorial compromise for some best outcome.

The construction of this shared world can make it seem that a merely personal world—*my* world, as opposed to *the* world—is nothing but a back-formation from the real world, that prior world which is objective and shared. Captain Ahab, seeking revenge, commandeers the common world of a ship, built, operated, and financed by many hands for common gain, taking it over for the personal fantasy of angry vengeance. The common world of ships and whaling is temporally prior to the kidnapping of that world and its conversion to the armed extension of a single passion that has to be called Ahab's world. The individual, centered world in time can appear, as it does in *Moby Dick*, as no more than a defection or deformation of this powerful shared human project.

The passions, as I have tried to define them—grief, anger, fear, shame, and joy—insist on *moments of experience in time* as prior to any integrative act like a rational life plan. They insist on the differential reality of life in time. Time's distinct parts—the past, the present, the future, the immediate past, and the imminent future—are details not to be surrendered or blended somehow into any objective, larger abstraction of time. The passions, above all anger, insist on the wider sphere of injury and retaliation that is local, everyday, composed of ongoing repeated actions among those who live together through time. Anger, understood as militancy about a perimeter of the self, includes as one small part the gross crimes and losses that have been assigned to our impersonal legal system, but includes them only as one kind of insult to the will and one kind of diminution of the border of self-esteem.

Through anger the part played by diminution in grief, fear, shame, and many other passions appears under magnified focus. It was by means of anger that the connection could be made clear of the passions to the topic of the will, the perimeter of the will, the finite but indefinite radius of the will, along with the connection of small-scale injury to the will to everyday preliminary experiences of our own mortality, along with the enhanced energy of each passion because of the undertone of awakened memory of mortality. It was by means of anger and the concept of a spirited self—*thumós*—that these inner themes of attention to the passions and the kind of experience in time that the passions force into awareness was possible.

If no other passion could resist the skepticism and hostility directed historically toward the passions, then the unnegotiable legitimacy of mourning (even if we wanted to discredit anger, fear, pity, shame, and envy) would restate the claims of a personal world made evident in the line we find drawn within ourselves between those whose sudden death would just be news or just a fact to us, and those for whom spontaneous sorrow and mourning would begin, making clear to us that *their* loss diminishes *my* world, and that I know it to be my world by the fact that some but not all deaths arouse mourning whether I expect them to or not. All losses, all deaths diminish the objective world understood as a census count. Only some diminish, or, in some cases, seem to reduce to almost nothing, my world. John Donne's well-known, but untrue, words "any man's death diminishes me" attend to the instruction of reason, but not to the instruction of grief. The phrase "any man's death" slides over the important, nonuniversal or inequitable fact that some, but only some, deaths do bring about the felt diminution of my self in ways that anticipate my own death, no matter how far in the future my own death might stand.

The passions are evidence in us for the prior importance of my own world over *the* world. For that reason they are the strongest evidence that we have of the fact that *the* world has been a costly, and only partially effective, necessary sacrifice, and that it has been won, stage by stage, by means of ingenious and effective disabling techniques addressed to the energy of the passions and to our individual sense of ourselves as spirited, temporal beings.

The Stoic technique of repeated practice, in advance of unexpected events like the news of the sudden death of a friend or a child, so that the impassioned response of the moment when we find ourselves surprised by that news is defeated in advance by our practice and preparation, is only one form of dismantling the mechanisms of the passions piece by piece. The cost in this case lies in the choice no longer to permit singular experiences, because we rehearse each possible event to numb its uniqueness when and if it actually occurs, like a judge numbed by presiding over too many murder trials. The cost is borne by the defeated notion of "having an experience," which Stoic rehearsal and preparation thin out.

The active life of the passions in all of its details was reconsidered in the last chapter in the mirror of all of those brilliant techniques, like Stoic practice or Spinoza's veil over time—techniques designed to prevent or diminish impassioned moments of response within experience. But as we attend to this successful dismantling, we need to be prepared to change sides and restate the other claims, those of the *thumós*, the part with which we get angry. I have tried to show the connections between the line drawn by anger or fear, the line drawn by self-interest—defensive lines, we might argue—and the line drawn by pity or sympathy, no less decisive in articulating my world, but now in terms of those injuries that I see done to others by which my own particular concern and pity are aroused. I have tried to show, in the case of shared fear, just how the most self-interested of states, intense fear of imminent death, can create community, because of the odd feature that we are often part of a group like the passengers on a falling airplane or the members of a village being taken out to a field where one of every ten will be executed—a group where each person is at the same time threatened identically, but where some will survive and others will not. Shared fear leads to the natural path within the passions from fear to pity or to the ability to feel the losses of another as having the same weight as one's own.

Throughout I have claimed that the passions provide our best, most immediate template for our idea of "having an experience" and lead beyond that to the meaning of experience within a precisely articulated landscape of time. Literature is one location for the necessary representation of full experiences, of experience in time, and of a world centered on a certain person, at a certain location in time. Literature defends the priority of such person-centered experiences in time over any idea we might be able to describe of a common world or an objective world or even a world where reciprocity obtains. Literature could be called our most important anti-Kantian domain, because in literature universality and reciprocity are structurally excluded. Narrative is innately perspectival in time and circumstance.

King Lear's world, or the world of Juliet that forms the subject of the play *Romeo and Juliet*, the world of Achilles after his anger begins, or the world of Marcel in Proust's novel, or of Swann in the section *Un Amour de Swann* within that larger novel: we cannot begin to think through the experiences represented in these works without acknowledging whose world this is.

Narrative has inevitable and unbreakable links to the subject of the passions because narrative must begin from the act of taking up a position in the world. *Pride and Prejudice* takes up the position of Elizabeth Bennet and no other person, and that position is also a position within the unfolding time of a marriageable young woman with an imminent future structured by hope, shame, regret, and joy. Novels and stories are accounts of my own world or of someone's world, and not of the world per se. When Tolstoy and George Eliot multiply the positions by using several centers, and when they alternate between them, they only underline the narrative fact that any larger narrative world is made up of Lydgate's world plus Fred Vincy's plus Casaubon's, plus Dorothea Brooke's, but only one at a time.

In the epic, the tragedy, or the novel, at any moment it is always somebody's world. Narrative and the passions are, from different directions, systems for the articulation of a personal world, along with that world's claim to be prior to and, finally, more essential than any shared, common world or "mere world." Thus narrative and the passions share a common interest in the moments of time, however exceptional they might be among lived moments, in which the vehemence of grief or anger or fear or shame or joy makes unmistakable once again the structure of a world in which there is one and only one will, one and only one person.

NOTES

1. René Descartes, *Oeuvres philosophiques* (Paris: Garnier, 1967), 3:1009–10.

2. *Webster's New International Dictionary*, 3d ed., s.v. "pathology."

3. Cicero, *De Finibus Bonorum et Malorum*, 2d ed., trans. H. Rackham (Cambridge: Harvard University Press, 1931), 3.10.35.

4. Edmund Burke, *A Philosophical Enquiry into the Origin of Our Ideas of the Sublime and Beautiful*, ed. James T. Boulton (Oxford: Basil Blackwell, 1987). See pt. 2, secs. 3, 7, 12, 17, 19–22.

ONE Passions, Strong Emotions, Vehement Occasions

1. Charles Darwin, *The Expression of the Emotions in Man and Animals* (Chicago: University of Chicago Press, 1965), 69.

2. William James, *Collected Essays and Reviews*, ed. Ralph Barton Perry (New York: Russell and Russell, 1969), 244–45.

3. See, for example, Antonio R. Demasio, *Descartes' Error: Emotion, Reason, and the Human Brain* (New York: G. P. Putnam, 1994), esp. chap. 7, "Emotions and Feelings" (127–64). For more on the role of fear in brain-emotion research see J. S. Morris et al., "A Differential Neural Response in the Human Amygdala to Fearful and Happy Facial Expressions," *Nature* 383 (1996): 812–15. See also Sophie K. Scott et al., "Impaired Auditory Recognition of Fear and Anger following Bilateral Amygdala Lesions," *Nature* 385 (1997): 245–57.

4. Thomas Hobbes, *Leviathan* (New York: E. P. Dutton, 1950), 43.

5. Plato, *Republic*, trans. G.M.A. Grube (Indianapolis: Hackett, 1974), 9.590.

6. Cicero, *De Finibus* 3.10.35.

7. See A. A. Long and D. N. Sedley, *Translations of the Principal Sources with Philosophical Commentary*, vol. 1 of *The Hellenistic Philosophers* (Cambridge: Cambridge University Press, 1987), 411.

8. Plato, *Republic*, Loeb Classical Library, 4.439E.

9. See Peter L. Bernstein, *Against the Gods: The Remarkable Story of Risk* (New York: John Wiley and Sons, 1996), 227.

10. David Hume, "Of the Direct Passions," sec. IX in *A Treatise of Human Nature*, ed. Ernest C. Mossner (Baltimore: Penguin, 1969). Here Hume concludes, "Thus we still find, that whatever causes any fluctuation or mixture of passions, with any degree of uneasiness, always produces fear, or at least a passion so like it, that they are scarcely to be distinguish'd" (494).

11. Darwin, *Expression of the Emotions*, 306.

12. Ibid., 280.

13. Immanuel Kant, *Anthropology from a Pragmatic Point of View*, trans. Victor Lyle Dowdell, ed. Hans H. Rudnick (Carbondale: Southern Illinois University Press, 1978), 156.

14. Hobbes, *Leviathan*, 43–50.

15. "The Emotions are all those feelings that so change men as to effect their judgments, and that are also attended by pain or pleasure. Such are anger, pity, fear and the like, with their opposites." Aristotle, *Rhetoric* 2.1.1378a20–25, in *Rhetoric and Poetics*, trans. W. Rhys Roberts and Ingram Bywater (New York: Modern Library, 1954). Unless noted otherwise, further references to *Rhetoric* and to *Poetics* are to this edition.

16. See, for example, Joseph E. LeDoux, "Emotion, Memory and the Brain," *Scientific American*, June 1994, 32–39.

17. Algirdas Julien Greimas and Jacques Fontanille, *The Semiotics of Passions: From States of Affairs to States of Feeling*, trans. Paul Perron and Frank Collins (Minneapolis: University of Minnesota Press, 1993).

18. Ronald de Sousa, *The Rationality of Emotion* (Cambridge: MIT Press, 1991), 110.

19. Ibid., 117.

TWO **Paths among the Passions**

1. Aristotle, *Rhetoric* 2.1.1378a20–25.

2. Descartes, *Oeuvres philosophiques*, 3:1009–10.

3. Baruch Spinoza, *Ethics*, trans. Andrew Boyle (New York: J. M. Dent, 1963), pt. 3, def. 4, pp. 129–30.

4. Aristotle, *Rhetoric* 2.3.1380a30–35.

5. Albert O. Hirschman, *The Passions and the Interests* (Princeton: Princeton University Press, 1981). See esp. 32 and 132.

6. Michel de Montaigne, "Of Fear," in *The Complete Essays of Montaigne*, trans. Donald M. Frame (Stanford: Stanford University Press, 1958), 53.

7. François de La Rochefoucauld, *Maximes*, ed. Jean Lafond (Paris: Gallimard, 1995), 123.

8. Aristotle, *Rhetoric* 2.8.1386a15–20.

9. Aristotle, *Poetics* 14.53b1–10.

THREE **Thoroughness**

1. Lucretius, *On the Nature of Things*, trans. H.A.J. Munro (Garden City, N.Y.: Doubleday, Dolphin Books, n.d.), 35.

2. John Locke, *An Essay Concerning Human Understanding*, collated and annotated by Alexander Campbell Fraser (New York: Dover, 1959), vol. 1, 2.27.11.

3. Stanley Cavell, *In Quest of the Ordinary: Lines of Skepticism and Romanticism* (Chicago: University of Chicago Press, 1988).

4. Marcus Aurelius, *The Meditations*, trans. G.M.A. Grube (Indianapolis: Hackett, 1983), bk. 11, pp. 110–21.

5. Spinoza, *Ethics*, pt. 3, propositions 9–10, p. 92. See also Harry Austryn Wolfson, *The Philosophy of Spinoza* (Cambridge: Harvard University Press, 1962), 195–208.

FOUR **Privacy, Radical Singularity**

1. Lucretius, *On the Nature of Things*, 68.

2. Hume, *Treatise of Human Nature*, 462–63.

3. Homer, *Iliad*, trans. Martin Hammond (New York, Penguin Books, 1987), 18.1–36.

4. Sigmund Freud, "Mourning and Melancholy" (1917), in *Collected Papers*, trans. under the supervision of Joan Riviere (New York: Basic Books, 1959), 4:153.

5. Ibid.

FIVE **Time**

1. Marcus Aurelius, *Meditations* 7.61.

2. Hume, *Treatise of Human Nature*, bk. 2, sec. 7, 474–79.

3. Ibid., 466.

4. Ibid., 473.

5. John Rawls, *Theory of Justice* (Cambridge: Harvard University Press, Belknap Press, 1971), sec. 63–64, pp. 407–24.

6. Hume, *Treatise of Human Nature*, bk. 2, sec. 7, p. 475.

7. Derek Parfit, *Reasons and Persons* (Oxford: Oxford University Press, 1984), 161. See also Robert H. Frank, *Passions within Reason* (New York: Norton, 1988), 76–80, 84–88.

8. See similar examples in Derek Parfit, "Different Attitudes to Time," in *Reasons and Persons*, 149–86.

9. Examples are similar to those found in Frank's *Passions within Reason*, 77–80.

10. Rawls, *Theory of Justice*, 420.

11. David Hume, "Of the Passions," in *Treatise of Human Nature*, bk. 2, secs. 7–8, pp. 478, 481–82.

12. Freud, "Mourning and Melancholia," in *Collected Papers*, 4:166.

13. Aristotle, *On the Soul* 1.1.403a15–25, in *Introduction to Aristotle*, ed. Richard McKeon (New York: Random House, Modern Library, 1947).

SIX **Rashness**

1. Adam Smith, *The Theory of Moral Sentiments*, ed. A. L. Macfie and D. D. Raphael (Oxford: Clarendon Press, 1976), pt. 6, sec. 3, pp. 237–64.

2. William Shakespeare, *King Lear* 1.1.214–16 (Boston: Riverside/Houghton Mifflin, 1974). All subsequent Shakespeare references are to this edition.

3. Ibid., 1.1.150–51.

4. Aristotle, *Nicomachean Ethics* 3.6–9, in McKeon, *Introduction to Aristotle*.

5. *Romeo and Juliet* 3.5.156, 183–84, 192.

6. Aristotle, *Nicomachean Ethics*, Loeb Classical Library, 7.7.1150b15–25.

7. *King Lear* 5.3.271–75.

8. Kafka, *The Blue Octavo Notebooks*, trans. Ernst Kaiser and Eithne Wilkins, ed. Max Brod (Cambridge, Mass.: Exact Change, 1991), 90.

SEVEN **Mutual Fear**

1. Robert Nozick, "Prohibition, Compensation, and Risk," in *Anarchy, State, and Utopia* (New York: Basic Books, 1974), 54–87.

2. Parfit, *Reasons and Persons*.

3. Frank H. Knight, *Risk, Uncertainty and Profit* (Boston: Houghton Mifflin, Riverside Press Cambridge, 1921), 273, 199.

4. Mark Blaug, *Economic Theory in Retrospect* (Cambridge: Cambridge University Press, 1997), chap. 10, sec. 3, pp. 359–61.

5. Hume, *Treatise of Human Nature*, bk. 2, sec. 9, p. 492.

6. Knight, *Risk, Uncertainty and Profit*, 245.

7. Shakespeare, *The Merchant of Venice* 1.1.33–34.

8. Judith N. Shklar, "Bad Characters for Good Liberals," in *Ordinary Vices* (Cambridge: Harvard University Press, Belknap Press, 1984), 238.

9. Thomas Hobbes, *Man and Citizen*, ed. Bernard Gert, trans. Charles T. Wood, T.S.K. Scott-Craig, and Bernard Gert (Garden City, N.Y.: Doubleday, Anchor Books, 1972), 113.

10. Ibid., 113n.

11. See Roland Barthes, *The Pleasure of the Text*, trans. Richard Miller (New York: Farrar, Straus and Giroux, Hill and Wang, 1975), 48.

12. See Long and Sedley, *Translations of the Principal Sources with Philosophical Commentary*, 411.

13. Brad Inwood, *Ethics and Human Action in Early Stoicism* (Oxford: Clarendon, 1985), 175–81.

14. Burke, *A Philosophical Enquiry into the Origin of Our Ideas of the Sublime and Beautiful*, 57.

15. Aristotle, *Nicomachean Ethics* 3.6–9; Saint Augustine, *City of God*, trans. Henry Bettenson (Harmondsworth: Penguin, Pelican Classics, 1972), 9.4.4.

16. See Thomas C. Schelling, *Strategy and Conflict* (Cambridge: Harvard University Press, 1980).

17. Aristotle, *Nicomachean Ethics* 3.6–9.

18. Ibid., 3.8.1117a15–25.

19. Augustine gives the most extended account of Aristotle's example of a sinking ship in *City of God* 9.4.4.

20. Epictetus, *Discourses of Epictetus*, in *The Stoic and Epicurean Philosophers*, ed. Whitney J. Oates (New York: Random House, 1940), bk. 2, chap. 5, pp. 288–89.

21. Homer, *Iliad* 10.358–404.

22. Ibid., 10.221–65.

23. G.W.F. Hegel, *Phenomenology of Spirit*, in Alexandre Kojéve, *Introduction to the Reading of Hegel*, ed. Allan Bloom, trans. James H. Nicols, Jr. (1969; reprint, Ithaca: Cornell University Press, Agora Paperbacks, 1980), 3–30 (esp. 26).

24. Thomas C. Schelling, "The Reciprocal Fear of Surprise Attack," in *Strategy of Conflict*, 207.

25. Ibid., 207.

26. Ibid., 83–84.

27. William Poundstone, *Prisoner's Dilemma* (New York: Doubleday, Anchor Books, 1992).

28. Blaise Pascal, *Pensées*, trans. A. J. Krailsheimer (Harmondsworth: Penguin, 1966), I.15.198h5.

29. Hume, *Treatise of Human Nature*, bk. 2. sec. 9, p. 492.

30. Kenneth Arrow, "The Economics of Agency," in *Principals and Agents: The Structure of Business*, ed. John W. Pratt and Richard J. Zeckhauser (Boston: Harvard Business School Press, 1985), 37–51.

EIGHT **The Aesthetics of Fear**

1. Aristotle, *Poetics* 14.1453b1–14.

2. Homer, *Iliad* 18.85–131.

3. Ibid., 24.491–537.

4. Aristotle, *Rhetoric* 2.8.1386a25–30.

5. Jean-Jacques Rousseau, "Discourse on the Origin and Foundations of Inequality among Men," in *The First and Second Discourses*, ed. Roger D. Masters, trans. Roger D. Masters and Judith R. Masters (New York: St. Martin's Press, 1964), 104–20.

6. Aristotle, *Rhetoric* 2.8.1386a15–20.

7. Ibid., 2.8.1386a15–25.

8. Ibid., 1.14.1375a5–10.

9. Ibid., 1.14.1375a1–5.

10. Aristotle, *Poetics* 14.1453b1–15.

11. Ibid., 11.1452b10–15.

12. Rousseau, "Discourse on the Origin and Foundations of Inequality among Men," in *The First and Second Discourses*, 131. Rousseau borrows the image from Mandeville's *The Fable of the Bees*. His analysis is striking because the image is one of the only ones in the "Discourse on Inequality."

13. Hume, *Treatise of Human Nature*, bk. 2, sec. 7, pp. 417–20.

14. Immanuel Kant, *Critique of Judgment*, trans. Werner S. Pluhar (Indianapolis: Hackett, 1987), 129.

15. Ibid., 128.

16. Ibid., 120.

17. Martin Heidegger, *The Fundamental Concepts of Metaphysics: World, Finitude, Solitude*, trans. William McNeill and Nicholas Walker (Bloomington: Indiana University Press, 1995), 74–184.

NINE **The Radius of the Will**

1. La Rochefoucauld, *Maximes*, 65.

2. Saint Augustine, *Confessions*, trans. R. S. Pine-Coffin (Harmondsworth: Penguin, 1961), I.7.

3. Darwin, *Expression of the Emotions*, 196–310.

4. Ibid., 152–56.

5. Epictetus, *The Manual of Epictetus*, in *The Stoic and Epicurean Philosophers*, sec. I, p. 468.

6. See Hannah Arendt, *Willing* (New York: Harcourt Brace Jovanovich, 1978), 37.

7. Plato, *Laws*, in *The Collected Dialogues*, ed. Edith Hamilton and Huntington Cairns, Bollingen Series (New York: Pantheon Books, 1961), 9.864d–74e; Aristotle, *Rhetoric* I.13–14.

8. See Bernard Williams, "Centres of Agency," in *Shame and Necessity* (Berkeley and Los Angeles: University of California Press, 1993), 21–49.

9. Jean-Pierre Vernant, *Myth and Tragedy in Ancient Greece*, trans. Janet Lloyd (New York: Zone Books, 1990).

10. Locke, *An Essay Concerning Human Understanding*, vol. I, bk. 2, chap. 27, pp. 439–70.

11. Vernant, *Myth and Tragedy*, 47.

12. Ibid., 49.

TEN **Anger and Diminution**

1. Homer, *Iliad* 1.262–309.

2. Aristotle, *Nicomachean Ethics* 4.5.1125b30–35.

3. Ibid.

4. Aristotle, *Rhetoric* 2.8.1386a15–20.

5. Aristotle, *Nicomachean Ethics* 4.5.1126a1–10.

6. Aristotle, *Rhetoric* 2.2.1378a30–1378b.

7. See Hume, "Of Pride and Humility," pt. I of bk. 2 in *A Treatise of Human Nature*, 327–78.

8. Plato, *Republic* (Loeb) 4.440C–440D.

9. Plato, *Laws* 5.731b.

10. Hume, *Treatise of Human Nature*, bk. 2, sec. 3, pp. 462–63.

11. Plato, *Laws* 864d–874e; Aristotle, *Rhetoric* 1.13–14.

12. Aristotle, *Rhetoric*, ed. J. H. Freese, Loeb Classical Library, 174–75n.

13. Robert Axelrod, "The Success of TIT FOR TAT in Computer Tournaments," in *Evolution of Cooperation* (n.p.: Harper Collins, Basic Books, 1984), 27–54.

14. Aristotle, *Rhetoric* 2.2.1378a30–1378b.

15. Robert C. Ellickson, *Order without Law* (Cambridge: Harvard University Press, 1991).

16. Aristotle, *Politics*, in *The Complete Works of Aristotle*, ed. Jonathan Barnes, Bollingen Series (Princeton: Princeton University Press, 1984), vol. 2, bk. 7, sec. 7.

17. Epictetus, *Manual of Epictetus*, sec. 11, p. 470.

18. Rawls, *Theory of Justice*, 445.

ELEVEN **Grief**

1. *Oxford English Dictionary*, 2d ed., s.v. "mood."

2. Plutarch, "Coriolanus," in *Makers of Rome* (Harmondsworth: Penguin Books, 1965), 16.

3. Augustine, *Confessions* 9.12.

4. David Hume, *Dialogues Concerning Natural Religion* (London: Penguin Classics, 1990), 67–68, 132.

5. Spinoza, *Ethics*, pt. 3, propositions 9–10, p. 92.

6. Homer, *Iliad* 24.1–37.

7. Shakespeare, *Hamlet* 1.2.133–34.

8. Homer, *Iliad* 1.305–97.

9. Aristotle, *Rhetoric* 2.2.1379b–1380b.

10. The term "bright lines" comes from George Ainslie's article "Beyond Microeconomics," in Jon Elsir's collection *The Multiple Self* (Cambridge: Cambridge University Press, 1987), 146 ff. Ainslie is commenting on Schelling's idea in *The Strategy of Conflict* that we use focus points to eliminate ambiguity in strategies.

11. Shakespeare, *Hamlet* 1.2.68, 88, 93–94, 107.

12. Epictetus, *Discourses of Epictetus*, 231.

13. Epictetus, *Manual of Epictetus*, sec. 11, p. 470.

14. Marcus Aurelius, *The Meditations* 9.35.

15. Ibid., bk. 11.

16. Hirschman, *The Passions and the Interests*.

TWELVE **Spiritedness**

1. *Diagnostic and Statistical Manual of Mental Disorders*, 3d ed., s.v. "Dysthymic Disorder."

2. Darwin, "Low Spirits, Anxiety, Grief, Dejection, Despair," in *Expression of Emotions*, 176–95.

3. Darwin, "Joy, High Spirits, Love, Tender Feelings, Devotion," in *Expression of Emotions*, 197–219.

4. W.H.S. Jones, general introduction to *Hippocrates*, vol. I, Loeb Classical Library, lvii–lviii.

5. Aristotle, *Problems*, in *The Complete Works of Aristotle*, vol. 2, 30.1–14.

6. *A Greek-English Lexicon*, comp. Henry George Liddell and Robert Scott (Clarendon: Oxford University Press, 1968), 809–10.

7. Spinoza, *Ethics*, pt. 4, proposition 42, p. 171.

8. Spinoza, "Concerning the Power of the Intellect or Human Freedom," pt. 5 of *Ethics*, esp. pp. 213–19.

9. Immanual Kant, "Passage from Ordinary Rational Knowledge of Morality to Philosophical," in *Groundwork of the Metaphysic of Morals*, trans. H. J. Paton (New York: Harper and Row, 1964), 61.

10. Ibid., 61.

11. Immanuel Kant, "The Incentives of Pure Practical Reason," pt. I, bk. I, chap. 3, of *Critique of Practical Reason*, trans. Lewis White Beck (New York: Bobbs-Merrill, 1956), 89–90.

12. Kant, *Critique of Practical Reason*, pt. 2, p. 165.

13. Ibid., 90.

14. Ibid., 24.

15. Kant, *Groundwork*, 61.

16. Ibid., 69.

17. Kant, *Critique of Practical Reason*, 77.

18. Ibid., 166.

19. Ibid., 86.

20. Ibid., 77–78.

21. Kant, *Groundwork*, 67.

22. Kant, *Critique of Practical Reason*, 79.

23. Kant, *Groundwork*, 102.

24. Ibid., 70.